SCHOOL LAW
for TEACHERS

CONCEPTS AND APPLICATIONS

Julie Underwood, J.D., Ph.D.
University of Wisconsin–Madison

L. Dean Webb, Ph.D.
Arizona State University

PEARSON

Merrill
Prentice Hall

Upper Saddle River, New Jersey
Columbus, Ohio

Library of Congress Cataloging-in-Publication Data

Underwood, Julie.
    School law for teachers: concepts and applications/Julie Underwood, L. Dean Webb.
        p. cm.
    Includes index.
    ISBN 0-13-119242-6
        1. Teachers—Legal status, laws, etc.—United States—Popular works. 2. Educational law
and legislation—United States—Popular works. I. Webb, L. Dean. II. Title.

KF4175.Z9U53 2006
344.73′071—dc22

2005047950

Vice President and Executive
  Publisher: Jeffery W. Johnston
Executive Editor: Debra A. Stollenwerk
Senior Editorial Assistant: Mary Morrill
Assistant Development Editor: Elisa Rogers
Production Coordination: Lisa Garboski, bookworks
Senior Production Editor: Linda Hillis Bayma

Design Coordinator: Diane C. Lorenzo
Cover Designer: Ali Mohrman
Cover image: Getty Images
Production Manager: Susan Hannahs
Director of Marketing: Ann Castel Davis
Marketing Manager: Darcy Betts Prybella
Marketing Coordinator: Brian Mounts

This book was set in Frutiger by Pine Tree Composition. It was printed and bound by R.R. Donnelley
& Sons. The cover was printed by R.R. Donnelley & Sons.

Portions of all chapters in this text originally appeared in Chapters 11 and 12 of *Foundations of American
Education,* 4th Edition, by L. Dean Webb, Arlene Metha, and K. Forbis Jordan, copyright © 2003 by
Pearson Education, Inc.

Pearson Education Ltd.
Pearson Education Singapore Pte. Ltd.
Pearson Education Canada, Ltd.
Pearson Education—Japan

Pearson Education Australia Pty. Limited
Pearson Education North Asia Ltd.
Pearson Educación de Mexico, S.A. de C.V.
Pearson Education Malaysia Pte. Ltd.

10 9 8 7 6 5 4 3 2 1
ISBN: 0-13-119242-6

We dedicate this book for teachers

To our teachers:
S. Kern Alexander and K. Forbis Jordan

SCHOOL LAW *for* TEACHERS

PREFACE

This text is written for preservice teachers. It provides a concise explanation of the legal framework of education, presents the legal requirements for the teaching profession, and explains the state and federal laws and court decisions that govern the everyday life of the classroom teacher. It simply and clearly explains and summarizes the most current and important legal principles, with examples of their application to classroom practice. We have limited the coverage of the text to those issues of greatest concern to the classroom teacher; we do not address those issues that typically are not central to daily classroom practice, including topics such as school funding and compulsory attendance.

We expect that through a more complete understanding of the law governing their profession, practicing teachers will be better prepared to carry out their duties and responsibilities, exercise their rights, and protect those of their students.

Education is rife with laws, rules, regulations, processes, and procedures. Educators are expected to know and act within all of these boundaries. Classroom teachers face a daunting array of legal responsibilities and confront myriad legal issues on an almost daily basis. School board minutes as well as the popular press record the legal ramifications when teachers fail to follow the laws and regulations that regulate their conduct or protect the rights of students.

America has become an increasingly litigious society. The growing number of lawsuits in the United States is particularly apparent in our public education system. According to a survey of the American Tort Reform Association,[1] 25% of all secondary schools were involved with lawsuits of all kinds—from accidental injuries to disciplinary disputes. The survey also showed a dramatic increase in litigation within the public schools in the last 10 years. A research report released by Public Agenda[2] provided the following conclusions:

1. For many teachers and principals, the possibility of being sued for or being accused of physical or sexual abuse of a student is ever present in their minds.

2. For many principals and superintendents, avoiding lawsuits and fulfilling regulatory and due process requirements is a time-consuming and often frustrating part of the job. Special education, discipline, sexual harassment, and staff issues seemed to be the most problematic areas.

3. Many teachers and school leaders believe that litigation and due process requirements often give unreasonable people a way "to get their way" even when their demands are unwarranted. School leaders appeared divided over whether agreeing to an unjust settlement is preferable to going to battle in the courts.

4. Litigation and the threat of litigation often take a personal toll on educators. An unwarranted charge and/or the prospect of dealing with litigation can create enormous anxiety and anguish, sometimes enough to derail a career.

We have concluded from our many years of experience in training teachers and administrators and representing school districts in various legal forums that these legal conflicts often stem from a lack of understanding of the law or a misunderstanding of the application of the law in specific situations in the school setting. The intent of this text is to provide a broad legal background for teachers as they enter the profession. We have designed it to serve as a resource for prospective and practicing teachers in understanding and assuring their rights and responsibilities and the rights of their students.

Key Features

Each chapter includes the following features to help students understand and apply key concepts:

- *Links to state and federal education statutes and regulations.* This major feature of the text links to the education statutes for most states as well as to many federal statutes and regulations. For every important topic in each chapter, through the Companion Website the student and instructor are able to access state education statutes specific to that topic. This allows students and professors to see how broad legal principles and court decisions have been adopted and adapted in the education codes of their state.

- *In the News.* This feature presents an issue related to chapter content that is currently in controversy and whose outcome is likely to have an important impact on teachers or students.

- *Landmark cases decided by the U.S. Supreme Court.* To highlight their importance, text boxes strategically present case summaries of the facts and the U.S. Supreme Court decisions of landmark cases related to chapter content.

- *Guiding Legal Principles.* Students can use a summary list of guiding legal principles at the end of each chapter for study and review as well as a guide to classroom discussion.

- *You Be the Judge.* This feature presents real-life cases reflecting the legal issues discussed in the chapter and illustrating the complexity of cases involving a balance of the conflicting interests of teachers, students, parents, the school administration, and the public. This section asks students to apply the legal principles presented in the chapter in suggesting the resolution to the case. Then the text refers students to the Companion Website for the actual court decision and rationale.

Acknowledgments

The authors wish to recognize and express our appreciation to our professional colleagues who have provided critical comments and suggestions in the preparation of this text. We extend our special thanks to Executive Editor Debbie Stollenwerk and her assistant Mary Morrill and to Production Coordinator Lisa S. Garboski of bookworks. Special thanks are also extended to the reviewers for their constructive comments and recommendations. For their efforts, we extend appreciation to Morris L. Anderson, Wayne State College; Tony Armenta, Southeastern Louisiana University; Steven S. Goldberg, Arcadia University; David Jelinek, California State University, Sacramento; Venitta C. McCall, Mary Washington College; John L. Strope, Jr., University of Louisville (emeritus); and Willis Walter, Jr., Florida A&M University.

Companion Website

A user-friendly Companion Website extends and reinforces chapter content. The website is organized by chapter and provides both the student and the professor with a variety of meaningful resources, including a **Syllabus Manager**™, Message Board, and resources to extend coverage of the subjects addressed in each chapter. Other information on the Companion Website builds on features in the text itself:

- *Cases.* For every landmark case summarized in the chapters, the Companion Website offers the full version of the case for deeper perusal.
- *You Be the Judge.* The Companion Website extends this feature beyond the text by offering readers more information about the cases in question, including the actual court decisions.
- *More on the Web* contains Internet activities based on websites that relate to each chapter's content, with convenient web links for each.
- *Chapter Objectives* and *Guiding Legal Principles* are available online to be used as study guides.

Endnotes

1. Joyce, Sherman. (1999). *Educators fear liability: Survey of principals.* Washington, DC: American Tort Reform.
2. Public Agenda. (2004). *Teaching interrupted: Do discipline policies in today's public schools foster the common good?* Retrieved May 3, 2005, from **http:cgood.org/assets/attachments/22.pdf**

DISCOVER THE COMPANION WEBSITE ACCOMPANYING THIS BOOK

The Prentice Hall Companion Website: A Virtual Learning Environment

Technology is a constantly growing and changing aspect of our field that is creating a need for content and resources. To address this emerging need, Prentice Hall has developed an online learning environment for students and professors alike—Companion Websites—to support our textbooks.

In creating a Companion Website, our goal is to build on and enhance what the textbook already offers. For this reason, the content for each user-friendly website is organized by chapter and provides the professor and student with a variety of meaningful resources.

For the Professor—

Every Companion Website integrates **Syllabus Manager**™, an online syllabus creation and management utility.

- **Syllabus Manager**™ provides you, the instructor, with an easy, step-by-step process to create and revise syllabi, with direct links into Companion Website and other online content without having to learn HTML.
- Students may log on to your syllabus during any study session. All they need to know is the web address for the Companion Website and the password you've assigned to your syllabus.
- After you have created a syllabus using **Syllabus Manager**™, students may enter the syllabus for their course section from any point in the Companion Website.
- Clicking on a date, the student is shown the list of activities for the assignment. The activities for each assignment are linked directly to actual content, saving time for students.
- Adding assignments consists of clicking on the desired due date, then filling in the details of the assignment—name of the assignment, instructions, and whether it is a one-time or repeating assignment.
- In addition, links to other activities can be created easily. If the activity is online, a URL can be entered in the space provided, and it will be linked automatically in the final syllabus.

- Your completed syllabus is hosted on our servers, allowing convenient updates from any computer on the Internet. Changes you make to your syllabus are immediately available to your students at their next logon.

Common Companion Website features for students include:

For the Student—

- **Chapter Objectives**—Outline key concepts from the text
- **Cases**—Provide full versions of the landmark case summaries in the text
- **Guiding Legal Principles**—Summary lists of chapter content that can be used for class discussions or as study guides
- **You Be the Judge**—Provides the authors' responses to the questions posed in the text or gives a summary of the actual court decision and rationale
- **Resources**—Extend and reinforce topics discussed in the chapters
- **More on the Web**—Links to Internet sites that relate to chapter content
- **Message Board**—Virtual bulletin board to post or respond to questions or comments from a national audience

To take advantage of the many available resources, please visit the *School Law for Teachers* Companion Website at

www.prenhall.com/underwood

EDUCATOR LEARNING CENTER:
An Invaluable Online Resource

Merrill Education and the Association for Supervision and Curriculum Development (ASCD) invite you to take advantage of a new online resource, one that provides access to the top research and proven strategies associated with ASCD and Merrill— the Educator Learning Center. At **www.educatorlearningcenter.com**, you will find resources that will enhance your students' understanding of course topics and of current educational issues, in addition to being invaluable for further research.

How the Educator Learning Center Will Help Your Students Become Better Teachers

With the combined resources of Merrill Education and ASCD, you and your students will find a wealth of tools and materials to better prepare them for the classroom.

Research

- More than 600 articles from the ASCD journal *Educational Leadership* discuss everyday issues faced by practicing teachers.
- A direct link on the site to Research Navigator™ gives students access to many of the leading education journals, as well as extensive content detailing the research process.
- Excerpts from Merrill Education texts give your students insights on important topics of instructional methods, diverse populations, assessment, classroom management, technology, and refining classroom practice.

Classroom Practice

- Hundreds of lesson plans and teaching strategies are categorized by content area and age range.
- Case studies and classroom video footage provide virtual field experience for student reflection.
- Computer simulations and other electronic tools keep your students abreast of today's classrooms and current technologies.

Look into the Value of Educator Learning Center Yourself

A four-month subscription to Educator Learning Center is $25 but is **FREE** when packaged with any Merrill Education text. In order for your students to have access to this site, you must use this special value-pack ISBN number **WHEN** placing your textbook order with the bookstore: 0-13-221693-0. Your students will then receive a copy of the text packaged with a free ASCD pincode. To preview the value of this website to you and your students, please go to **www.educatorlearningcenter.com** and click on "Demo."

BRIEF CONTENTS

CONTENTS

11 **Religion in the Schools   209**

Note: Every effort has been made to provide accurate and current Internet information in this book. However, the Internet and information posted on it are constantly changing, and it is inevitable that some of the Internet addresses listed in this textbook will change.

CASE SUMMARIES

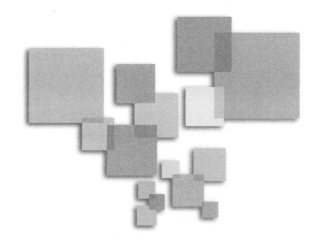

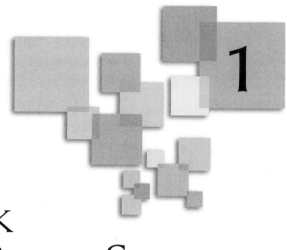

LEGAL FRAMEWORK FOR THE PUBLIC SCHOOLS

The legal foundation of education comes from state and federal constitutions, the laws enacted by state and federal legislatures, the rules and regulations adopted by state and federal agencies, school board policies, and court decisions. Although the federal Constitution does not mention education, a number of its provisions affect education and provide protection to school personnel, pupils, and patrons. Moreover, numerous federal statutes significantly impact the operation of the schools and the conduct of teachers and students.

Unlike the federal Constitution, which is silent on education, every state constitution provides for the establishment of a system of education. The wording of the education clause in the state constitution is important in determining the state's obligation in providing for education and in determining the constitutionality of legislative action. In meeting their constitutional obligation to provide for a system of education, state legislatures have enacted and continue to enact numerous statutes to regulate the state education system, have established state departments of education or public instruction, and have created local school districts. They also have delegated to these agencies and districts the responsibilities for the administration and daily operation of the public elementary and secondary schools.

Before discussing the specifics of the law as they relate to the various topics addressed in the remainder of this text, this chapter provides a brief overview of the major sources of school law, the federal and state court systems, and their interrelationship in forming the legal basis for public education. After reading this chapter you will be able to

- Identify the federal constitutional provisions affecting education.
- Discuss the importance of state constitutional provisions affecting education.
- Distinguish between statutory law and case law.
- Describe the importance of administrative law to the operation of the schools.
- Explain the purpose of school board policies and rules.
- Describe the functions and powers of the courts.
- Compare the levels of the federal court system with those of a typical state court system.
- Explain how to locate a case using West's reporter system.

FEDERAL CONSTITUTIONAL PROVISIONS AFFECTING EDUCATION

A constitution is the original agreement under which a group of people form a government. It consists of the fundamental laws of the people of a state or nation, establishing the very character and concept of their government, its organization and officers, its sovereign powers, and the limitations of its power. Constitutions are the highest level of law. Constitutions are written broadly so as to endure changing times and circumstances. Although constitutions can be changed by amendment, the process is normally difficult and seldom utilized. The Constitution of the United States, written over 200 years ago, has served the needs of a fledgling nation and a world power with only 26 amendments.

The U.S. Constitution, though, does not mention education. It is therefore considered to be one of the powers reserved to the states by the Tenth Amendment. Although the provision of education is considered one of the powers of the state, the supremacy clause of the Constitution (Article VI, Section 2) declares the federal Constitution and the laws enacted by the U.S. Congress to be the supreme law of the land. Thus the states, in exercising their authority, may not enact any laws that violate any provisions of the federal Constitution.

Several important sections of the federal Constitution affect the schools. Among these are

- Article I, Section 8, the general welfare clause;
- Article I, Section 10, the obligation of contracts clause; and
- the First, Fourth, Fifth, Eighth, Ninth, Tenth, and Fourteenth Amendments.

These constitutional provisions serve as the basis for the majority of education-related cases being filed in the federal courts.

General Welfare Clause

Article I, Section 8 of the Constitution, known as the general welfare clause, gives Congress the power to tax and to "provide for the common Defence and general Welfare of the United States." The Supreme Court has interpreted the general welfare clause as authorizing Congress to tax and spend money for a variety of activities deemed to be in the general welfare. However, the general welfare clause does not give Congress the authority to do anything it pleases to provide for the general welfare, only to tax and spend for that purpose. This means, for example, that while Congress may levy taxes to provide support for education, it may not legislate control of education. However, the Supreme Court has ruled that the federal government can attach conditions to the use of federal education funds, which, if not complied with, may result in the denial or withdrawal of the funds.

Under its authority to provide for the general welfare, Congress has enacted a large body of legislation that provides direct federal support for a variety of instructional programs, services, and programs for identified special needs students; financial assistance to prospective teachers; and professional development and higher education to practicing teachers and administrators. The general welfare clause has also served as the federal government's authority to establish the U.S. military academies; operate overseas schools for dependents of military and civilian personnel; establish schools on Indian reservations, in the U.S. territories, and in the District of Columbia; operate libraries, such as the Library of Congress; and conduct a variety of other activities and operations deemed educational in nature.

Obligation of Contracts Clause

Article I, Section 10 of the Constitution, the obligation of contracts clause, declares: "No state shall . . . pass any Bill of Attainder, ex post facto Law, or Law impairing the obligation of Contracts." This clause prohibits a state legislature from passing a law that attempts to invalidate or change the terms of an existing contract. For example, in a case that the Fifth Circuit Court of Appeals characterized as representing "a collision between the Contract Clause of the United States Constitution and the state of Mississippi," the state of Mississippi attempted to invalidate the lease agreements that various individuals held for use of the state education trust lands. The rental agreements had been first signed in 1821 for a period of 99 years with a "renewal forever" provision. The state argued that the rental agreements, which required the payment of only pennies per year, amounted to the donation of public property for public use, a violation of the state constitution. While not disagreeing that the rental fees represented only a very small fraction of fair market value, the circuit court agreed with the lower court that to violate the leases would be a violation of the contract clause of the Constitution.[1]

As discussed more fully in chapter 4, the obligation of contracts clause protects school personnel who have contracts from arbitrary dismissals. That is, a teacher who has a contract cannot be dismissed during the term of that contract without a showing of cause and without due process. The obligation of contracts clause also protects both the school board (or the state) and those businesses and individuals with whom it does business from nonperformance relative to the terms of a contract.

For example, a Louisiana school district entered into a contract for the building of a junior high school to replace one that had burned down. The contract provided that the building was to be substantially completed by August 1 and that the contractor would pay the school board $200 for every day after August 1 that the building was not completed. The building was not completed until September 4, and so the school board withheld $6,600 from its final payment to the contractor. The contractor sued for recovery, claiming that the delay was excused under a clause in the contract that allowed for extensions caused by adverse weather conditions. The school board's action was upheld on appeal because the contractor did not present proof that the rain and cold weather experienced were in excess of what an experienced contractor should have taken into account in estimating time for weather losses when bidding on contracts that have a term for performance.[2]

First Amendment

The First Amendment addresses several basic personal freedoms. It provides that

> Congress shall make no law respecting an establishment of religion, or prohibiting the free exercise thereof; or abridging the freedom of speech, or of the press; or of the right of the people peaceably to assemble, and to petition the Government for a redress of grievances.

In recent years the first clause of the First Amendment, the Establishment and Free Exercise of Religion clause, has become the focus of litigation in education. As discussed in chapter 11, these cases have dealt with numerous issues surrounding school practices objected to on the basis of promoting or inhibiting religion (e.g., prayer and religious displays and observances) and curriculum content.

The second clause of the First Amendment, which deals with the freedom of speech and the press, has also been the subject of a growing number of education cases. Both teachers and students have protested violations of their rights to express themselves in ways ranging from personal attire to publicly criticizing school board practices. Teachers have also become more concerned with what they consider attempts to infringe upon their academic freedom to select textbooks and other teaching materials and to practice certain teaching methodologies.

The third clause of the First Amendment, which deals with the rights of citizens to assemble, has been invoked in a number of education cases in which students and teachers have asserted their right to belong to various organizations, including those that may have goals contrary to that of the school system (see, e.g., **Melzer v. New York City Bd. of Educ.**,[3] in which the court rejected a teacher's complaint that his constitutional right to freedom of association was violated when the board terminated him in retaliation for his membership in the North American Man/Boy Love Association). The question of freedom of association has also been at issue in a number of cases dealing with teachers' associations or unions. However, questions of non-school-sponsored student assemblies, such as prayer meetings or antiwar protest rallies, are usually not addressed under this clause but under the freedom of religion or freedom of expression clause.

Fourth Amendment

The Fourth Amendment provides that the right of the people to be "secure in their persons, houses, papers, and effects, against unreasonable searches and seizures, shall not be violated and no Warrants shall issue, but upon probable cause." The growing problem of student possession of drugs and weapons has led to an increase in student searches. Discussion in subsequent chapters will cover how the Fourth Amendment has served as the basis for a number of employee as well as student challenges to searches of their lockers, backpacks, desks, automobiles, or persons by school officials and others.

Fifth Amendment

The Fifth Amendment provides that no person shall be "compelled in any criminal case to be a witness against himself, nor be deprived of life, liberty, or property, without due process of law; nor shall private property be taken for public use, without just compensation." Teachers have invoked the first clause of the Fifth Amendment, the self-incrimination clause, in refusing to answer questions about their affiliations and activities in criminal proceedings. The second clause, the due process clause, is not usually involved in education cases. Instead, education cases use the due process clause of the Fourteenth Amendment because it relates directly to the states.

The last clause of the Fifth Amendment is relevant in those few cases in which the state or school system seeks to obtain private property for school purposes in the exercise of the government's right of *eminent domain,* the right to take private property for public use. Thus a school district attempting to gain property to enlarge a school may find it necessary to exercise its power of eminent domain (if the state has given it such power) if it has not been able to negotiate a voluntary purchase of the needed property. Whenever the power of eminent domain is exercised, fair and just compensation must be given to the owners of the property that is taken.

Eighth Amendment

The Eighth Amendment, in part, provides protection against "cruel and unusual punishments." Over the years students challenging the use of corporal punishment in schools have invoked this amendment. The Supreme Court has held, however, that disciplinary corporal punishment per se is not cruel and unusual punishment as anticipated by the Eighth Amendment.[4] This does not mean, however, that state or school district regulations may not prohibit corporal punishment or that punishment can be excessive.

Tenth Amendment

The Tenth Amendment states that "The powers not delegated to the United States by the Constitution, nor prohibited by it to the States, are reserved to the States respectively, or to the people." Because education is not mentioned in the Constitution, it comes under the terms of this amendment that education is considered one of the powers reserved to the state.

Fourteenth Amendment

Section 1 of the Fourteenth Amendment states:

> No State shall make or enforce any law which shall abridge the privileges or immunities of citizens of the United States; nor shall any State deprive any person of life, liberty, or property, without due process of law; nor deny to any person within its jurisdiction the equal protection of the laws.

The Fourteenth Amendment is the federal constitutional provision most often involved in education-related cases because it is directed specifically to state actions and, as previously stated, education is a state function. As discussed throughout the remainder of this text, the due process clause of the Fourteenth Amendment has been invoked in a wide array of issues involving student and teacher rights.

STATE CONSTITUTIONAL PROVISIONS AFFECTING EDUCATION

Like the federal Constitution, state constitutions have provided the foundation for the enactment of the numerous state statutes that govern the activities of the state and its citizens. However, unlike the federal Constitution, which makes no mention of education, every state constitution includes a provision for education, and all but one expressly provides for the establishment of a system of public schools. The language of these provisions ranges from a very general statement that the legislature must provide for a free system of education to very specific mandates. Their overall intent is to ensure that schools and education be encouraged and that a uniform system of schools be established. For example, Article X, Section 3 (as amended, April 1972) of the Wisconsin constitution provides:

> The Legislature shall provide by law for the establishment of district schools, which shall be as nearly uniform as practical; and such schools shall be free and without charge for tuition to all children between the ages of 4 and 20 years.

The constitutions of 45 states provide for the establishment of "common schools" and 35 states establish specific methods for financial support.[5] The constitutions of 30 states expressly prohibit the use of public funds for the support of religious schools, and the constitution of every state except Maine and North Carolina contains a provision prohibiting religious instruction in the public schools, and some of these also specifically prohibit any religious or political requirements for admission or employment. For example, Article XI, Section 7 of the Arizona constitution provides:

> No sectarian instruction shall be imparted in any school or State educational institution and no religious or political test or qualification shall ever be required as a condition of admission into any public educational institution of the State, as teacher, student, or pupil.

The wording of the education clause in specific state constitutions has proven to be very important to the courts in determining whether particular legislative enactments were constitutionally permissible or required. For example, an Arizona court of appeals ruled that the constitutional requirements that the state legislature provide for a system of "free common schools" did not require that free textbooks be provided to high school students.[6] The basis for the court's decision was its interpretation that at the time the constitution was adopted the common schools consisted of only grades 1 through 8.

Go to the Companion Website at **http://www. prenhall.com/underwood,** select Chapter 1, then choose the Resources module to find the education clause in state constitutions.

The language of the state constitution has also proven important in a number of cases challenging the constitutionality of state funding systems. In some of these cases the courts have ruled that phrases in the constitution such as "a thorough and efficient system of education" or "a thorough and uniform system of education" required that the state establish a finance system that provides some degree of equity in expenditures per pupil across districts as well as one that did not make the quality of a child's education dependent on the wealth of the school district.

Although state constitutions give state legislatures broad power to directly control public education, they do not grant unlimited power to state legislatures in providing for the public schools. Rather, they establish the boundaries within which the legislatures may operate. Individual legislatures may not enact legislation that exceeds these boundaries or that violates any provisions of the federal Constitution, the supreme law of the land.

STATUTORY LAW

Statutory law is that body of law consisting of the written enactments of a legislative body. These written enactments, called statutes, are the second highest level of law, following constitutions. Whereas constitutions provide broad statements of policy, statutes establish the specifics of operation. Both the U.S.

Congress and state legislatures have enacted innumerable statutes affecting the provision of education. Successive legislatures have continually reviewed and often revised or supplemented these statutes. They are also subject to review by the courts to determine both their intent and whether they are in violation of the state or federal constitution.

Federal Statutes

Despite the federal constitutional silence on education, during each session the U.S. Congress enacts or renews numerous statutes that have a considerable impact on the public schools. Some of these, such as the Occupational Safety and Health Act,[7] which requires employers to furnish a safe working environment, or the Fair Labor Standards Act,[8] which regulates wages and working conditions, are not directed specifically at school districts but do have a significant effect on their operation. Many of the statutes enacted by Congress grant funds to states and local school districts based on their adoption and implementation of plans, performance programs, policies, or procedures that the federal government promotes or supports (see Table 1.1).

One of the most recent and far-reaching pieces of federal education legislation is the No Child Left Behind (NCLB) Act of 2001.[9] NCLB requires that by

Table 1.1 Federal Funding Statutes

Federal Statute	Purpose	Citation
Title IV of the Civil Rights Act	Provides funds for technical assistance and training regarding race, national origin, and sex equity issues	42 U.S.C. § 2000c
Carl Perkins Vocational Education Act	Provides funds for quality vocational education programs with attention to special needs populations	20 U.S.C. § 2301
Title I of No Child Left Behind Act of 2001	Provides funds to improve the academic achievement of disadvantaged students	20 U.S.C. § 6301 *et seq.*
Title II of No Child Left Behind Act of 2001	Provides funds to improve the preparation, training, and recruiting of high-quality teachers and principals	20 U.S.C. § 6601 *et seq.*
Title III of No Child Left Behind Act of 2001	Provides for language instruction for students who have limited English proficiency	20 U.S.C. § 6801 *et seq.*
Individuals With Disabilities Education Act (IDEA)	Ensures appropriate special education and related services	20 U.S.C. § 1400 *et seq.*
Child Abuse Reporting and Prevention Act	Ensures mandatory reporting of suspected child abuse and neglect	42 U.S.C. § 5101 *et seq.*

Go to the Companion Website at **http://www. prenhall.com/underwood,** select chapter 1, then choose the Resources module to find the full text of the No Child Left Behind Act.

the end of the 2005–2006 school year all students in grades 3 through 8 be tested each year in reading and math using state prescribed tests, that the tests be aligned with state-developed curriculum standards, and that schools make *adequate yearly progress* (AYP) toward reaching grade-level proficiency on the state test. All students are expected to reach the state proficient level by 2014. Schools that fail to make AYP, termed *schools in need of improvement,* are subject to increasingly serious consequences ranging from being required to develop improvement plans to state takeover. Each state determines what test(s) will be used and what level of performance will be necessary to achieve proficiency. As a result considerable variation exists among the states both in the rigor of the tests as well as in the setting of proficiency levels.

The NCLB Act also specifies that by 2003 all new teachers (and paraprofessionals) hired with Title I funds be highly qualified and by 2005–2006 all teachers be highly qualified, regardless of the funding source. NCLB defines *highly qualified* differently for new and experienced teachers and for elementary and secondary teachers. It requires that new elementary teachers pass a state test in the core elementary subjects and that new middle and high school teachers either pass a state test in the academic subject matter or have an academic major, graduate degree, or advanced certification in the subject(s) they teach. Experienced teachers may demonstrate content knowledge by any of these means or by meeting the requirements of a state standard of evaluation, which vary significantly among the states.

Go to the Companion Website at **http://www. prenhall.com/underwood,** select Chapter 1, then choose the Resources module to find the state standards of evaluation for new and experienced teachers.

The far-reaching impact of NCLB demonstrates the power that the federal government can have over education without directly mandating that states or school districts act in certain ways. That is, although the federal government does not have the authority to mandate that schools test students or hire only teachers with certain qualifications, it can say that, as a condition of receiving federal funds, states or school districts must meet certain requirements or adhere to certain conditions. (See the In the News feature for state challenges to NCLB.)

Still other federal statutes, federal civil rights statutes, are directed at the eradication of discrimination and the protection of the civil rights of all Americans. Table 1.2 provides an overview of the major civil rights statutes affecting the schools. Relevant sections of this text discuss these in more detail.

State Statutes

State legislatures enact most of the statutory laws affecting the public schools. The authority of the state legislature to enact legislation regulating the operation of the schools is plenary, or absolute, and the legislature may enact any legislation that is not contrary to federal and state constitutions. Moreover, local school districts challenge the principle every year. The courts have clearly established that

Table 1.2   Major Civil Rights Statutes Affecting Education

Statute	Major Provision
Civil Rights Act of 1866, 1870 42 U.S.C. § 1981	Provides all citizens equal rights under the law regardless of race.
Civil Rights Act of 1871 42 U.S.C. § 1983	Any person who deprives another of his or her rights may be held liable to the injured party.
Civil Rights Act of 1871 42 U.S.C. § 1985 and 1986	Persons conspiring to deprive another of his or her rights, or any person having knowledge of any such conspiracy, are subject to any action to recover damages.
Civil Rights Act of 1866, 1870 (as amended) 42 U.S.C. § 1988	Courts may award reasonable attorney fees to the prevailing party in any action arising out of the above acts and Title VI of the Civil Rights Act of 1964.
Civil Rights Act of 1964, Title VI 42 U.S.C. § 2000d	Prohibits discrimination on the basis of race, color, or national origin.
Equal Pay Act of 1963 29 U.S.C. § 206(D)	Prohibits sex discrimination in pay.
Civil Rights Act of 1964, Title VII 42 U.S.C. § 2000e	Prohibits discrimination in employment on the basis of race, color, religion, gender, or national origin.
Age Discrimination in Employment Act of 1967 29 U.S.C. § 621	Prohibits discrimination against any individual with respect to employment unless age is a bona fide occupational qualification.
Education Amendments of 1972, Title IX 20 U.S.C. § 1681	Prohibits sex discrimination in any education program or activity receiving federal financial assistance.
Rehabilitation Act of 1973 (as amended) 29 U.S.C. § 791	Prohibits discrimination against any "otherwise qualified" individual with a disability.
Equal Educational Opportunities Act of 1974 20 U.S.C. § 1703	Prohibits any state from denying equal educational opportunities to any individual based on his or her race, color, gender, or national origin.
Americans With Disabilities Act of 1990 42 U.S.C. § 12112	Prohibits discrimination against persons with disabilities.
Individuals With Disabilities Education Act of 1990 20 U.S.C. § 1400–1485	Individuals with disabilities must be guaranteed a free appropriate education by programs receiving federal financial assistance.
Civil Rights Restoration Act of 1991 42 U.S.C. § 1981 *et seq.*	Amends the Civil Rights Act of 1964, the Age Discrimination in Employment Act of 1967, and the Americans With Disabilities Act of 1990 with regard to employment discrimination.

Source: Webb, L. D.; Metha, A.; Jordan, K. F., *Foundations of American Education* © 2003. Reprinted by permission of Pearson Education, Inc., Upper Saddle River, NJ.

IN THE NEWS . . .

The nation's largest teachers union (NEA) and school districts in three states (Michigan, Vermont, and Texas) sued the Bush administration on Wednesday over the No Child Left Behind law. . . . The lawsuit, filed in the U.S. District Court for eastern Michigan, is the first major challenge to President Bush's signature education policy. The outcome would apply directly to the districts in the case, but it could affect how the law is enforced in schools across the country. . . .

The lawsuit is built upon one paragraph in the law that says no state or school district can be forced to spend its money on expenses the federal government has not covered.

The lawsuit accuses the government of shortchanging schools by at least $27 billion, the difference between the amount Congress authorized and what it has spent . . . the suit, citing a series of cost studies, outlines billions of dollars in extra expenses to meet the law's mandates. They include the costs of adding testing, getting children up to grade level in reading and math, and ensuring teachers are highly qualified.

The plaintiffs want a judge to order that states and schools don't have to spend their own money to pay for the law's expenses and that the Education Department cannot yank federal money from a state or school that refuses to comply based on those grounds.

Source: From "Bush Plan's Funding Falls Short, Suit Says," by B. Feller, April 21, 2005, *Arizona Republic,* p. A10.

education is a function of the state, not an inherent function of the local school district, and that the local district has only those powers the state legislature delegates to it. The courts have also affirmed the authority of the state to regulate such matters as certification, powers of school boards, accreditation, curriculum, the school calendar, graduation requirements, facilities construction and operation, and raising and spending of monies. In fact, the courts have made it clear that school districts have no absolute right to exist; they exist only at the will of the legislature and can be created, reorganized, or abolished at the will of the legislature.

In practice most state legislatures have delegated the administration of the state education system to an administrative agency, such as the state department of education or the state department of public instruction, and the actual operation of schools to the local school districts. However, while delegating the operation of most schools (the state often retains operation of certain types of specialized schools, such as schools for the deaf and blind) to local school districts, the legislature still must enact legislation to administer the system as a whole and to provide for its financing and operation. Consequently, numerous education statutes exist in every state, and in every legislative session new statutes are enacted that affect education.

CW

Go to the Companion Website at **http://www. prenhall.com/underwood,** select Chapter 1, then choose the Resources module to find the state-specific education code.

CASE LAW

Case law is that body of law originating with historical usages and customs, including court decisions. Also referred to as common law, case law is based on the doctrine of *stare decisis,* which means "let the decision stand." The doctrine requires that once a court has laid down a principle of law as applicable to a certain set of facts, it will apply it to all future cases in which the facts are substantially the same, and other courts of equal or lesser rank will similarly apply the principle.[10] However, adherence to the doctrine of *stare decisis* does not mean that all previous decisions may never be challenged or overturned. In fact, courts of appeals commonly reject the reasoning of a lower court and reverse its decision in whole or part. It also happens, though not as commonly, that a court will reverse an earlier decision of the same court.

ADMINISTRATIVE RULES AND REGULATIONS

Both state and federal agencies adopt rules and regulations that affect education. These administrative rules and regulations carry the force of law and are, in fact, sometimes referred to as administrative law. Like other laws they are subject to review by the courts and will be upheld unless found to be in conflict with federal or state constitutional provisions, statutes, or court decisions.

As the primary federal agency most directly concerned with education, the U.S. Department of Education issues regulations to implement federal education statutes and monitors compliance. Its ultimate power is the authority to withhold federal funds from states or districts found to be in noncompliance. Courts grant a good deal of discretion to the administrative agencies charged with implementing and monitoring federal statutes. Thus, the Department of Education exerts a significant amount of control over public education across the nation. The regulations issued by the Office of Civil Rights of the Department of Education in regard to the implementation of Title IX of the Education Amendments of 1972, the law prohibiting sex discrimination in the schools, are a prime example of the profound impact that administrative law can have on the operations of the schools. Among the other federal agencies that have significant interaction with schools are the Department of Agriculture, which administers the National School Lunch Act, and the Department of the Health and Human Services, which administers Head Start.

The state agency that has the most direct control over and responsibility for education is the state department of education. This agency generates a large body of administrative law as a result of the promulgation of numerous rules and regulations relating to such areas as certification of teachers and administrators, accreditation of schools, adoption of textbooks, curriculum standards, teacher and student testing, graduation requirements, and distribution of state funds.

SCHOOL BOARD POLICIES AND RULES

As previously stated, in all but one state—Hawaii, which has only one school district—state constitutions and statutes delegate the actual day-to-day operation of public elementary and secondary schools to the approximately 15,000 local school districts in the United States. The constitutions and statutes in these states also give to local school districts the authority to enact policies and rules necessary to carry out the responsibilities delegated to them. Each state defines somewhat differently the powers and duties of school boards. Some statutes are very general, others very specific; some outline mandatory duties, others discretionary duties. Some states with a tradition of strong local control may give school boards much more discretion than those with a tradition of more centralized control.

The school board acts through its adopted policies. The policies also spell out how the school district will operate. Policies impact virtually every aspect of district operations—employment of staff, administration of pupil services, curricular requirements, student discipline, school facilities, equipment, transportation, finance, and support services. School board policies guide the everyday actions of administrators, teachers, staff, and students. Unless the school board policy is arbitrary or in violation of federal or state constitutions, statutes, or department of education guidelines, the courts will not declare it invalid.

POWERS AND ORGANIZATION OF THE COURTS

Courts have three basic functions: (1) settle disputes between parties, (2) interpret laws and policies, and (3) determine the constitutionality of governmental actions. In school-related matters, the courts have generally taken the position that they will not intervene in a dispute unless all internal appeals have been exhausted. For example, when school board policy provides teachers with specific procedures and avenues of appeal for a disciplinary action (e.g., dismissal), these procedures and avenues of appeal must be exhausted before the courts will hear the appeal. The exception to this requirement is if the case involves an alleged violation of a constitutionally protected right.

Courts cannot become involved in education cases on their own initiative even if the situation seems to warrant judicial action. Some party affected by the action, law, or policy being challenged must bring a case to the court for resolution. The most common type of school case brought to the court requires the court to interpret laws within its jurisdiction. Another common type of education case requires the court to determine the constitutionality of state statutes or administrative rules or regulations.

The Federal Court System

Only two kinds of issues generally involve federal courts: those involving questions of interpretations of the federal Constitution or federal statutes, and those involving parties of different states. Certain cases will involve questions of both federal and state law. When this occurs, the federal court can decide on the state issue, but it must do so according to the rules governing the courts of that state. Most education cases that come to federal courts involve alleged violations of constitutionally protected rights or interpretations of federal statutes.

The federal court system consists of three levels of courts of general jurisdiction: a supreme court, courts of appeals, and district courts. In addition, the federal court system includes courts of special jurisdiction, such as the Customs Court or the Tax Court. Courts of special jurisdiction would normally not be involved in education cases.

The lowest level federal courts are district courts. There are over 100 district courts: at least one in each state, and in the more populated states, such as California, New York, and Texas, as many as four. The names of federal district courts reflect the geographic area they serve; for example, S.D. Ohio indicates the Southern District of Ohio. District courts are the courts of initiation or original jurisdiction for most cases filed in the federal court system, including most education cases. That is, they are where the cases begin or are initially filed. District courts are trial courts, meaning that evidence is heard in the case. The decisions of federal district courts have an automatic right of appeal to the next level of federal courts, U.S. circuit courts of appeals. The appeal is made to the circuit court by a filing of a *writ of certiorari,* a petition asking the case be moved to the higher court for review.

There are 13 circuit courts of appeals in the federal court system. Twelve of the circuit courts have jurisdiction over a specific geographic area (see Figure 1.1). A thirteenth, the Federal Circuit, has jurisdiction to hear appeals in specific areas of federal law (e.g., customs, copyright, international trade). A circuit court hears appeals from the decisions of federal district courts as well as certain federal administrative agencies. It hears arguments from attorneys, but it does not retry the case. A panel of judges, usually three, hears the case and can affirm, reverse, or modify the decision of the lower court. It can also send the case back to the lower court for determination of the facts or retrial.

The decision of a federal circuit court is binding only on federal district courts within its geographic jurisdiction. Circuit courts have no power over state courts and do not hear appeals from them, nor does the decision of one circuit court bind other circuit courts or the district courts in other circuits. Thus it is possible, and indeed it happens quite often, that one circuit court will rule one way on an issue, whereas another circuit court will rule in the reverse. For example, in the First, Fourth, Seventh, and Eighth circuits the appeals courts have said that school board policies restricting hair length violate students' First Amendment rights of symbolic expression, whereas courts in the Third, Fifth, Sixth, Ninth, and Tenth circuits have found no constitutional violations.

Figure 1.1 The Thirteen Federal Districts

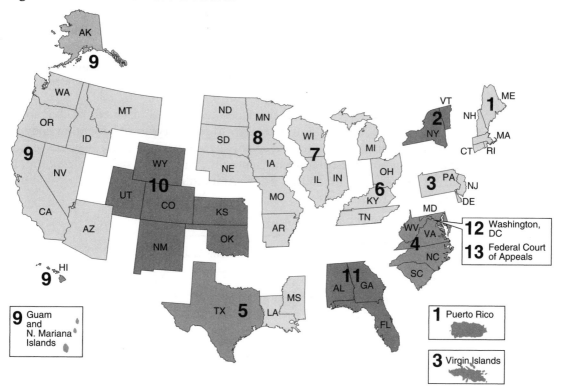

The highest federal court, indeed the highest court in the land, is the U.S. Supreme Court. Decisions of the Supreme Court are absolute: There is no appeal. If Congress or citizens do not agree with a decision of the Supreme Court, the only way they can mediate against the effect of the decision is to pass a law or to get the Court to reconsider the issue in a later case. A notable example in education of the Supreme Court reversing itself is the case of **Brown v. Board of Education of Topeka.**[11] In 1896, in **Plessy v. Ferguson,**[12] the Supreme Court had said that "separate but equal" public railcars for blacks and whites were constitutionally permissible. But in 1954, in the *Brown* decision, the Court reversed this position and ruled that separate educational facilities for blacks and whites were inherently unequal.

The Supreme Court hears cases on appeal not only from lower federal courts but also from state supreme courts if the state case involves a question of federal law. Thousands of cases are appealed to the Supreme Court each year but only a small number are heard. However, in recent years the number of education cases being appealed to the Supreme Court and heard by it has increased.

State Courts

Because most education cases do not involve the federal Constitution or federal statutes, state courts rather than federal courts handle them. Although the specific structure of the court system and the names given to courts vary from state to state, in most respects state court systems resemble the federal court system in terms of having courts of special jurisdiction, general jurisdiction, and courts of appeal (see Figure 1.2).

Most states have courts that are designated as courts of limited or special jurisdiction. The limitation may be related to the types of cases they may handle (e.g., probate courts or juvenile courts) or the amount in controversy (e.g., small claims courts or traffic courts). Generally, state court systems do not allow appeal of decisions from courts of limited jurisdiction.

Figure 1.2   State and Federal Court Systems

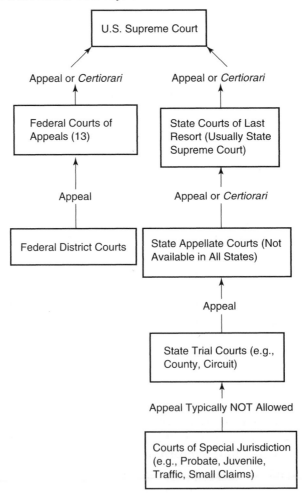

Go to the Companion Website at **http://www. prenhall.com/underwood,** select Chapter 1, then choose the Resources module to find a description of the court system in your state.

All states have courts of general jurisdiction, which are typically trial courts that hear witnesses, admit evidence, and, when appropriate, conduct jury trials. Depending on the state, courts of general jurisdiction may be referred to as district courts, county courts, circuit courts, superior courts, or supreme courts (in New York State). Appeals from decisions of state courts of general jurisdiction are made to state appellate courts, often referred to as courts of appeals. Like the federal appellate courts, state appellate courts do not retry cases but sit as a panel of judges to review the record of the trial court and hear attorneys' arguments.

The final appeal in state court systems is to the state supreme court. State supreme courts function as the final authority on questions related to the state constitution, state law, or school district policies. If the case involves federal issues, however, appeal may be taken to the U.S. Supreme Court. Decisions of state supreme courts have legally binding effect only in their own states, although their analysis and rationale may influence federal courts or courts in other states.

LOCATING AND READING EDUCATION CASES

The term *case* refers to the written opinions of judges. Cases are named for the parties to the litigation. The party bringing the suit is called the *plaintiff* and the party against whom the suit is brought is called the *defendant*. The plaintiff's name is always listed first. If the case is appealed the name of the party appealing is listed first and may be in reverse order from how it was listed in the original suit.

Soon after a case is decided the opinion is published in an official reporter. Opinions of the United States Supreme Court are published in the *United States Reporter* (U.S.), the official reports of Supreme Court decisions, as well as in two unofficial reports, the *Supreme Court Reporter* (S. Ct.), published by West Publishing Company, and the *United States Supreme Court Reports, Lawyers Edition* (L.Ed.), published by Lawyers Cooperative Publishing Company. Opinions by the U.S. Circuit Courts of Appeal are published in a series of *Federal Reporters* (F., F.2d, F.3d, and F.4d), and decisions of the federal district courts are reported in the *Federal Supplement Reporter* (F. Supp. and F. Supp.2d).

A case is referenced, or cited, by the name of the case, the volume and page number of the reporter in which it appears, the name of the reporter, and the year of the decision. For example, the citation for **Anderson v. City of Boston,** 375 F.3d 71 (1st Cir. 2004), a case dealing with the use of race in determining school assignment, means that the case can be found in volume 375 of the *Federal Reporter, Third Series,* on page 71, and the decision was made by the First Circuit Court of Appeals in 2004. The citation for the case **Bell v. Marseilles Elementary School,** 160 F. Supp.2d 883 (N.D. Ill. 2001) means that the case was decided by the Northern District Court of Illinois in 2001 and can be found in volume 160 of the *Federal Supplement, Second Series,* on page 883.

Decisions of state supreme and appellate courts are published in each state's official state reporter, as well as one of the regional reporters that are part of the West National Reporter System. The citation system is similar to that used for the federal courts. For example, a case citation of **Desilets v. Clearview Regional Bd. of Educ.**, 265 N.J. Super. 370, 627 A.2d 667 (N.J. Super. A.D. 1993) would mean that this New Jersey case can be found in the reports of the New Jersey Superior Court, volume 265, page 370, as well as in the *Atlantic Reporter, Second Series,* volume 627, page 667.

The regional reporters and the states they cover are as follows:

Atlantic Reporter (A.2d)
Connecticut, Delaware, District of Columbia courts of appeal, Maine, Maryland, New Hampshire, New Jersey, Pennsylvania, Rhode Island, and Vermont
North Eastern Reporter (N.E.2d)
Illinois, Indiana, Massachusetts, New York, and Ohio
North Western Reporter (N.W.2d)
Iowa, Michigan, Minnesota, Nebraska, North Dakota, South Dakota, and Wisconsin
Pacific Reporter (P.2d)
Arizona, California, Colorado, Hawaii, Idaho, Kansas, Montana, Nevada, New Mexico, Oklahoma, Oregon, Utah, Washington, and Wyoming
South Eastern Reporter (S.E.2d)
Georgia, North Carolina, South Carolina, Virginia, and West Virginia
Southern Reporter (So.2d)
Alabama, Florida, Louisiana, and Mississippi
South Western Reporter (S.W.2d)
Arkansas, Kentucky, Missouri, Tennessee, and Texas
California Reporter (Cal.Rptr.2d)
New York Supplement (N.Y.2d)

If you know the citation of a particular case, you can retrieve the full text of the decision from a university or public law library or from one of several online legal research sites, such as WestLaw or LEXIS/NEXIS available through university and law school libraries as well as many public libraries and most law firms. The reported case looks like that in Figure 1.3. As can be seen, the name of the case is typically followed by the name of the court rendering the decision and the date of the decision. What follows next, before the actual decision is presented, are two important features that West adds to the opinion of the court: (1) a case synopsis, which includes the name of the judge writing the decision and ends with the decision, and (2) the West topic headings and key numbering system. The topic heading and number are important to doing legal research as they enable

Figure 1.3 Case in West Reporter

393 U.S. 503   TINKER V. DES MOINES INDEPENDENT COM. SCH. DIST.
Cite as 80 S.Ct. 733 (1969):

393 U.S. 503
John F. TINKER and Mary Beth Tinker,
Minors, etc., et al., Petitioners,

v.

Case name DES MOINES INDEPENDENT COM-
MUNITY SCHOOL DISTRICT et al.
No. 21

Argued Nov. 12, 1968.

Date of decision Decided Feb. 24, 1969.

Synopsis Action against school district, its board of directors and certain administrative officials and teachers to recover nominal damages and obtain an injunction against enforcement of a regulation promulgated by principals of schools prohibiting wearing of black armbands by students while on school facilities. The United States District Court for the Southern District of Iowa, Central Division, 258 F.Supp. 971, dismissed complaint and plaintiffs appealed. The Court of Appeals for the Eighth Circuit, 383 F.2d 988, considered the case en banc and affirmed without opinion when it was equally divided and certiorari was granted. The United States Supreme Court, Mr. Justice Fortas, held that, in absence of demonstration of any facts which might reasonably have led school authorities to forecast substantial disruption of, or material interference with, school activities or any showing that disturbances or disorders on school premises in fact occurred when students wore black armbands on their sleeves to exhibit their disapproval of Vietnam hostilities, regula-

tion prohibiting wearing armbands to schools and providing for suspension of any student refusing to remove such was an unconstitutional denial of students' right of expression of opinion.

Reversed and remanded. **Court decision**

Mr. Justice Black and Mr. Justice Harlan dissented.

1. Constitutional Law ☛90
Wearing of armband for purpose of expressing certain views is type of symbolic act that is within free speech clause of First Amendment. U.S.C.A. Const. Amend. 1.

2. Constitutional Law ☛90
Pure speech is entitled to comprehensive protection under the First Amendment. U.S.C.A.Const. Amend. 1.

3. Constitutional Law ☛90
First Amendment rights, applied in **Headnotes** light of special characteristics of school environment, are available to teachers and students. U.S.C.A.Const. Amend. 1. **West topic and key number**

4. Constitutional Law ☛90
Neither students nor teachers shed their constitutional rights to freedom of speech or expression at the schoolhouse gate. U.S.C.A.Const. Amend. 1.

5. Schools and School Districts ☛169
State and school authorities have comprehensive authority, consistent with fundamental constitutional safeguards, to prescribe and control conduct in the schools.

Source: West Reporter.

the researcher to find related cases that have one or more of the same topics or key numbers. The number of topics and key numbers presented will vary by case. Each topic and key number is followed by a brief headnote.

Although reading law cases can sometimes be challenging for the novice, the more one reads cases, the easier it becomes to understand the language of the law, a task that references such as *Black's Law Dictionary* can make easier. Throughout this text we encourage students to read cases in their entirety by going to the Companion Website at **http://www.prenhall.com/underwood**, selecting the chapter number, than choosing the Cases module. We hope they will take advantage of this opportunity.

GUIDING LEGAL PRINCIPLES

- The U.S. Constitution is the supreme law of the land, and although it does not mention education many of its provisions, particularly several key amendments—First, Fourth, Fifth, Eighth, Tenth, and Fourteenth—have significant impact on the operation of schools and the conduct of teachers and students.
- By accepting federal education funds, school boards agree to comply with specific programmatic conditions and certain civil rights laws.
- Within the boundaries of the federal and state constitutions a state legislature has the absolute power to enact laws regulating the operation of the schools.
- The wording of the education clause in the state constitution is important to the courts in determining whether particular legislative actions are permissible or required.
- School districts are created by the state and exercise only that authority the state delegates to them.
- Courts cannot initiate cases; they must be brought to them.
- In deciding the cases before them, courts must follow past case law made by courts superior to them in the state or federal court system.
- Decisions by the U.S. Supreme Court apply to everyone. Other court decisions apply only to those within their geographic jurisdiction.

MORE ON THE WEB

*Go to the Companion Website at **http://www.prenhall.com/underwood**, select Chapter 1, choose the More on the Web module to connect to the site mentioned.*

Look on the United States Supreme Court multimedia website, **http://www.oyez.org**, to see whether any of the cases listed under The Pending Docket are education cases. If so, what are the facts of the case and what is the question(s) before the court? While at the site, take the "Virtual Tour" of the Supreme Court and discover which other justice is on the elephant in the picture with Justice Ruth Bader Ginsberg.

Click on "More Featured Audio" and then "Most Popular Audio." Listen to the oral arguments for ***Tinker v. Des Moines***. What other important case involving religious expression is mentioned as having been decided that same day. In the *Tinker* case, which one of the students did not wear a black armband on the first day? What was the argument given by the school district in support of the suspension of John and Mary Beth Tinker and Christopher Echardt?

ENDNOTES

1. *Clark v. Libscomb,* 269 F.3d 494 (5th Cir. 2001).
2. *S. J. Lemoine v. St. Landry Parish School,* 527 So.2d 1150 (La. App. 3d Cir. 1988).
3. 336 F.3d 185 (2nd Cir. 2003).
4. *Ingraham v. Wright,* 430 U.S. 651 (1977).
5. Collins, G. J. (1969). Constitutional and legal basis for state action. In E. Fuller & J. B. Pearson (Eds.), *Education in the states, Nationwide development since 1900.* Washington, DC: National Education Association; Underwood, J. (1995). School finance adequacy. *University of Michigan Journal of Law Reform, 28*(3).
6. *Carpio v. Tucson High Scool District No. 1 of Pima County,* 517 P.2d 1288 (1974).
7. 29 U.S.C.A. § 651 (2005).
8. Fair Labor Standards Act of 1938, 29 U.S.C. § 201 *et seq.* (2004).
9. No Child Left Behind Act of 2001, 20 U.S.C. § 6301 *et seq.* (2005).
10. Black, H. C. (1990). *Black's law dictionary.* St. Paul, MN: West.
11. 347 U.S. 483 (1954).
12. 163 U.S. 537 (1896).

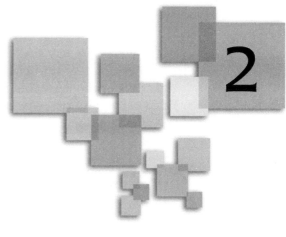

EMPLOYMENT AND TENURE

As discussed in chapter 1, within the framework provided by state and federal constitutions and statutes, the state has complete power to operate and regulate public education. Through its legislature, state department of education, local school boards, and in some instance school-based councils, the state promulgates the rules and regulations for the operation of the schools. Among these rules and regulations are those establishing the terms and conditions of employment. The areas most often covered by state statutes and regulations are those dealing with certification, citizenship and residency requirements, health and physical requirements, competency testing, contracts, tenure, reductions in force, and the collective negotiations process. This chapter discusses each of these briefly. After reading this chapter you will be able to

- Identify the most common requirements for certification of prospective teachers.
- Discuss the arguments in favor of requiring teachers to be U.S. citizens and residents of the employing district.
- Explain the health and physical requirements to which teachers may be held.
- Evaluate the issues surrounding teacher assessment.
- Outline the elements of an employment contract.
- Explain the process in obtaining tenure and the legal issues surrounding the major steps in the process.
- Review the major legal challenges to reductions in force.
- Discuss teachers' rights in relation to collective negotiations.

CERTIFICATION

To qualify for most teaching, administrative, and other professional positions in the public schools, an individual must hold a valid certificate or license. The intent of the certification requirement is to ensure that the holder has met established state standards and is qualified for employment in the area for which the certificate is issued. The courts have held that states have not only the right but also the duty to ensure that school district employees meet certain minimum qualifications for employment. As previously discussed, the NCLB Act of 2001 requires that by 2005–2006 all newly hired teachers in schools receiving Title I funds be certified in the level or subject to be taught. A certificate does not guarantee employment; it only makes the holder eligible for employment.

All states have established the requirements necessary for prospective teachers to obtain certification. Although these will vary some from state to state, these requirements typically include a college degree with minimum credit hours in specific curricular areas, evidence of specific job experience, "good moral character," a specified age, U.S. citizenship, the signing of a loyalty oath, good health, and a minimum score on a test of basic skills. Most states require some type of standardized test or performance assessment for teacher education programs, initial certification, or renewal, the most common being the National Teachers Exam.

Go to the Companion Website at http://www. prenhall.com/underwood, select Chapter 2, then choose the Resources *module to find the state-specific teacher certification requirements.*

An applicant can obtain state certification in two ways. First, the candidate can make an application to the state certification agency, which will assess the candidate's transcripts and experiences against the state requirements. Or, second, the applicant can be recommended for certification after graduation from a state-approved teacher preparation program.

In cases involving whether candidates for certification meet the required state standards, the courts have generally strictly interpreted the standards and have overturned the denial of certification only when unsupported by substantial evidence or if the statutory or constitutional rights of the applicant have been violated. In a case from Florida a local district recommended that a prospective candidate not be granted state certification because he had failed to finish the requirements of the certification program. The state board agreed with the recommendation and denied him certification. The applicant challenged the decision. The court found that the state board and the school had based their decisions on reasonable evidence.[1]

Where specified certification requirements exist, failure to meet the requirements or giving untruthful responses on the application can result in termination of employment or other adverse employment decision. For example, in a Texas case a prospective teacher entered into a contract with a school district conditioned on him filing his certificate with the personnel director no later than the issuance of the first payroll check (in this case, September 20). The prospective teacher had failed the exam required for certification twice before the school year began, but eventually passed it and so informed the district on October 20. In the meantime the district had hired another teacher. The prospective teacher sued the district for breach of contract but did not win.[2] In another case a teacher who had been convicted of two felonious counts of cocaine delivery 20 years previously indicated on his application for a professional teaching certificate that he had never been convicted of a felony. When the state department of education later discovered the statement was untrue, it suspended his teaching certificate for two years.[3]

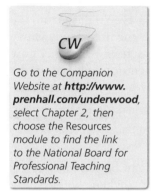

Go to the Companion Website at *http://www. prenhall.com/underwood*, select Chapter 2, then choose the Resources module to find the link to the National Board for Professional Teaching Standards.

Acquiring a certification does not mean that a teacher is certified for life. The initial certificate, as well as any renewed certificate, is good for only a limited number of years, typically 10. In order to be recertified in most states teachers are required to earn a specified number of continuing education units (CEUs). As discussed later, a few states and school districts have imposed a testing requirement for recertification. Teachers may earn CEUs by taking approved college courses or by attending workshops, in-service training, or other activities approved by the school district. In about half the states, obtaining certification by the National Board for Professional Teaching Standards (NBPTS) will qualify a teacher for recertification.

In addition the agency responsible for granting certification can also suspend and revoke certification. State statute or regulations generally set out the reasons for suspension and revocation, which typically are parallel to the reasons for dismissing a teacher for cause (e.g., immorality, dishonesty). For example, in **Prof. Standards Commission v. Denham**[4] the court upheld the state agency's suspension of a teacher's certificate for changing a student's answers on a standardized exam and in **Stelzer v. State Board of Educ.**[5] the court upheld the agency's revocation of a teacher's certificate after she was convicted of welfare fraud.

CITIZENSHIP AND RESIDENCY REQUIREMENTS

The courts have upheld both citizenship and residency for certification and/or as a condition of employment. With regard to the citizenship requirement, the U.S. Supreme Court has held that education is among those governmental functions that is "so bound up with the operation of the state as a governmental entity as to permit the exclusion from those functions of all persons who have not become part of the process of self-government."[6] The Court also acknowledged a rational relationship between the citizenship requirement and a legitimate state purpose: The Court found the requirement justified because of the critical part teachers play "in developing students' attitudes toward government and understanding the role of citizens in our society."[7]

Not only may U.S. citizenship be required for certification; if state statutes permit, school districts may also require employees to reside within the districts. (See the Residency Requirement for Apple Valley School District.)

RESIDENCY REQUIREMENT FOR APPLE VALLEY SCHOOL DISTRICT

Because there is value in having school employees committed to the community, the educational atmosphere is enhanced by the increased opportunities for parent–teacher communication when employees are residents of the community and because the staffing of extracurricular programs is jeopardized by the employment of nonresidents, it shall be the policy of this district to hire only persons who will become residents of the district. Residency as a condition of employment shall be included on every contract offered to newly hired personnel. When a nonresident is appointed, he or she will have 90 days from the beginning of the school term to establish residency. Only the Board may waive this policy and then only for a critical reason. Current school personnel now living outside the District are encouraged to establish their domicile within the District. The Board will hire only persons who are, or who will become, residents of the school district.

These residency requirements have been upheld if it can be shown that a rational basis exists for the requirement. In a case on point, when the Pittsburgh school district adopted a residency requirement for all future employees of the district, the Pittsburgh Federation of Teachers challenged it. The court upheld the requirement and agreed that the district's stated reasons for it—that employees would have an increased personal knowledge of conditions in the district, would feel a greater personal stake in the district, would pay taxes in the district, and would have reduced absenteeism and tardiness—were all rational, legitimate, and justifiable.[8] In another case with the same results, the Arkansas Supreme Court upheld a school district requirement that teachers live in the district or within 10 miles of city limits. The court ruled that the policy did not violate equal protection, even though the policy did not apply to noncertificated personnel, and that the policy was "rationally related to community involvement and district identity as it related to tax base support of district tax levies, and [the] 10 mile limit was reasonable commuting distance and was not arbitrary."[9]

HEALTH AND PHYSICAL REQUIREMENTS

Most states and school boards have adopted health and physical requirements for teachers. The courts have recognized such requirements are necessary to ensure that employees can meet their contractual obligations and to protect the health and welfare of students and other employees. In districts that have adopted health and physical requirements, the courts have upheld the release or reassignment of employees when their physical or mental condition made it impossible

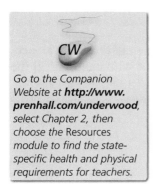

*Go to the Companion Website at **http://www. prenhall.com/underwood**, select Chapter 2, then choose the* Resources *module to find the state-specific health and physical requirements for teachers.*

for them to meet their contractual duties. The courts have also upheld school districts in requiring medical examinations to determine employees' fitness to perform their duties. For example, the court supported the school board against a claim of violation of the Americans With Disabilities Act when it denied tenure to a guidance counselor who suffered from depression, panic attacks, and dermatological symptoms associated with stress, and who had missed 41 days of work during the probationary period.[10]

The courts have also upheld school districts when they have required employees to take medical examinations to determine their fitness to perform their duties. For example, a Michigan court upheld a school board that suspended a teacher for 3 years and required the teacher to undergo physical and mental examinations at the board's expense before returning to work. The court determined that the district had a legitimate concern, following several instances of misconduct and insubordination, that the teacher might be experiencing a breakdown.[11]

Although the courts have upheld school district health and physical requirements, they require that such requirements not be arbitrarily applied, be specific to the position, and not violate state and federal laws intended to protect the rights of the disabled. For example, Section 504 of the Rehabilitation Act of 1973, which protects "otherwise qualified" handicapped individuals from discrimination, served as the basis for the U.S. Supreme Court decision in **School District of Nassau County v. Arline,**[12] which overturned the dismissal of an Arkansas teacher with tuberculosis. (For further discussion and summary of *Arline* see chapter 10.) According to the Court, when discrimination is based solely on *fear of contamination* it is considered discrimination against those with disabilities. The Supreme Court instructed the lower court to determine whether the teacher posed a "significant risk" that would preclude her from being "otherwise qualified" and whether the district could reasonably accommodate her condition. Ultimately the court found the teacher posed little risk and was otherwise qualified, and ordered her reinstated with back pay.

The significant risk standard articulated by the court in *Arline* and the provisions of Section 504 have been relied on by teachers in cases involving AIDS. In the leading case, **Chalk v. U.S. District Cent. Dist. of California,**[13] the U.S. district court relied heavily on the significant risk standard to determine when a contagious disease would prevent an individual from being "otherwise qualified." In applying the "significant risk of communicating" standard in this instance, the court found that the overwhelming consensus of medical and scientific opinion regarding the nature and transmission of AIDS did not support a conclusion that Chalk posed a significant risk of communicating the disease to children or others through casual social contact.

As an example of typical requirements imposed before hiring, see the Caanan District Hiring Policy.

CANAAN DISTRICT HIRING POLICY

Persons interested in securing employment with the Board of Education shall complete all necessary information forms before employment is finalized. The applicant who can best fill the requirements of the position shall be employed.

Administrative Implemental Procedures

1. A written application form must be completed.
2. Applicant shall possess established educational requirements.
3. The Division of Personnel Services shall administer and the applicant shall achieve a passing score on any proficiency and/or aptitude tests considered relevant to the position for which application is being made.
4. First consideration shall be given to qualified, current employees in filling vacancies. Unless an emergency exists, notice of vacancies will be posted at the Education Management and Resource Center.
5. In all hiring and assigning of employees and in all compensation, benefits, and other terms and conditions of employment, the school district shall comply with all applicable federal and state laws with regard to nondiscrimination on account of race, color, religion, sex, age, handicap, national origin, or ancestry.
6. Employment requirements relating to special programs will be followed.
7. A medical exam, including substance abuse testing for illegal drugs, shall be required of all persons offered employment who are to be assigned half-time or more positions, and evidence of good health and the absence of disqualifying impairments and/or deficiencies must be submitted including a medical examination and health certification forms.
8. Applicants being offered a permanent position must pass a physical examination prior to being employed.
9. Applicants being employed in a temporary or part-time position are required to submit a Health Certification form.
10. All forms and requirements necessary to secure entry on payroll and personnel records (including Loyalty Oath and Race Statement) must be completed.
11. At the time of employment, a copy of the applicant's Social Security Card must be made and placed in the respective personnel file.
12. An employee who has falsified any preemployment information is subject to immediate dismissal.
13. Employees eligible for State Public Employees Retirement System benefits shall provide the Personnel Services Division with a copy of their birth certificate. A photographic copy of the birth certificate will be made and placed in the employee's personnel file.

CANAAN DISTRICT HIRING POLICY

14. An employee shall provide the Personnel Services Division with a recent photograph or snapshot.
15. Identification cards will be issued to all employees. ID cards will be distributed by administrators or supervisors, and it will be their responsibility to return invalid ID cards to the Personnel Services Division.
16. New employees must complete the I-9 Employment Eligibility Verification Form, which is required by the Immigration Reform and Control Act of 1986. All new employees hired by Canaan School District must be United States citizens or lawfully authorized alien workers.

TEACHER TESTING

Public concern about the quality of the teaching force in recent years, combined with the influence of the No Child Left Behind Act, has led to an increase in state testing of teachers. As of 2002, some form of state testing for initial certification of teachers is required in 43 states (see Table 2.1 to see the requirement in your state). In over one-half the states prospective teachers are tested in professional pedagogy and subject area competency. The No Child Left Behind Act requires that all newly hired teachers in schools that receive Title I funds be highly qualified. For new elementary teachers this means they must pass a rigorous state test of the elementary curriculum and teaching skills. New middle and high school teachers must pass a rigorous state test in the academic subject they are to teach or complete an academic major in every subject they will teach. The most commonly used tests are the customized state tests developed by National Evaluation Systems and the Praxis series developed by the Educational Testing Service.

Challenges to the use of tests for certification purposes have been made in several states because they tend to disproportionately disqualify more minorities than nonminorities. (As an example, see the In the News feature.) In these cases the courts have upheld the use of the tests if they are significantly related to the job for which applicants are being evaluated and are rationally related to a legitimate state purpose.[14] For example, a recent case in California involved a challenge to the use of the California Basic Education Skills Test (CBEST) by Mexican American educators who were disqualified by the test. The Ninth Circuit Court of Appeals upheld the use of the test and ruled that the state had established the validity of the test by setting cutoff scores that were "reasonable and consistent with normal expectations of acceptable proficiency with the workforce."[15]

In addition to testing for initial certification or recertification, in an isolated number of cases school districts have sought to test practicing teachers to determine their competency. The Massachusetts State Board of Education, for example, enacted a regulation requiring math teachers in low-performing schools and teachers teaching math but not certified in math to take a math assessment test.

Table 2.1 States Requiring Testing for Initial Certification of Teachers and Test Used, 2002

| State | Assessment for Certification | | | | |
	Basic Skills Exam	Subject Matter Exam	General Knowledge Exam	Knowledge of Teaching Exam	Assessment of Teaching Performance
1	2	3	4	5	6
Alabama	(^{1})	(^{2})		(^{2})	X
Alaska	X				
Arizona		X		X	X
Arkansas	X	X		X	X
California	X	(^{3})			
Colorado		X			
Connecticut	X	X			
Delaware	X				
District of Columbia	X	X			X
Florida	X	X	X	X	X
Georgia	X	X			
Hawaii	X	X		X	
Idaho					
Illinois	X	X			
Indiana	X	X	X	X	
Iowa				X	
Kansas				X	
Kentucky	(^{1})				X
Louisiana	X	X	X	X	X
Maine	X		X	X	
Maryland	X	X		X	X
Massachusetts		(^{4})			
Michigan	X	X	(^{5})		
Minnesota	X		X	X	
Mississippi		X		X	
Missouri	(^{1})	X		(^{6})	
Montana	X				
Nebraska	X				
Nevada	X	X		X	
New Hampshire	X	X			

| State | Assessment for Certification | | | | |
	Basic Skills Exam	Subject Matter Exam	General Knowledge Exam	Knowledge of Teaching Exam	Assessment of Teaching Performance
1	2	3	4	5	6
New Jersey		x	([7])		x
New Mexico	x		x	x	
New York			x	x	
North Carolina	([1])	x			
North Dakota	([1])		x	x	
Ohio		x		x	x
Oklahoma	x	x	x	([8])	x
Oregon	x	x			([9])
Pennsylvania	x	x	x	x	
Rhode Island			x		
South Carolina	x	x		x	x
South Dakota	x	x			x
Tennessee	([10])	x		x	x
Texas		x		x	
Utah				([11])	
Vermont	x				
Virginia	x	x			
Washington	([1])				
West Virginia	x	x		x	x
Wisconsin	x				
Wyoming					

[1]For admission to teacher education program.
[2]Institution's exit exam.
[3]Subject matter exam or completion of an approved subject matter program.
[4]Two-part exam covers communication and literacy skills and the subject matter knowledge for the certificate.
[5]Elementary certificate exam (subject-area exam).
[6]If no subject knowledge assessment is designed.
[7]For elementary education.
[8]Required for standard certificate.
[9]For Oregon graduates.
[10]Basic skills exams in reading, math, and writing are covered in the Praxis Pre-professional Skills Test.
[11]Entry year requirement.
Source. From *Digest of education statistics, 2003,* by U.S. Department of Education, National Center for Education Statistics, 2004, Washington, DC: NCES.

An obscure trial challenging New York State rules requiring teachers to pass competency tests wrapped up testimony in a federal court in New York City last month. More than 3,300 black and Latino teachers sued the state, saying their careers were derailed after they flunked certification exams.

To the teachers, the issue is about fairness. They claim the tests for basic math and literacy skills have nothing to do with their performance in the classroom. And they say because minority teachers failed at far higher rates than whites, the tests were biased. . . .

Certainly, many of the New York teachers who are suing the state deserve sympathy. They were already on the job—some with many years of classroom experience. But the general-knowledge tests they failed are important. During the testimony, education experts established links between testing—for both basic skills and subject content—and classroom competency. . . .

Test scores are not the only factor in determining a good teacher. But they are a gauge school reformers can't afford to lose.

Source: From "Teacher Tests Key to Reform, May 13, 2005, *Education Week,* p. 14A.

It used the results in developing individual professional development plans. On challenge by the Massachusetts Federation of Teachers, the court upheld the regulation finding it was within the board's authority and did not violate the teachers' rights of due process and equal protection.

THE EMPLOYMENT CONTRACT

Both tenured and nontenured teachers hold their positions under a contract. The contract defines the rights and responsibilities of the teachers and the school board. The general principles of contract law apply to a teacher's employment contract. That is, for the contract to be valid it must contain the basic elements of (1) offer and acceptance, (2) legally competent parties, (3) consideration, (4) legal subject matter, and (5) proper form. In addition, the employment contract must meet the specific requirements of applicable state law.

Offer and Acceptance

To be valid, a contract must contain an offer by one party and an acceptance by another. "For a communication to be an offer, it must create a reasonable expectation in the offeree that the offeror is willing to enter a contract on the basis of the offered terms."[16] Typically the offer of employment specifies that acceptance of the offer must be made within a certain period of time of the offer. Until the teacher to whom the offer is made accepts the offer (i.e., acceptance cannot be made by a spouse or relative), the contract is not in force. For this reason it is important that the prospective employee render the acceptance in writing and within the specified period of time.

Legally Competent Parties

Only a school board has the legal authority to contract. The superintendent or other authorized employee may recommend employment but only the school board may enter into the contract. Unfortunately, every year there are instances where prospective teachers have relied on the presumed authority of a principal, superintendent, or other employee to offer a contract only to discover that that person lacked the authority to enter into a binding contract. Moreover, a school board can enter into a contract only when it is a legally constituted body. That is, contracts issued when a quorum of the board was not present or at an illegally called meeting of the board (e.g., the meeting was illegal because adequate notice of the school board meeting was not given) are not valid. In these instances the law does not consider the board a competent party because it lacks legal status. By the same token, a teacher or other employee who lacks the necessary certification or other requirements (e.g., has not reached a specified age) is not considered to be competent party for contractual purposes, nor are individuals who are mentally ill, impaired by drugs or alcohol, or under duress at the time of entering into the contract.

Consideration

Consideration is something of value or importance that persuades a contracting party to enter into a contract. As it relates to teacher contracts, consideration is the teacher salary. The salary offered by the school district must be clear and definite. Although school boards have considerable latitude in the matter of employee compensation, they must abide by any state statutes regarding minimum salary levels as well as the terms of any contracts negotiated with employee associations. In the absence of any teacher performance pay or career ladder program, school boards apply teacher salary offers uniformly to individuals who have the same preparation and experience and perform the same duties.

Legal Subject Matter

To be valid a contract must be for a legal subject matter. That is, a contract for the commission of a crime (e.g., the purchase of illegal substances or the performance of illegal services) is not enforceable. Nor can the terms of the contract circumvent state or federal requirements or statutes, common law, or public policy.[17] For example, districts cannot contract with employees to pay less than the federal minimum wage.

Proper Form

To be enforceable, the contract must be in the form required by state statute or regulations. Most states require that the employment contract be signed and in writing. Some statutes also specify the provisions that are to be included in the contract. Figure 2.1 provides an example of a contract for a nontenured teacher.

CW

Go to the Companion Website at **http://www. prenhall.com/underwood**, select Chapter 2, then choose the Resources module to find the state-specific requirements for valid teacher contracts.

Figure 2.1 Teacher Contract

2004–2005
Certificated Teacher Contract

Name   Base Salary   Degree

The Contract ("Contract") is made the   day of   between the above-name person ("Employee") and the Governing Board of Tempe School District No. 3, of Maricopa County, Arizona ("District"), and supersedes any and all previously issued contracts.

The Employee, who holds a legal certificate to teach in the public elementary schools of Arizona during the period of this Contract, hereby agrees to teach such grade, grades, or subjects in the District as the Superintendent of the District may assign for the 2004–2005 school year. The school year is to be determined by the Governing Board. The Employee is expected to fulfill the terms of the Contract unless s/he has been released from the Contract by the Governing Board. Policies, procedures and regulations prescribed or approved by the Governing Board shall be a part of this Contract. Loss of certificate for any reason and at any time during the term of this Contract shall constitute grounds for immediate termination of this contract.

In consideration of services rendered satisfactorily, the Governing Board agrees to pay the Employee the sum listed above as a Base Salary established by the Teacher Salary Schedule for the 2004–2005 school year that incorporates the 20% of monies allocated by Proposition 301 for teacher base salary increases. In addition to the Base Salary, Employee may receive Performance Pay and Classroom Site Fund compensation if Employee qualifies for such monies as determined by the district in accordance with the District's Proposition 301 Performance Pay Plan ("Plan"). The amount of Performance Pay and Classroom Site Fund compensation, and the method and timing of payment of such monies, shall be specified in the Plan.

Employee expressly acknowledges and agrees that if the Legislature fails to fund fully or partially the amounts appropriated for the salary and benefits categories of the District budget, and/or the estimated amounts for Proposition 301 sales tax collection do not materialize during the contract year, the Board shall reduce pro rata the total amount of compensation due under the Contract in accordance with A.R.S. 15–544, and Plan. This includes, but is not limited to, monies earned pursuant to the District's Plan, Base Salary and Classroom Site Fund monies, all of which have been derived from said Proposition 301 sales tax collections. Such Compensation from Proposition 301 monies must be renewed each year and is not subject to the provisions of A.R.S. 15–544 since Classroom Site Fund and Performance Pay is not considered general or base salary.

To be valid, this Contract must be returned without modification within thirty (30) days from the date written above.

Done at a legally convened meeting of the said Governing Board.

_____   _____

              Date   Signature of Teacher

Approved by the Governing Board
Tempe School District No. 3
Maricopa County, Arizona

Please return the original and one copy to the Human Resources Department.

Source: Tempe School District No. 3, Maricopa County, Arizona.

Terms of the Contract: Duties and Responsibilities

The teacher's rights and obligations of employment are derived from the employment contract. The contract will typically include those rules and regulations of the school district applicable to employment conditions. Even if the rules and regulations of the school board have not been specifically included in the contract, the courts have held that the rules and regulations, as well as all applicable state statutes, are part of the contract. However, before employees can be held accountable for adherence to the rules and regulations, the school board must inform employees of its rules and regulations, not only at the time of initial employment but also on an ongoing basis as they are revised. This point is especially important because the courts have held that, even though a teacher has tenure, each yearly contract is considered a new contract and includes whatever rules and regulations are in effect at the time of the new contract.

In most states state law controls certain terms of the contract, and so they are not subject to negotiation or to the discretion of the local school board. For example, tenure and due process rights granted by state statutes cannot be changed by the contract offered by the local school district. A number of states require that certain terms (e.g., salary, beginning and ending date of the contract, and duties) be detailed in the contract. In addition, the terms of the contract cannot conflict with the terms or rights of employees detailed in any collective bargaining agreement.

Whether they are detailed in the contract or not, the courts have held that employees may be required to perform certain tasks incidental to classroom activities (e.g., supervision of field trips, playground, study hall, bus, and cafeteria; supervision of extracurricular activities; and attendance at open houses). Teachers cannot, however, be required to drive a bus, perform janitorial duties, or perform duties unrelated to the school program. The primary consideration of the courts in reviewing duty assignments is whether the duty has been expressly provided for in the contract and whether the duty in question can be considered part of normal school operations and is reasonable.[18] If an employee refuses to perform extracurricular duties required as a condition of employment, regardless of whether the duties are specified under contract, the court may construe such refusal as insubordination justifying removal.[19] For example, in an Alabama case a guidance counselor was dismissed for refusing to perform his assigned rotational supervision duty before school. He maintained that counselors should be exempt from such supervision. The court upheld the dismissal.[20]

OUTSIDE EMPLOYMENT

It is not uncommon for teachers to be employed outside the school during the summer, on the weekend, or even after school hours during the week. Although school districts cannot interfere with teachers' employment during the summer when they are not on contract, some schools districts have adopted policies regulating or forbidding employment during the school year. (See the example Sunshine School District Policy on Outside Employment on page 25.) The courts have upheld such school board policies that regulate outside employment as long as they are not arbitrary and are uniformly applied to all teachers.

TENURE

Typically tenure is a status conferred by state statute upon teachers who have served a specified probationary period that guarantees them continued employment unless the district can establish "good and just cause" for dismissal (chapter 4 treats dismissal of both tenured and nontenured teachers), or as a necessary reduction in force as discussed later in this chapter. (When tenure is not created by state statute or regulation, the local school district itself may create it.) Tenure benefits the state by helping to create a permanent and qualified teaching force. Tenure benefits teachers by providing them stability of employment and greater rights than those held by nontenured teachers. Tenure is a right conferred upon teachers by statute; it is not a constitutional right. However, once a teacher is granted tenure the teacher is said to have a "property right" to continued employment, which cannot be taken away without due process. Tenure is awarded for teaching

---

SUNSHINE SCHOOL DISTRICT POLICY ON OUTSIDE EMPLOYMENT

The board believes the primary responsibility of employees is to the duties of their position within the school district as outlined in their job description. The board considers an employee's duties as part of a regular, full-time position as full-time employment. The board expects such employees to give the responsibilities of their positions in the school district precedence over any other employment.

assignments, not for extracurricular assignments such as coaching. Depending on state law, administrative positions may or may not be eligible for tenure.

Because state statute typically creates the tenure status (referred to in some states as "continuing" status), specific provisions vary from state to state. Most tenure statutes specify the requirements and procedures both for acquiring tenure and for dismissing a tenured teacher. Generally, tenure can be acquired only in the area of certification. When tenure is created by the state, the local school board cannot alter the terms of its acquisition and the procedures and grounds for dismissal.

Tenure statutes normally require the successful completion of a probationary period before the awarding of tenure, usually 3 years. During this period the probationary teacher is issued a contract valid for a fixed period of time (e.g., 1 or 2 years). Renewal of the contract at the end of each term is at the discretion of the school board.

Legal issues surrounding the probationary period primarily have involved questions of what constitutes service during the probationary period and what protections are afforded probationary teachers. Most tenure statutes require "regular and continuous" teaching service during the probationary period. When teachers have spent a part of the probationary period as guidance counselors, administrators, homebound teachers, social workers, or other positions outside the regular classroom, questions have arisen as to their eligibility for tenure under the "regular" service requirement. Similar issues have arisen when service was as a substitute teacher, less than full time, less than the full school year, or interrupted by a leave. In deciding each of these cases the courts have attempted to interpret the state tenure statutes to protect the teacher's rights while maintaining the discretion and flexibility of school officials in the administration of personnel matters. For example, in **Scheer v. Independent School District**,[21] the Oklahoma Supreme Court held that a teacher was not credited with years of service toward tenure during the time she was teaching under a temporary contract. She had previously taught under a regular appointment for 3 years, but for her fourth (and final year toward tenure) year she was offered only a temporary contract. When she was not granted tenure after the fourth year she filed suit. The court found that teachers who teach under temporary contracts are exempt from the tenure statutes.

The successful completion of the probationary period does not guarantee a probationary teacher continued employment. In an Alabama case a probationary teacher had received a positive evaluation each of her 3 years and had been recommended for retention but was not continued. When the teacher challenged the board's action the court said that the fact that the district had adopted an

Go to the Companion Website at *http://www. prenhall.com/underwood*, select Chapter 2, then choose the Resources module to find state-specific teacher tenure provisions.

evaluation policy for teachers and that the nontenured teacher had received a favorable evaluation under the policy did not create a right of employment.[22] However, although school districts are not required to continue the employment of a teacher who has successfully completed the term of a contract, most states do require that the school board give a nontenured teacher whose contract will not be renewed timely notice (typically no later than April 1) of the nonrenewal. (See Table 4.1 for an overview of the due process rights of nontenured teachers.)

In some states tenure is automatically awarded at the end of the probationary period unless the school board gives notice of nonrenewal. In other states the school board must take formal action to award tenure. In cases in which school officials fail to follow applicable state laws, the courts will attempt to balance the public policy interests of employing competent and qualified teachers against the rights of the individual teacher. As a result, in a number of cases in which the school board did not give timely notice of nonrenewal, the courts have ordered that the teacher be rehired, but still as a probationary teacher, until the proper evaluation and notification take place. In an equal number of other cases in which the school board failed to follow state tenure laws, the courts have said, "It is the school district, not the teacher, that must bear the consequences," and the teacher has been granted full tenure status.[23] However, trifling or insignificant violations of policy or state statutes have been decided in favor of school boards.

REDUCTION IN FORCE

Declining enrollments, school reorganizations or consolidations, financial cutbacks, curriculum changes, and other reasons may result in a reduction in the number of employees needed by a school district. Forty-six states have adopted statutes that address reductions in force (RIF). Typically, these statutes address the accepted reasons for a RIF, the order of release of employees, and the order of their reinstatement. Some statutes also provide detail as to the procedures to be followed and the protections that are to be given teachers in the RIF process. School board policies and collective bargaining agreements often address these same issues. These statutes, policies, or agreements usually require that the school board give the employee adequate and timely notice of an imminent RIF and the right to a hearing.[24]

The legal challenges to reductions in force usually involve three issues: (1) whether the abolishment of the position is justified, (2) whether the release of the particular individual is justified, and (3) the retention, reassignment, and callback of employees. As a general rule, an employee has no right to a position no longer deemed necessary by the district. However, the reasons articulated by the district must be reasonable and supported by adequate justification to support the RIF decision. In **Strasburger v. Board of Education,** the

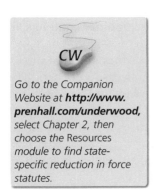

*Go to the Companion Website at **http://www. prenhall.com/underwood,** select Chapter 2, then choose the Resources module to find state-specific reduction in force statutes.*

Seventh Circuit Court of Appeals upheld the school district's decision to release an industrial arts teacher as a part of reduction in force. It affirmed the board's stated reasons that it needed to conserve funds and that enrollment in industrial arts was too low to justify continuing to offer it.[25]

Unlike the other terminations discussed in chapter 4, the burden of proof for a RIF is on the employee to show the reason given by the school district is a ruse for an impermissible act (e.g., discrimination, retaliation for union activity, or the exercise of a constitutionally protected right). Moreover, the board does not need to prove that it made the perfect decision in the particular set of circumstances, only that the decision is rational and not arbitrary or capricious.[26]

School boards may not use the RIF process to circumvent state tenure laws. When an Oklahoma school board dismissed an elementary school librarian, citing declining enrollments and budgetary constraints, and then rehired nontenured teachers for positions for which the librarian was certified and had previously taught, the court ruled that the district could not "manipulate job assignments in a manner that defeats the rights of tenured teachers and circumvents the purpose and spirit of the tenure law."[27] On the other hand, a Connecticut court upheld the elimination of a nurse–teacher position even though the elements of the job (i.e., clinical nursing and health education) were maintained. The court decision was based on the fact that no one employee was assigned both clinical nursing and health education.[28]

The second issue, who should be released, involves questions of preference and has been the subject of most of the litigation related to RIF. State statutes, school board policies, and employment contracts often specify the order of release in terms of tenure, seniority, or other criteria, as well as the procedures to be followed (notice, appeal, etc.). When the order of release and due process requirements are specified, the courts require that they be followed. When statutes, policies, or agreements do not address or are ambiguous about the order of release, the courts almost unanimously have given qualified tenured teachers priority over nontenured teachers in similar positions. In determining the "qualifiedness" of teachers, certification has been the major, but not the exclusive, criterion considered by the courts. Between tenured and nontenured teachers holding similar positions, seniority has been the primary, but not the only, factor in determining the order of release. Seniority preference may be mitigated by factors such as performance evaluations, years of teaching experience in the subject matter,[29] or collective bargaining agreements.[30]

The order of reassignment, reinstatement, and recall of employees who have been RIFed is basically the inverse of the order of release. That is, qualified tenured teachers would be called back before qualified nontenured teachers, in the order of seniority within each group. Again, though, the courts have been fairly consistent in stating that neither tenure nor seniority provides an absolute right to recall over certification or other evidence of qualification. For example, a New York court held that a tenured guidance counselor whose position was abolished was not entitled to reemployment as a school social worker. Although some of the duties of the two positions were similar, the positions were sufficiently dissimilar to require a separate certification, which the guidance counselor did not hold.[31]

COLLECTIVE NEGOTIATIONS

In most districts a contract negotiated with the local teacher organization controls many important aspects of teacher employment. In fact, 75% of the teachers in the United States are working under an agreement negotiated between the school board and a teacher organization. Although no federal labor laws cover school district employees, the federal courts have confirmed that the right of school district employees to form and join a union is protected by the First Amendment.[32] The courts have also affirmed the right to fully participate in union activities without reprisal or interference, as long as the activities do not interfere with the performance of their contractual duties. For example, in an Illinois case the school board discharged a custodian who was an outspoken union advocate and acting chief shop steward for violating the district's employment policy prohibiting custodial employees from leaving and reentering school buildings without punching out the time clock. During the term of his employment in the district, the custodian had been involved in union activities, but only after he assumed the chief shop steward's position did his union activities and work-related conduct became of greater interest to the school board. Based on an incident in which he was observed not punching out on the time clock, he was discharged. The union filed an unfair labor practice on behalf of the custodian, alleging that the school district took the action in retaliation for union activity in violation of state law protecting employees engaged in union activity. The court found that the board's reason for the dismissal was really just a pretext and that the custodian had been unjustly dismissed for his union activities and ordered his reinstatement.[33]

Although the federal courts have guaranteed teachers' rights to join and be actively involved in a union, the right to engage in collective bargaining is controlled by state labor laws and as such, varies considerably, from being prohibited in North Carolina to being detailed in great specificity in New York. More than a dozen states have no legislation addressing the bargaining rights of public employees. Unless required by state law, school boards do not have to negotiate with teacher unions. If, however, they do agree to negotiate and begin the negotiation process, they are then bound by applicable judicial standards (e.g., good-faith bargaining, impasse resolutions, contracts).

Among the most common items negotiated by teacher unions are salary, benefits, hours, evaluations, leaves of absence, reassignments and transfers, reductions in force, and grievance procedures. Once again, the actual scope of the negotiations varies considerably depending on state statute, which may be restrictive, broad, or silent.

Go to the Companion Website at **http://www. prenhall.com/underwood**, select Chapter 2, then choose the Resources module to find state-specific collective negotiation statutes.

In the private sector, when negotiations fail, employees often go on strike. However, in almost all states, the law prohibits public employees, including teachers, from striking. Nonetheless, in a number of well-publicized cases teachers' unions have gone on strike (and there are many more in which strikes have been threatened), some even though the school board has obtained an injunction prohibiting the strike. Teachers who participate in such strikes are subject to fines or dismissal. In upholding the right of school boards to dismiss such teachers the U.S. Supreme Court held that not only could the school board dismiss teachers who had participated in an illegal strike, but it also could act as the neutral body in making that dismissal decision.[34]

GUIDING LEGAL PRINCIPLES

- All states have set certification requirements for teachers that typically include professional preparation, good moral character, and passing a standardized examination. These requirements must be reasonable and related to the educational interests of the state.
- The school district may require teachers to live within the district in which they are employed once they have accepted a position.
- The school district may require a medical examination as a part of the application/hiring process.
- The employment contract defines the rights and responsibilities of the teachers and the school board. To be valid the contract must include an offer and acceptance, legally competent parties, consideration, legal subject matter, and proper form.
- Tenure requirements are generally determined by state statute.
- Most state statutes specify the requirements and procedures for acquiring and losing tenure.
- Most states allow districts to dismiss teachers through a reduction in force procedure for reasons of program changes, declining enrollment, or financial exigency.
- Teachers have a right to form and join professional organizations such as unions.
- Negotiations are generally on topics such as wages, hours, and other terms and conditions of employment. Although most states allow teachers to negotiate in some way, most of them do not allow teachers to strike.

YOU BE THE JUDGE

*Go to the Companion Website at **http://www.prenhall.com/underwood**, select Chapter 2, choose the You Be the Judge module, and click on the name of the case for more information about the case and the court's decision and rationale.*

When Is Writing Better than Talking?

Williams, a teacher in the Little Rock School District (AR) told his principal that he quit. The principal responded that he had to submit a written resignation. However, the next day after Williams had changed his mind and wanted to take back the verbal resignation, the principal said his resignation had already been accepted by the central administration. Approximately 3 weeks later, the school board met and formally accepted Williams's verbal resignation. Williams filed suit asking the court to give him his job back.

Questions for Discussion and Reflection

1. Should the verbal resignation have been enough to end the contract?
2. Would the decision have been different if Williams were a tenured or nontenured teacher?
3. How likely is Williams to be successful in getting his job back?

Visit the Companion Website for a more detailed description of the facts in the case **Williams v. Little Rock School District.**

* * *

Let It Snow

During the school year the South Newton (IN) school district canceled eight student instructional days due to hazardous weather. Under state law, the school district was required to provide 180 instructional days. South Newton received a waiver for 2 of the days, leaving it with 6 days to make up. The teachers' collective bargaining contract required teachers to work a total of 185 days. The agreement did not specify whether these were instructional days or noninstructional days. The school district decided that the teachers should be required to make up the 2 days that were waived during the summer as noninstructional professional days. The teachers' union filed suit, claiming a violation of the teachers' collective bargaining agreement.

Questions for Discussion and Reflection

1. Did the district change the terms of the contract?
2. Do you think the union would have filed suit if the days had not been waived and the school district had to make up instructional days? Why?
3. What alternatives might the school district have chosen?

Visit the Companion Website for a more detailed description of the facts in the case **South Newton School Corp. Bd. of School Trustees v. South Newton Teachers Ass'n.**

* * *

Show Me the Money

Chartiers Valley is a public school district. Generally, salaries are determined through a collective bargaining agreement that includes pay scale increases based on number of years of employment. However, with respect to starting salaries of newly hired teachers, Chartiers Valley has discretion. It bases its starting salary decision on various factors, including budgetary concerns, the type of teaching certification an applicant possesses, whether an applicant had any lapses in teaching service, relevant years of teaching experience for the particular position sought, and whether past experience was full time or part time. Henderson was hired in 1994 as a high school chemistry teacher. She had 13 years of experience at the time of hire. Howard was hired in 1997 as a middle school librarian. She had 4 years of experience as a librarian and 12 years of total experience in education when hired. Neither Henderson nor Howard was paid commensurate with her total years of experience: Both were paid as if they possessed 5 years of experience. This was inconsistent with two male Chartiers Valley teachers who, hired in 1992 and 1999, were given full credit for their past experience. Henderson and Howard filed suit for a violation of the Equal Pay Act, alleging that they had received lower starting salaries than two of their male counterparts because of their gender.

Questions for Discussion and Reflection

1. What, if any, justification could the district have for offering the two women lower starting salaries?
2. Two of the factors considered in determining starting salaries is whether there was a break in the applicant's teaching history and whether the work was part time. How could these factors have a discriminatory impact on women?
3. What factors do you believe should be included in determining a teacher's starting salary?

Visit the Companion Website for a more detailed description of the facts in the case **Henderson v. Chartiers Valley School.**

MORE ON THE WEB

Go to the Companion Website at **http://www.prenhall.com/underwood**, select Chapter 2, choose the More on the Web *module to connect to the site mentioned.*

The Education Commission of the States (ECS) provides information and policy analysis on a broad range of topics of interest to educators and policy makers, including multistate reports and data on a variety of current topics and policy developments in each state. Go to the ECS website, **http://www.ecs.org,** and click on "50 State Databases." Follow the link to "Teacher Preparation" and then to "Recruitment and Retention." What is the average salary in the state(s) where you are considering working? Is there an alternative to standard licensure/certification in these states? How long is the probationary period? Does the state have license reciprocity with other states? Why might this be important to you?

ENDNOTES

1. *Smith v. School Board of Polk County,* 205 F. Supp.2d 1308 (M.D. Fla. 2002).
2. *Grand Prairie Independent School District v. Vaughn,* 792 S.W.2d 944 (Tex. 1990).
3. *Adkins v. W.Va. Dept. of Educ.,* 556 S.E.2d 72 (W.Va. 2001).
4. 556 S.E.2d 920 (Ga. Ct. App. 2001).
5. 595 N.E.2d 489 (Ohio Ct. App. 1991).
6. *Ambach v. Norwick,* 441 U.S. 68, 73–74 (1979).
7. Ibid., p. 78.
8. *Pittsburgh Federation of Teachers Local 400 v. Aaron,* 417 F. Supp. 94 (Pa. 1976).
9. *McClelland v. Paris Public Schools,* 742 S.W.2d 907, 908 (Ark. 1988).
10. *Mexcall v. Marra,* 49 F. Supp.2d 365 (S.D. N.Y. 1999).
11. *Sullivan v. River Valley Sch. Dist.,* 20 F. Supp.2d 1120 (W.D. Mich. 1998).
12. 480 U.S. 273 (1987).
13. 840 F.2d 701 (9th Cir. 1988).
14. See, e.g., the lead case in education, *United States v. South Carolina,* 434 U.S. 1026 (1978).
15. *Association of Mexican-American Educators v. State of California,* 231 F.3d 572 (9th Cir. 2000).
16. Sperry, D. J., Daniel, P. T. K., Huefner, D. S., & Gee, E. G. (1998). *Education law and the public schools: A compendium* (2nd ed., p. 4). Norwood, MA: Christopher Gordon.
17. Ibid.
18. Valente, W. D., & Valente, C. M. (2001). *Law in the schools* (5th ed.). Upper Saddle River, NJ: Merrill/Prentice Hall.
19. Beckham, J. (1983). Critical elements of the employment relationship. In J. Beckham & P. A. Zirkel (Eds.), *Legal issues in public school employment* (pp. 1–21). Bloomington, IN: Phi Delta Kappa.
20. *Jones v. Alabama State Tenure Commission,* 408 So.2d 145 (Ala. Civ. App. 1981).
21. 948 P.2d 275 (1997).
22. *King v. Jefferson County Board of Education,* 659 So.2d 686 (Ala. Civ. App. 1995).

23. *Nixon v. Board of Cooperative Educational Services,* 564 N.Y.2d 903 (App. Div. 1990).

24. Hartmeister, F., & Russo, C. J. (1990). "Taxing" the system when selecting teachers for reduction in force. *Education Law Reporter, 130,* 989–1007.

25. *Strasburger v. Board of Education, Hardin County Community Unit School District No. 1,* 143 F.3d 351 (7th Cir. 1998).

26. *Palmer v. Board of Trustees of Crook County School District No. 1,* 785 P.2d 1160 (Wyo. 1990).

27. *Babb v. Independent School Dist. No. 1–5,* 829 F.2d 973 (10th Cir. 1987).

28. *Ballanto v. Board of Education of Stonington,* 663 A.2d 323 (Com. App. 1993).

29. See *State ex rel. Melchiori v. Board of Educ.,* 425 S.E.2d 251 (W. Va. 1992).

30. See *Underwood v. Henry County Sch. Bd.,* 427 S.E.2d 330 (1993).

31. *Brown v. Board of Education, Morrisville-Eaton Central School District,* 621 N.Y.2d 167 (App. Div. 1995).

32. See, e.g., *McLaughlin v. Tilendis,* 398 F.2d 287 (7th Cir. 1968).

33. *Bloom Township High School District 206 v. Illinois Educational Labor Relations Board,* 728 N.E.2d 612 (Ill. App. 2000).

34. *Hortonville Joint School District No. 1 v. Hortonville Education Association,* 426 U.S. 482 (1976).

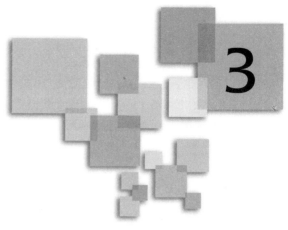

TEACHERS' RIGHTS

School boards in the United States have historically considered it their right, indeed their responsibility, to control the personal as well as the professional conduct of teachers. School boards have sought to regulate teachers' dress, speech, religion, association, and instructional content and practices. However, in the last several decades teachers have increasingly sought to exercise and expand the rights conferred upon them by state and federal constitutions, state and federal statutes and regulations, and employment contracts. As they have done so, the courts have confirmed that school districts cannot take negative actions against a teacher for exercising his or her constitutional or statutory rights. At the same time, a teacher cannot use the Constitution as a shield from all negative actions taken by the school district. If the school district can show that it would have made the same decision even in absence of the protected conduct, the decision is constitutionally permissible.[1]

Although all constitutional protections apply to teachers, this chapter focuses on the freedoms of expression, association, and religion; the right to be free from unreasonable search and seizure and self-incrimination; the right to privacy; and the freedom to discuss the subject matter discipline and determine the most appropriate instructional strategies without unwarranted governmental interference. After reading this chapter you will be able to

- Distinguish between protected and unprotected speech.
- Describe the conditions under which a district may place limits on a teacher's organizational membership or political activity.
- Discuss the limits that may be placed on a teacher's free exercise of religion.

- Outline the teacher's expectations of privacy and freedom from unreasonable search and seizure in the workplace.
- Provide an overview of the circumstances under which the drug testing of teachers is permissible.
- Discuss the limits of a teacher's right to refuse to give self-incriminating testimony.
- Explain how the concept of academic freedom applies to questions of who controls the curriculum and instruction.

FREEDOM OF EXPRESSION

The U. S. Supreme Court has made it clear that neither "students or teachers shed their constitutional rights to freedom of speech or expression at the schoolhouse door."[2] In this case the Supreme Court was not referring only to verbal communication. Speech also includes written and symbolic expression. Symbolic speech is an action intended to convey a particular message, such as dancing or painting.

Freedom of association is often closely related to symbolic speech. For example, a teacher wears a cross as a symbol of his or her religious affiliation; written speech may also be associational, such as union newsletters. According to the courts, the test for whether expressive conduct or symbolic speech is "speech" entitled to First Amendment protection is to ask: (1) Was the conduct "intended to convey a particularized message"? and (2) Was "the likelihood great that the message would be understood by those who viewed it"?[3]

Generally, a school district may not make an adverse employment decision as a result of a teacher's exercise of the constitutionally protected right to free speech.[4] However, this does not mean that teachers are free to say or write anything they wish. Rather, the courts attempt to balance the rights of the teacher against the harm caused to the school.

What Is Protected Speech?

In the employment context the First Amendment protects communication and expressive activities when the teacher speaks on matters of public concern. In the lead case involving teachers' freedom of speech, Marvin Pickering, a high school teacher, was terminated after writing a letter to the newspaper severely criticizing the superintendent and school board over their handling of school funds (see boxed case summary of **Pickering v. Board of Education**). The Supreme Court overturned his dismissal and ruled that teachers, as citizens, do have the right to make critical public comments on matters of public concern. The Court further held that unless the public expression undermines the effectiveness of the working relationship between the teacher and the teacher's superior or coworkers, the teacher's ability to

> "Congress shall make no law . . . abridging the freedom of speech."
>
> U.S. Const. Amend. I

perform assigned duties, or the orderly operation of the schools, such expression may not furnish grounds for reprisal. Finding that the issue of school board spending is an issue of legitimate public concern, that Pickering's statements were not directed at people he normally worked with, nor that there was any disruption to the operation of the schools (in fact, the letter had been greeted with apathy by everyone but the board), the Supreme Court overturned Pickering's dismissal.

PICKERING v. BOARD OF EDUCATION

A teacher criticized the school board and superintendent's actions regarding a school tax levy in a letter to the editor published by the local newspaper. The board dismissed the teacher. The Supreme Court found the school had violated the teacher's rights to free speech.

*Go to the Companion Website at **http://www. prenhall.com/underwood**, select Chapter 3, choose Cases module, and click on **Pickering v. Board of Education** to read the entire opinion of the court.*

In a more recent example, the Fifth Circuit reached the same conclusion and held that teachers' speech during a meeting about a school improvement plan that criticized the principal for not effectively implementing the plan was on a matter of public concern and therefore entitled to First Amendment protection because the district had failed to present evidence that the teachers' speech disrupted school operations.[5] Examples of topics that may involve matters of public concern include

- comments on instructional methods;
- comments on curriculum;
- comments on administrative or board action on general issues of management and policy[6];
- advocacy of political or social views outside the work site.

As opposed to speech on matters of public concern, speech that involves purely personal concern is not protected. Examples of such unprotected speech include

- personal attacks on administrators, board members, and/or other teachers; and
- grievances and complaints relating to individual personnel actions.

Is the Speech Disruptive?

Even if expression does involve a matter of public concern, it is still not protected, and the teacher may still be disciplined based on that expression, if the school district reasonably believes that the speech would significantly undermine the teacher's ability to perform his or her duties, disrupt the normal operation of the school, undermine supervisory authority, or destroy the effectiveness of working relationships.[7] For example, the Fourth Circuit upheld the dismissal of a teacher who wrote and circulated a letter to fellow teachers objecting to a delay in receiving summer pay, complaining about budgetary management, and encouraging teachers to stage a "sick-out" during final examination week. The Court ruled that any First Amendment interest inherent in the letter was outweighed by the public interest in having public education provided by teachers loyal to that service (i.e., not causing a disruption of exams by a sick-out that was in violation of both district policy and the teachers' contract and that represented professionally questionable behavior), and by the employer's interest "in having its teachers abide by reasonable policies adopted to control sick leave and maintain morale and effective operation of the schools."[8]

FREEDOM OF ASSOCIATION

The Constitution does not specifically mention the right to freedom of association but it has been recognized as inherent in the freedoms of speech, assembly, and petition. Accordingly, the courts have ruled that teachers have the right of free association and cannot be disciplined for nondisruptive participation in political, labor, religious, or social organizations or activities.

Membership

The courts are unanimous in their rulings that rules and statutes specifically *banning* members of controversial organizations from public employment are unconstitutional. Any rules or statutes that attempt to *inhibit* membership must be justified by a compelling state interest or need. For example, in **Melzer v. Bd. of Educ. of the City Sch. Dist. of the City of N.Y.,**[9] the court upheld the school district's decision to terminate a teacher because of his membership and active participation in the North American Man/Boy Love Association (NAMBLA), a group that advocates sexual relations between men and boys. The court found that Melzer's membership and participation in the group was potentially disruptive to school operations and undermined his effectiveness as a teacher because students may not feel comfortable having a teacher who advocates such views.

However, membership in a controversial organization cannot be used as a shield against negative employment actions. The teacher must show that membership was the primary motivating factor in the district's decision in order to prevail on this ground.[10] The question would be whether the negative employment action would have been taken even absent the teacher's membership in a controversial organization.

Political Activity

Teachers have the right to engage in political activities and hold public office; however, school boards may place restrictions on the exercise of this right. For example, teachers may discuss political issues and candidates in a nonpartisan manner in the classroom and even wear political buttons, badges, or armbands outside of the classroom. However, they may not make campaign speeches in the classroom or otherwise take advantage of their position of authority over a captive audience to promote their own political views. Political activity in the schools that would cause divisiveness among the faculty or otherwise be disruptive also may be restricted if the school can demonstrate the restriction is necessary to meet the compelling public need to protect efficiency and integrity in the school.

The authority of school boards to restrict teachers' political activities outside the school setting is far less than their authority to restrict activities in the schools. The courts have upheld teachers' rights to support candidates or issues of their choice, display political buttons and stickers, and participate in demonstrations. In addition, the courts generally have upheld the right of teachers to run for and hold public office. However, the courts also have indicated that if the time and activities associated with running for or holding office interfere with the performance of teaching duties, then the school board may require the teacher to take a leave of absence (but only if such were required for any other time-consuming activity). In addition, the courts have found the holding of certain political offices (e.g., school board member in the employing school district) to present a conflict of interest and therefore forbid the joint occupancy of the positions.

Go to the Companion Website at **http://www. prenhall.com/underwood**, select Chapter 3, choose Cases module, and click on **Connell v. Higginbotham** to read the entire opinion of the court.

Loyalty Oaths

The courts have upheld state and district requirements that as a condition of certification or employment teachers pledge support of the U.S. Constitution and opposition to subversive action and illegal or unconstitutional overthrow of the government by force. However, teachers cannot be required to disavow membership in particular groups or organizations that espouse such overthrow[11] (see boxed case summary of **Connell v. Higginbotham**). Teachers who refuse to take a loyalty oath may be denied employment in the public schools.

CONNELL v. HIGGINBOTHAM

A teacher was dismissed from her position after she refused to sign a loyalty oath required of all public employees. The oath required employees to swear allegiance to the United States and state constitutions, and that they do not believe in the overthrow of the state or federal government. The Court upheld the first oath of allegiance, but found the second was a violation of the employees' rights because it permitted dismissal from public employment without a hearing.

FREE EXERCISE OF RELIGION

The First Amendment protects the right to free exercise of religion. Generally, school districts may not pursue adverse employment action against a teacher because of his or her religious beliefs.[12] Whereas the right to believe as one chooses is absolute, the right to act on those beliefs is not. The Supreme Court held in **Employment Division v. Smith**[13] that Oregon could constitutionally deny unemployment benefits to two drug rehabilitation counselors discharged for ingesting peyote during a religious ceremony of their Native American church. The Court said that the right of free exercise does not relieve an individual of the obligation to comply with a valid and neutral law of general applicability. The government need not have a compelling interest to deny an exemption to the law based on the individual's religious beliefs.

In cases involving the teachers' right to free exercise of religion, the teachers' right to a belief must be balanced against the school's interests. For example, in **Palmer v. Board of Education**,[14] a teacher refused to follow certain parts of the curriculum on religious grounds. The court stated that the school's interest in delivering the curriculum to students outweighed any interference with the teacher's constitutional right. A teacher "has no constitutional right to require others to submit to their views" and force students "to forego a portion of their education they would otherwise be entitled to enjoy."[15] Similarly, in **LeVake v. Independent School District No. 656**[16] the court rejected a biology teacher's free speech and religion claims after he was reassigned following his refusal to teach the theory of evolution in his class.

Sometimes rules regarding religion are based on the public employer's need to ensure that it does not engage in the establishment of religion. An example of such a rule would be one that prohibits teachers from proselytizing to students during class time or at other school activities.

The Oregon Supreme Court went so far as to uphold the revocation of the certificate of a female Sikh teacher for wearing religious garb in the classroom. The court stated, "the teacher's appearance in religious garb may leave a conscious or unconscious impression among young people and their parents that the school endorses the particular religious commitment of the teacher."[17] However, a different conclusion was reached by the Mississippi Supreme Court, which ruled in favor of a teacher who wore a religious garb, finding that the First Amendment protected the teacher's dress.[18]

In a more recent case, while not involving religious garb but expressive dress with a religious message, a federal district court in Connecticut rejected the free speech claims of a teacher who wore a "JESUS 2000—J2K" shirt to class.[19] The court concluded that whatever free speech rights that were implicated by wearing the shirt must give way to the school's legitimate concern about a potential Establishment Clause violation in a public school.

> "Congress shall make no law . . . prohibiting the free exercise [of religion]."
>
> U.S. CONST. AMEND. I

Reasonable Accommodation Under Title VII

In general, a school district has an affirmative obligation to attempt to reasonably accommodate a teacher's religious observance or practice provided it can do so without undue hardship on the conduct of the educational enterprise. Title VII of the Civil Rights Act of 1964[20] requires employers to make reasonable accommodations for teachers' religious beliefs, observances, and practices unless it would cause the employers undue hardship. The law requires the employer to provide a reasonable accommodation, but not necessarily the accommodation preferred by the teacher.

Because it is not possible for the schools to be closed on the holy days of all religions, when feasible, schools typically allow teachers to use leave for religious purposes. The leave, however, does not have to be paid personal leave, unless the school district provides paid leave for all other purposes.[21]

FREEDOM FROM UNREASONABLE SEARCH AND SEIZURE

The heightened concerns about substance abuse and school violence have led to an increase in searches of both students and teachers. The Fourth Amendment provides protection against unwarranted governmental intrusion into places, clothes, belongings, person, or anywhere an individual might otherwise have a reasonable expectation of privacy. Ownership is not essential to establish an expectation of privacy.

Workplace Searches

Generally public school teachers are deemed to have a reasonable expectation of privacy in their offices, lockers, personal effects, and in their person. Their expectation of privacy regarding desks, filing cabinets, and storage areas depends on the extent to which they share these items with others. When the expectation of privacy does exist, the employer may conduct a search only if (1) there is reasonable suspicion that the search will produce evidence of work-related misconduct, and (2) the scope of the search is reasonably related to the objectives of the search and not excessively intrusive in light of the nature of the misconduct.[22]

Generally courts will balance a school's need to discover the information sought by the search against the degree of intrusion involved in the search. The more personally intrusive the search, the more compelling the circumstances must be to justify the search. However, exigent circumstances obviating the need for a warrant exist when the possibility of extreme danger is present. For example, a shooting may create exigent circumstances to search an area for a gun. Under any

> "The right of the people to be secure . . . against unreasonable searches and seizures, shall not be violated, and no Warrants shall issue, but upon probable cause."
>
> U.S. CONST. AMEND. IV

circumstances, searches may be conducted when an individual freely gives consent to do so.

Teachers have a "reasonable expectation of privacy" in their desks and files at work. Because of an employer's need to provide a safe environment and enforce its own rules, it does not need a warrant to search the workplace for noninvestigatory, work-related purposes. For example, in **Shaul v. Cherry Valley–Springfield Central School District**[23] a federal district court rejected the illegal search and seizure claims of a suspended teacher after school officials found incriminating personal items when opening a cabinet and desk while preparing the classroom for instructional use. The court concluded that the teacher did not have a reasonable expectation of privacy in his desk and filing cabinets based on the fact that coworkers, students, school officials, parents, and custodians had access to the classroom.

Urinalysis

Urinalysis (the most common form of drug testing) is considered a search under the Fourth Amendment. Historically employees have successfully challenged such tests as violating their rights of privacy and the Fourteenth Amendment prohibition against searches without an "individualized reasonable suspicion" of substance abuse. For example, in **Warren v. Bd. of Educ. of the City of St. Louis**[24] a federal district court determined that a principal acted unreasonably by ordering a teacher to undergo a drug test after the teacher exhibited "aggressive, erratic and argumentative" behavior. The court concluded that for a search to be reasonable, the employer must base it on an individualized suspicion of wrongdoing, and concern that the individual was using or under the influence of drugs.

Generally, the only exception to the individualized suspicion standard was when an employee's job duties involve student safety. For example, federal law requires school districts to conduct alcohol and drug testing of school bus drivers, in accordance with established regulations.[25] Teachers who regularly use hazardous substances or operate potentially dangerous equipment may also be subjected to random alcohol and drug testing.[26]

The major departure from the individualized suspicion standard that allowed drug testing of the general teacher population occurred in 1999 in **Knox County Educ. Ass'n v. Knox County Board of Educ.**[27] in which the Supreme Court let stand a decision of the Sixth Circuit that allowed mandatory urinalysis of all applicants (including principals) for positions or transfers in the district. The court reasoned that the policy was justified because educators were on the "frontline of school security" and because they occupy so-called "safety sensitive" positions (i.e., positions in which even a momentary lapse of attention could have serious consequences).[28] Also important in the court's decision was that the testing program was narrowly prescribed and not overly intrusive (it was a one-time test with advance notice), as well as the fact that educators were involved in a "heavily regulated industry," so their expectations of privacy were diminished. The district, however, has withdrawn the requirement. As of this writing only one other published case[29] documents a

> "No person . . . shall be compelled in any criminal case to be a witness against himself."
>
> U.S. Const. Amend. V

district's use of this type of testing, which possibly indicates that few districts have followed the lead of Knox County, but in the Sixth Circuit the courts would uphold such action. (See the In the News feature.)

FREEDOM FROM SELF-INCRIMINATION

The Fifth Amendment to the Constitution protects individuals from being forced to give self-incriminating testimony. The right against compelled self-incrimination applies only in courtroom or court-like situations. At a disciplinary or dismissal hearing, a teacher may not invoke the privilege and may be required to answer direct questions related to his or her employment.[30] Refusal to do so may be considered insubordination and may serve as grounds for dismissal.

If a teacher refuses to answer a question during the hearing, the district may draw adverse inferences from his or her silence. However, the district may not draw such inferences if the teacher has properly invoked the privilege in an appropriate forum, such as a criminal trial. Still, a school district does not have to postpone a dismissal hearing if a criminal action has been filed based on the same acts. Because these are separate actions, the results and evidence do not depend upon one another.

RIGHT TO PRIVACY

Although the Constitution does not mention the right to privacy, it has been deemed to be so basic and fundamental to individual freedom that it is assumed to be an *implied* fundamental right.[31] Situations that involve an individual's privacy rights generally relate to personal choices in procreation, marriage, family relations, child rearing, and activities in the home. Examples include

- procreation (e.g., right to use contraceptives[32] and right to abortion in the first trimester)[33];
- marriage (e.g., right to interracial marriage[34] and right of noncustodial parent to marry without court approval)[35];
- child rearing (e.g., right of parents to direct children's education)[36]; and
- certain activities within the home (e.g., right to possess obscene materials in one's home).[37]

A school district cannot base an employment decision on an individual's activity within these "zones of privacy" or attempt to interfere with the exercise of a privacy right unless the district can show a connection between the activity and the teacher's fitness to perform his or her duties and not cause an unreasonable disruption at school. For example, a principal in Florida refused to allow an elementary teacher to breastfeed her child, who was brought to school during her duty-free lunch period (in a private room) on the basis that it violated a school rule against teachers bringing their children to school. The court overruled the principal, saying that the right of personal privacy or personal liberty, included breastfeeding, "the most elemental form of parental care."[38] (See also the In the News feature.)

IN THE NEWS . . .

A Hartford Superior Court (CT) jury awarded $200,000 to a former teacher who claimed that his right to privacy was invaded when the school district's attorneys insisted that he sign a waiver regarding his medical records, including his sessions with a psychiatrist. Thomas O'Connor, an English teacher at Wethersfield High School, was accused of using lewd language in the classroom and other inappropriate conduct. An offhand remark O'Connor made about the Oedipus complex during a class discussion of the Greek tragedy *Oedipus the King* led to his being investigated. During the investigation, school district attorneys insisted that he undergo psychiatric testing and evaluation, to which he agreed. However, when the attorneys demanded that he sign a waiver that would allow the school board and anyone else involved in the investigation to review his medical records, including those of the psychiatrist, he refused. After spending a year on administrative leave, Mr. O'Connor was cleared of all charges and returned to the classroom in January 2002. He subsequently left the district and filed a lawsuit alleging a violation of his privacy rights.

Source: From "Jury Awarded $200,000 to a Former Teacher Who Claimed That His Right to Privacy Was Invaded," by Ann Marie Somma, October 2003, *Hartford Courant.*

ACADEMIC FREEDOM

Academic freedom is not a constitutional protection in and of itself but is "the desirable end to be achieved by the enforcement of the individual rights and freedom in the classroom as guaranteed by the Bill of Rights."[39] Academic freedom refers to the teacher's freedom to discuss the subject matter discipline and to determine the most appropriate instructional methodology. Academic freedom is not without limits. For example, teachers do not have the ultimate right to determine course content or select textbooks: that authority belongs to the school board. The school board may also require that teachers receive approval prior to the use of supplementary materials. Teachers also do not have the right to ignore prescribed content or to refuse to follow the designated scope and sequence of content or materials, even if the refusal is for religious reasons.

While teachers have limited freedom in determining the content of the curriculum, they have greater freedom in choosing the particular strategies to teach the prescribed content. When the school board challenges teaching strategies the courts consider:

> The adequacy of notice that use of specific teaching methodologies will result in disciplinary action, the relevance of the method to the course of study, the support for the strategy or materials by the teaching profession, and the threat of disruption posed by the method. The judiciary also has considered community standards in assessing challenges to various teaching methods. However, if a particular strategy is instructionally relevant and supported by the profession, it will probably survive judicial review even though it might offend some parents.[40]

In a case in point, a Texas teacher was discharged for failure to obey a school board warning that she refrain from using a role-playing simulation to teach about post–Civil War American history.[41] Parents had complained that the simulation aroused strong feelings about racial issues. When the teacher refused to obey the district's directive "not to discuss Blacks in American history," the district did not renew her contract. The Circuit Court reinstated the teacher, finding that the district violated her constitutional rights by basing the nonrenewal on classroom discussions that were protected by the First Amendment.

If, however, the teacher is discussing, showing, or distributing material that is lewd or not relevant, or using a teaching method that the profession does not support, the teacher may be sanctioned. Such was the case when a teacher was dismissed for refusing to stop using a classroom management technique she had developed called "Learnball," which included a sports format, dividing the class into teams, and a system of rewards that included radio playing and shooting foam basketballs in class. The teacher not only continued to use the technique but also advocated its use by others and in connection with this advocacy publicly criticized the school system. Although the court acknowledged the teacher's First Amendment right to advocate Learnball and to criticize school officials, it ruled that the teacher had no constitutional right to use Learnball in the classroom."[42]

GUIDING LEGAL PRINCIPLES

- Teachers have a First Amendment right to express their view on matters of public concern without fear of retaliation.
- Speech that involves matters of purely personal concern is not constitutionally protected.

- Disruptive speech is not protected and can serve as the basis for teacher discipline.
- Teachers have the right to join labor unions, political and religious organizations, and to participate in activities that cannot be interfered with without a showing of a compelling state interest.
- Teachers' right to hold political office may be limited if it presents a conflict of interest or interferes with the performance of teaching duties.
- Teachers' right to free exercise of religion does not include the right to refuse to follow certain parts of the curriculum or to express religious views during class time.
- School districts must attempt to reasonably accommodate a teacher's religious beliefs, observances, and practices unless to do so would put an undue hardship on the school district.
- Although teachers have a "reasonable expectation of privacy" in the workplace, the school district does not need a search warrant to search the workplace for work-related purposes.
- Teachers or other school employees who occupy safety-sensitive positions may be subjected to drug testing.
- Teachers cannot be forced to testify against themselves in a criminal proceeding.
- Teachers have the right to privacy in regard to procreation, marriage, child rearing, and other activities in the home, which the district may not abridge unless it can show the activity may negatively affect teaching performance or cause a disruption.
- Teachers have limited freedom in determining the content of the curriculum but have greater freedom in determining the most appropriate methodology to deliver the curriculum.

YOU BE THE JUDGE

Go to the Companion Website at **http://www.prenhall.com/underwood**, *select Chapter 3, choose the* You Be the Judge *module and click on the name of the case for more information about the case and the court's decision and rationale.*

Public Display of Discrimination

Jendra Loeffelman taught eighth-grade English at Crystal City Elementary School. When a student asked her view on interracial relationships, Ms. Loeffelman responded that she opposed them. She added that interracial couples should be "fixed" so they cannot have children, who are "racially confused." Her class included biracial children. The school board concluded that it had the authority to terminate her contract on the grounds that she had willfully violated board policy by engaging in discriminatory conduct and making disparaging racial comments. Ms. Loeffelman filed suit, alleging that the school board violated her free speech rights by terminating her for speaking on a matter of public concern.

Questions for Discussion and Reflection

1. How would you balance the teacher's right to her beliefs and right to speak with the school's interest in racial equity?
2. Are there some issues on which teachers should not have the right to voice their opinions even if they do not act on those beliefs?
3. Would your response be different if these comments had been made only outside the classroom?

Visit the Companion Website for a more detailed description of the facts in the case **Loeffelman v. Board of Education of the Crystal City School District.**

* * *

Right to Privacy

Laura Flaskamp, a physical education teacher at Fordson High School in Dearborn, Michigan, developed a close friendship with her student assistant, "Jane Doe," during which they exchanged letters and gifts. Their relationship continued after Jane graduated and turned 18, with Ms. Flaskamp occasionally visiting her at college. Jane's mother became aware of this and threatened to get Ms. Flaskamp fired unless she stayed away from Jane. When the relationship continued, the mother reported it to Fordson's principal and charged that it had begun while Jane was still a student. The principal's independent investigation found evidence that supported the mother's allegation. As a result, the principal recommended that the school board deny Ms. Flaskamp tenure. Based on the principal's recommendation, the board voted to deny her tenure. Ms. Flaskamp sued, alleging violation of her right to privacy.

Questions for Discussion and Reflection

1. How far should a teacher's right to privacy go?
2. Would this case have been different if the relationship had begun only after the student had graduated?
3. Is Ms. Flaskamp's allegation likely to be upheld? Why or why not?

Visit the Companion Website for a more detailed description of the facts in the case **Flaskamp v. Dearborn Public Schools.**

* * *

Three Speaks and You Are Out

The superintendent announced a new plan to improve student performance. Two teachers openly and publicly criticized the plan. The principal said these faculty members were not "team players" and were unlikely to support the proposed changes. The school district reassigned the teachers to different positions. The teachers' notice of transfer contained no reason for the action except "for good cause and extenuating circumstances." No hearing was provided other than the grievance process available under the collective bargaining agreement. The teachers filed suit, alleging violations of their free speech and procedural due process rights.

Questions for Discussion and Reflection

1. How are issues of public concern distinguished from issues of personnel concern?
2. What would be some school decisions that would not rise to the level of issues of public concern?
3. How can teachers constructively make their views known on important educational issues?

Visit the Companion Website for a more detailed description of the facts in the case **Leary v. Daeschner.**

MORE ON THE WEB

*Go to the Companion Website at **http://www.prenhall.com/underwood**, select Chapter 3, choose the More on the Web module to connect to the site mentioned.*

National and state teacher professional organizations are dedicated to not only improving the professional practice of teachers but also elevating the profession of teaching and protecting teacher rights. Go to the home page of the Association of Texas Professional Educators (ATPE), **http://www.atpe.org/index.html,** and click on "Legal Issues." Under "Employee Rights" click on "Religion in Schools" and summarize the discussion of the rights of employees in expressing their own beliefs. Do you believe this position is too restrictive? What does the ATPE state under "Due Process" regarding the type of due process that is due teachers in varying situations?

ENDNOTES

1. *Mt. Healthy City School Dist. v. Doyle,* 429 U.S. 274 (1977).
2. *Tinker v. Des Moines Independent* School District, 393 U.S. 503, 506 (1969).
3. *Spence v. Washington,* 418 U.S. 405 (1974).

4. *Pickering v. Board of Education,* 391 U.S. 563 (1968).
5. *Harris v. Victoria Independent School Dist.,* 168 F.3d 216 (5th Cir. 1999), *cert. denied,* 528 U.S. 1022 (1999).
6. See, e.g., *Givhan v. Western Line Consol. School Dist.,* 439 U.S. 410 (1979).
7. *Connick v. Myers,* 461 U.S. 138 (1983); *Waters v. Churchill,* 511 U.S. 661 (1994).
8. *Stroman v. Colleton County School District,* 981 F.2d 152 (4th Cir. 1992).
9. 336 F.3d 185 (2d Cir. 2003).
10. *Beilan v. Board of Public Education, School Dist. of Philadelphia,* 357 U.S. 399 (1958).
11. *Connell v. Higginbotham,* 403 U.S. 207 (1971).
12. *Sherbert v. Verner,* 374 U.S. 398 (1963).
13. 494 U.S. 872 (1990).
14. 603 F.2d 1271 (7th Cir. 1979).
15. Ibid. at 1274.
16. 625 N.W.2d 502 (Minn. App. 2001), *cert. denied,* 534 U.S. 1081 (2002).
17. *Cooper v. Eugene School District,* 723 P.2d 298 (Or. 1986).
18. *Mississippi Employment Security v. McGlothin,* 556 So.2d 324 (Miss. 1990).
19. *Downing v. West Haven Board of Education,* 162 F. Supp.2d 19 (D. Conn. 2001).
20. 42 U.S.C. § 2000e (2005).
21. *Ansonia Board of Educ. v. Philbrook,* 479 U.S. 60 (1986).
22. *O'Conner v. Ortega,* 480 U.S. 709 (1987).
23. 218 F. Supp.2d 266 (N.D. N.Y. 2002).
24. 200 F. Supp.2d 1053 (E.D. Mo. 2001).
25. Omnibus Transportation Teacher Testing Act of 1991, 49 U.S.C. § 31306 (2005).
26. *Aubrey v. School Board of LaFayette Parish,* 148 F.3d 559 (5th Cir. 1998).
27. 158 F.3d 361 (6th Cir. 1998), *cert. denied,* 528 U.S. 812 (1999).
28. See, e.g., *Skinner v. Railway Labor Executives Ass'n,* 489 U.S. 602 (1989); *National Treasury Teachers Union v. VonRaab,* 489 U.S. 656 (1989).
29. *Crager v. Board of Education of Knott County,* 2004 WL 813491 (E.D. Ky. April 8, 2004).
30. *Beilan v. Board of Public Education, School Dist. of Philadelphia,* 357 U.S. 399 (1958).
31. *Griswold v. Connecticut,* 381 U.S. 479 (1965).
32. Ibid.
33. *Roe v. Wade,* 410 U.S. 113 (1973).
34. *Loving v. Virginia,* 388 U.S. 1 (1967).
35. *Zablocki v. Redhail,* 434 U.S. 374 (1978).
36. *Pierce v. Society of Sisters,* 268 U.S. 510 (1925).
37. *Stanley v. Georgia,* 394 U.S. 557 (1969).
38. *Dike v. Sch. Bd.,* 650 F.2d 783 (5th Cir. 1981).

39. Alexander, K., & Alexander, M. D. (2001). *American public school law* (5th ed., p. 708). Belmont, CA: West/Thompson Learning.

40. McCarthy, M. (1989). Legal rights and responsibilities of public school teachers. In M. C. Reynolds (Ed.), *Knowledge base for the beginning teacher* (pp. 255–266). New York: Pergamon.

41. *Kingsville Independent School District v. Cooper,* 611 F.2d 1109 (5th Cir. 1980).

42. *Bradley v. Pittsburgh Board of Education,* 913 F.2d 1064 (3d Cir. 1990).

TEACHER DISCIPLINE

Teacher discipline is governed by state law, school board policies, administrative regulations, and collective bargaining agreements. In addition, when a teacher has tenure or

> "No State shall . . . deprive any person of life, liberty, or property, without due process of law."
>
> U.S. CONST. AMEND. XIV, Section 1

other form of expectation of continued employment, the teacher will have a constitutionally protected property right in his or her employment.[1] In these situations due process must be afforded before an adverse employment action can be taken. The protections provided to teachers depend on the proposed adverse employment action. These actions range from minor disciplinary actions, such as fines or reprimands, to more severe actions, such as dismissals or nonrenewals. In this chapter we examine the range of disciplinary actions that teachers may face, as well as the due process requirements that school districts must give before they can impose the discipline. After reading this chapter you will be able to

- Explain the most common forms of discipline imposed on teachers.
- Identify the categories of conduct that constitute immorality.
- Outline the categories of conditions or behaviors that constitute incompetence.
- Discuss the importance of establishing a nexus between a teacher's conduct and job performance in the disciplinary process.

- Enumerate the conditions that must be met to uphold the discipline of a teacher for insubordination.
- Compare the use of suspensions, reprimands, and fines in teacher discipline.
- Distinguish between a property interest and a liberty interest in the context of teacher employment.
- Describe the minimal due process rights of teachers.
- Differentiate between the due process rights of tenured and non-tenured teachers in dismissals and nonrenewals.

PROCEDURAL DUE PROCESS REQUIREMENTS

In keeping with the Fourteenth Amendment, if the dismissal of a teacher affects either a property or a liberty right, *due process* must be provided. *Substantive due process,* as a principle of fundamental fairness, requires that rules are reasonable and "not arbitrary, capricious, or without a rational basis."[2] *Procedural due process* deals with the process by which decisions are made. The more serious the disciplinary action, the more formal the due process procedures required. As previously noted, tenured teachers have a *property right* to employment and are therefore entitled to due process if the discipline constitutes a dismissal, demotion, suspension without pay, significant alteration of duties, or reduction of salary. On the other hand, nontenured teachers do not have a property right claim to due process unless the anticipated discipline takes place during the contract year.

Both tenured and nontenured teachers may have a *liberty interest* involved in disciplinary charges or actions for dismissal. A teacher has a liberty interest if the action creates a stigma, damages the teacher's reputation to the extent that it forecloses other employment opportunities, or damages the teacher's standing and associations in the community. Situations in which a liberty interest is implicated warrant some procedural due process as well.

The procedural due process that must be provided to teachers depends on the requirements of state statutes, school board policies, and the terms set forth in the employment contract. At a minimum the school district must provide the teacher with a notice of charges, a hearing, and a decision based solely on the evidence presented.[3] If the tenured teacher is facing a severe disciplinary action, the district will also typically give the teacher the right to testify, to provide evidence and cross-examine witnesses, to be represented by an attorney, and to appeal the decision. The following sections discuss the minimal due process requirements.

Notice

Notice of a proposed disciplinary action must inform the teacher of the specific charges being made and provide the teacher with sufficient time to prepare an adequate defense or rebut the charges. The notice should include the following elements:

- the allegations warranting disciplinary action;
- if applicable, the work rules that appear to have been violated;
- the range of disciplinary action seriously under consideration;
- that the employer will provide the teacher with a summary of the information the employer has concerning the allegations; and
- that at the meeting the employer will give the teacher an opportunity to dispute the information, provide additional information, and contest the form of discipline to be imposed.

No mandate or rule requires a particular time frame for notice. However, as a general rule, the school district will give the teacher 7 to 14 days of advance notice of the meeting. Depending on the number and complexities of the allegations, it may give more time, particularly if requested by the teacher. For simple misconduct, notice can be less formal and the meeting can be held immediately following the behavior in question.

Hearing

Due process guarantees a teacher at least a right to a predisciplinary meeting whenever the proposed discipline will affect the teacher's property or liberty interest[4] (see the boxed case summary of the landmark Supreme Court case **Cleveland Bd. of Educ. v. Loudermill**).

CLEVELAND BD. OF EDUC. v. LOUDERMILL

The school board terminated a school security guard after it discovered he had lied on his job application about his criminal record. The board did not give the guard an opportunity to respond to the charges prior to its termination decision. However, it did give him a posttermination hearing. Under the state law, the guard was classified as a civil servant who can be terminated only for cause and is entitled to administrative review of his termination. The guard appealed to the state civil service commission, which upheld the board's decision. The guard sued. He alleged that the statute providing for administrative review violated his due process rights because it did not provide a hearing prior to the board's decision to terminate employment. The U.S. Supreme Court held that the guard was entitled to a pretermination opportunity to respond to the charges because under state law he had a property interest in his continued employment. The Court observed that when a constitutionally protected property right is involved, the essential requirements of due process are notice and an opportunity to be heard before a decision is made.

Go to the Companion Website at **http://www. prenhall.com/underwood**, *select Chapter 4, choose Cases module, and click on* **Cleveland Bd. of Educ. v. Loudermill** *to read the entire opinion of the court.*

When the predisciplinary procedures do not afford an opportunity for a formal evidentiary hearing, the teacher should have a prompt postdisciplinary hearing when the discipline imposed deprives the teacher of a property or liberty interest. If a postdisciplinary hearing takes place its purpose is to determine whether the termination should stand or the teacher should be reinstated.

The form of the meeting and the applicable procedures usually will be specified in state law, school district regulations, or the teacher employment contract, and the courts will look to these services to determine what is required. For example, in **Board of School Commissioners of the City of Indianapolis v. Walpole**,[5] the Indiana Supreme Court held that a teacher facing a termination hearing by the school board was not entitled to formal discovery (an opportunity for each party to a lawsuit to request information and documents from the opposing side). Walpole, a permanent teacher, had been suspended with pay pending a termination hearing by the school board. Walpole requested that the board allow discovery involving document production and depositions. The Indiana Supreme Court found nothing in the Teacher Tenure Act that required discovery and pointed out that, although the Teacher Tenure Act defines the process due a permanent teacher during a termination hearing and creates a property interest in the teacher's job, due process does not include the right to discovery at a termination hearing.

The evidentiary hearing must be held before an impartial decision maker, which can be the school board or an independent hearing examiner. When the school board acts as the decision maker, it need not recuse itself just because it has some familiarity with the issues involved. In **Hortonville Joint Sch. Dist. No. 1 v. Hortonville Educ. Ass'n**[6] the U.S. Supreme Court concluded that a school board that had acted as a negotiator with its teachers was not disqualified from deciding to terminate teachers who participated in an illegal strike. The Court wrote, "The record does not support respondents' contention that the Board members had a personal or official stake in the dismissal decision sufficient to disqualify them." The opinion went on to state that "[M]ere familiarity with the facts of a case gained by an agency in the performance of its statutory role does not disqualify a decision maker . . . and here the School Board's participation pursuant to its statutory duty in the collective-bargaining negotiations was not a disqualifying factor."

During the hearing process, the school has the burden of proof; that is, the school must prove its case against the teacher. The strict rules of courtroom evidence do not apply, but the proceedings are often run much like a court hearing. Evidence is submitted to the board, and witnesses are presented and questioned.

At the close of the proceedings, the board must provide its conclusions and findings. These should be given in writing and clearly set out whether the charges made were proven.

*Go to the Companion Website at **http://www. prenhall.com/underwood**, select Chapter 4, then choose the* Resources *module to find the state-specific teacher dismissal regulations.*

DISMISSAL

Dismissal is defined as the termination of employment during the term of a contract. Both state laws and collective bargaining agreements set forth the reasons why teachers may be dismissed, as well as what procedures must be followed in the dismissal process. These reasons vary from state to state, from the very general to the very specific. In states that formally recognize collective bargaining, agreements often state that teachers may be dismissed only for "just cause." The behaviors that would justify dismissal apply equally to tenured and non-tenured teachers. Although the states use different labels, the grounds for dismissal most frequently cited in state statutes are immorality, incompetence, and insubordination. Other commonly cited reasons are neglect of duty, unprofessional conduct or conduct unbecoming a teacher, unfitness to teach, and the catchall phrase "other good and just cause." In this chapter we discuss the most frequently cited grounds for dismissal, as well as the requirements that the courts have established as necessary to support a disciplinary action against a teacher.

Immorality

Immorality, the most frequently cited reason for dismissal in state statutes, is broadly defined as unacceptable conduct that warrants removal from one's role as a teacher of children. The exact definition of immorality varies by state. Some states define immorality as conviction or commission of a crime of moral turpitude such as murder or embezzlement; others make no attempt to define immorality, but leave it up to the local school districts and perhaps, eventually, the courts. However, generally, immorality is considered actions that are contrary to commonly accepted moral principles or conduct unbecoming of a teacher, such as

- sexual conduct with students;
- sexually explicit remarks or talking about sex unrelated to the curriculum;
- distribution of sexually explicit materials to classes;
- use of obscene, profane, or abusive language;
- public lewdness;
- possession and use of controlled substances;
- criminal misconduct; and
- dishonesty.

Because it would be impossible to list in state statutes (or in this text) all the behaviors that might be considered to be "contrary to commonly accepted principles" or "conduct unbecoming a teacher," the courts apply certain standards that have evolved from case law to cases involving dismissal for immorality. First is the *exemplar standard.* Although this concept is not as universally accepted today as in the past, the courts do recognize that "there are legitimate standards to be expected of those who teach in the public schools."[7] A significant percentage of the public also believes that teachers should be good role models for their students, both in and out of school.[8]

A second standard that has emerged from contemporary court decisions in teacher dismissal cases is that in order to justify a charge of dismissal there must be a *nexus* or link between the personal conduct of the teacher and job performance. If the behavior has no connection to job performance, discipline may be considered an unwarranted intrusion into the teacher's private life. A nexus between the misconduct and the teacher's ability to perform professional duties exists when the behavior negatively affects the health, safety, welfare, or education of students. This can include behavior that makes the teacher an inappropriate role model for students, even if the misconduct is wholly unrelated to the work environment. For example, in a Pennsylvania case the court upheld the dismissal of a teacher after her third driving under the influence conviction and second driving with a suspended license conviction after ruling that her conduct set a bad example for her students and offended the community's morals.[9] And, in all states, some offenses are considered so extreme that they merit immediate termination, particularly when they violate a known policy and directly harm children.[10]

The link between the teacher's conduct and job performance may exist in one case involving a particular conduct and not in another case involving the same conduct. For example, the dismissal of a teacher in a small, rural town in Montana for living with a fellow teacher was upheld because his cohabitation had become a matter of public discussion in the community and at the school. (In fact, he had told his class that his girlfriend had to move from his home because of complaints from persons in the community.) In the judgment of the court, this affected his teaching effectiveness and adversely affected the school and his relationship with students and other employees.[11] On the other hand, the dismissal of a Florida teacher for living with her boyfriend was overturned by the courts. In this case the court found no evidence that her actions affected her ability to teach and that her relationship had not been commonly known until the school made the matter public.[12]

Homosexuality is another area in which the circumstances of the particular case very much dictate the ruling of the courts. In 2003, in **Lawrence v. Texas**[13] the Supreme Court found a Texas statute prohibiting intimate homosexual conduct unconstitutional. And, with the exception of the 1977 Washington Supreme Court ruling in **Gaylord v. Tacoma School District No. 10,**[14] most courts have ruled that homosexuality *per se* cannot be grounds for dismissal. To support a dismissal there must still be a nexus between a teacher's private sexual orientation and the performance of his or her duties as a teacher to justify dismissal. For example, in the previously mentioned case of **Melzer v. Bd. of Educ. of the City Sch. Dist. of the City of N.Y.**[15] the Second Circuit Court of Appeals concluded that Mr. Melzer's position as a teacher working with minors and his active involvement in the North American Man/Boy Love Association, which actively advocates pedophilia, sufficiently disrupted the educational mission to warrant his dismissal. However, in **Weaver v. Nebo School District**[16] the court overturned a teacher's dismissal as a girls' volleyball coach based only on her public discussion of her lesbian sexual orientation. The court found that the principal's decision not to continue her contract as volleyball coach because of her sexual orientation was unconstitutional. It stated that there was no evidence to indicate an inability to coach solely because of sexual orientation.

Although cases involving alleged immorality must often be settled on a case-by-case basis, the courts have agreed on the factors to be considered in determining whether a teacher's immoral conduct renders the teacher unfit to teach. The factors include (1) the age and maturity of the teacher's students, (2) the likelihood that the teacher's conduct will have an adverse effect on students or other teachers, (3) the degree of anticipated adversity, (4) the proximity of the conduct, (5) the extenuating or aggravating circumstances surrounding the conduct, (6) the likelihood that the conduct would be repeated, (7) the underlying motives, and (8) the chilling effect on the rights of teachers.[17]

Incompetence

Incompetence is often broadly defined to cover various forms of inadequate work performance. Courts typically describe incompetence as lack of ability, legal qualifications, or fitness to discharge the required duties. Those conditions or behaviors that have been considered to constitute incompetence fall into six broad categories: (1) inadequate teaching or supervision, (2) lack of knowledge of the subject matter, (3) failure to maintain classroom discipline or administration of unreasonable discipline, (4) failure to work effectively with colleagues, supervisors, or parents, (5) physical or mental incapacity, and (6) willful neglect of duty.

In dismissals for incompetence the courts require an established relationship between the teacher's conduct and the operation of the school. Additionally, the standard against which the teacher is measured must be one used for other teachers in a similar position, not some hypothetical standard of perfection. Dismissals for incompetence are usually based on a number of factors or a pattern of behavior, rather than an isolated incident or event. Most jurisdictions also require that before the teacher is terminated a school district make a determination as to whether the behavior in question is remedial, give a notice of deficiency, identify methods to improve, and provide reasonable time and opportunity to remediate. These steps are necessary to demonstrate that dismissal is the only alternative left to eliminate the teacher's incompetent performance.[18]

Insubordination

Regardless of whether it is specified in state statutes, *insubordination* is an acceptable cause for dismissal in all states. Insubordination is the persistent, willful, and deliberate disregard or disobedience of a reasonable school rule, regulation, or official order. Teachers can be dismissed for repeated or severe instances of insubordination even though their classroom performance is exemplary. For example, in one case a school district terminated a high school industrial arts teacher for repeated refusal to submit lesson plans to the principal even though the teacher had received positive performance evaluations.[19]

Generally, dismissal for insubordination is based on repeated incidents of minor violations of school rules or policies, repeated absences, or tardiness. However, a serious enough single incident (e.g., refusal to accept a teaching assignment), would support a dismissal. In all cases, the rule or policy that has been violated must not only be reasonable but also be clearly communicated to the teacher; and it cannot represent an infringement upon the teacher's constitutional rights. For example, rules that limit what teachers can say or write may, in some cases, violate their First Amendment right to free speech. In such cases violation of the rules would not be considered insubordination. Dismissal may also not be supported if the teacher tried, although unsuccessfully, to obey the rule or if no harm resulted from the violation of the rule.[20]

In cases involving alleged insubordination it is not necessary to establish a relationship between the insubordinate act and teaching effectiveness. The following actions are among those that have been held to constitute insubordination: refusal to obey the direct and lawful orders of school administrators or school boards, unauthorized absence from duty, abuse of sick leave, refusal to follow established policies and procedures, inappropriate use of corporal punishment, refusal to meet or cooperate with superiors, encouraging students to disobey school authority, refusal to perform assigned teaching or nonteaching duties, and failure to acquire required approval for use of instructional materials.

The courts have established certain conditions that must be met if the discipline of a teacher for insubordination is to be upheld, as listed here. (See also the In the News feature.)

ELEMENTS OF INSUBORDINATION

To uphold discipline due to insubordination the following must be proven:

- The conduct violated a rule or order.
- The rule may not be enforced in a discriminatory manner.
- The rule or order must be reasonable and valid (within the maker's authority).
- The violation had to have been willful.
- The discipline must be proportionate to the offense.

IN THE NEWS . . .

A bill making it easier for school districts to terminate a teacher's employment passed the New Hampshire House of Representatives. The bill's supporters argued that current state law, which allows a teacher to be dismissed for "incompetence," is not specific enough. This bill would allow for dismissal of teachers who had "not satisfactorily maintained the performance standards established by the school district." This would be the sole cause for dismissal. The state chapter of the National Education Association opposed the bill. But the New Hampshire School Board Association and the New Hampshire School Administrators' Association supported it.

Source: "Legislation Makes It Easier to Terminate N.H. Teachers," by Kathleen Bailey, April 5, 2005, *Exeter News Letter.* http://www.seacoastonline.com/news/exeter/04052005/news/35225.html

PROGRESSIVE DISCIPLINE

In general, for unionized teachers "just cause" requires the use of progressive discipline for immorality or insubordination. Progressive discipline involves using gradually more severe discipline with each violation. For example, the first step in progressive discipline might be an oral warning, the second step a written warning, then an unpaid suspension, and finally termination. However, if the misconduct or insubordination is particularly egregious, it may be possible for the district to disregard progressive discipline and terminate the teacher immediately.

NONRENEWAL

The annual contracts issued nontenured teachers typically include a provision that gives the school district the opportunity to renew the contract after the initial contract term has ended. A decision by the district not to offer an additional period of employment beyond the original specified time period is termed a nonrenewal. In states without collective bargaining, the district's decision not to renew the contract can be for any or no reason, as long as it is constitutionally permissible. In fact, in one third of the states the nontenured teacher does not have the right to be given the reasons for nonrenewal, and in one half of the states teachers do not have the right to meet with the school board or superintendent to argue for their job (see Table 4.1). The only requirement for nonrenewal is that the school district give timely notice to the teacher. However, in states with collective bargaining, the teachers' union can negotiate just cause protections for nontenured teachers, and in most of these states teachers who have completed the probationary period typically can be nonrenewed only for just cause. They must

Table 4.1 Employment Rights of Nontenured Teachers, K–12

	Right to Know Reasons for Nonrenewal	Right to Meet with Administration	Mandatory Evaluation of Job Performance	Mandatory Plan of Improvement	Violation of Evaluation Procedure Results in Contract Renewal	Union Can Bargain Just Cause Protection
Alabama						
Alaska	✓	✓	✓	✓		✓
Arizona	✓		✓			
Arkansas	✓	✓	✓	✓	✓	✓
California		✓				
Colorado	✓		✓	✓		
Connecticut	✓	✓	✓			
Delaware	✓	✓	✓	✓	✓	✓
Fed. Ed. Assn.			✓			
Florida			✓	✓		
Georgia	✓		✓	✓		
Hawaii		✓	✓		unclear	✓
Idaho	✓	✓	✓		✓	✓
Illinois	✓		✓			
Indiana	✓	✓	✓		✓	✓
Iowa	✓	✓	✓		unclear	✓
Kansas			✓			✓
Kentucky	✓		✓	✓	✓	✓
Louisiana	✓		✓	✓	✓	
Maine			✓			
Maryland			✓			
Massachusetts			✓			unclear
Michigan			✓	✓	✓	unclear
Minnesota	✓		✓			✓
Mississippi	✓	✓				
Missouri	✓		✓			
Montana						✓

	Right to Know Reasons for Nonrenewal	Right to Meet with Administration	Mandatory Evaluation of Job Performance	Mandatory Plan of Improvement	Violation of Evaluation Procedure Results in Contract Renewal	Union Can Bargain Just Cause Protection
Nebraska	✓	✓	✓	✓	✓	unclear
Nevada	✓		✓	✓	unclear	✓
New Hampshire						✓
New Jersey	✓	✓	✓	✓		✓
New Mexico	✓		✓			✓
New York	✓				✓	
North Carolina	✓		✓			
North Dakota	✓	✓	✓		unclear	unclear
Ohio	✓	✓	✓	✓	✓	✓
Oklahoma	✓	✓	✓	✓	✓	
Oregon	✓	✓	✓	✓		✓
Pennsylvania	✓	✓	✓		✓	✓
Rhode Island	✓	✓				unclear
South Carolina		✓	✓	✓		
South Dakota						unclear
Tennessee			✓	✓		✓
Texas		✓	✓		✓	
Utah			✓	✓		
Vermont	✓	✓				✓
Virginia	✓	✓	✓			
Washington	✓	✓	✓	✓		unclear
West Virginia	✓	✓	✓	✓	✓	
Wisconsin		✓				✓
Wyoming	✓		✓			

Source: From "NEA Examines the Rights of Nontenured Teachers. Rights Watch," May 2001, *NEA Today.* http://www.nea.org/neatoday/0105/rights.html

also be afforded due process and whatever other procedural and substantive requirements are available under state law.

SUSPENSION

A suspension occurs when school authorities remove a professional teacher from performing his or her duties for a limited time period because of the teacher's performance or conduct. School boards often use suspensions in a progressive discipline system as a form of punishment more severe than an oral or written warning but less severe than termination. Suspension is also often used while the district is investigating more serious accusations of misconduct. Suspensions may occur with or without pay.

The types of conduct that can give rise to suspension are generally the same as those for dismissal, though less serious in nature. A few states have statutory provisions related to suspension, but more often they do not. For this reason it is often difficult to define what procedural due process must be provided. For example, in one case an industrial arts teacher was suspended for four days without pay and then transferred after fighting with a student. During the course of the investigation into the matter, the board gave the teacher the opportunity to offer his version of events and granted an administrative review by the superintendent.[21] However, the court ruled that the teacher had a property interest in continued employment because of his tenure status, as well as a liberty interest because of the potential stigmatization resulting from a charge of child abuse, both of which warranted the granting of a due process hearing before the school board. The one thing that has evolved from court decisions is that if a suspension is for longer than 5 days the school board must provide the teacher a hearing with an opportunity to respond to the charges.

REPRIMAND/WARNING

A school district may place written documentation of performance deficiencies, misconduct, or insubordination in a teacher's personnel file. A reprimand/warning often includes a directive that specific improvement must be accomplished by a certain date or that the misconduct not be repeated in order to avoid more severe disciplinary measures.

FINES

Some states authorize the use of fines to penalize teachers for certain kinds of misconduct, such as theft. Teachers may also be subjected to fines (damages) for breach of contract if they resign their position during the term of the contract.

GUIDING LEGAL PRINCIPLES

- Teachers are entitled to due process whenever their property or liberty interests are involved.
- When a teacher's liberty or property interests are involved, courts have required adequate notice to the teacher and the teacher has a right to be heard and defend against the charges. However, this opportunity to be heard may take place as an appeal to the board after the termination.
- The most common reasons cited in state statutes for suspension and dismissal of teachers are immorality, incompetency, and insubordination. State statues also generally define reasons for discipline and procedures necessary for tenured teachers.
- The disciplining of a teacher for immorality requires proof of the immoral act and proof that the immorality has a connection or nexus to the teaching position.
- In most states, before a teacher can be dismissed for incompetency, not fulfilling the job responsibilities, the district must afford the teacher an opportunity to improve.
- If severe enough, a single act of insubordination can justify the dismissal of a teacher.
- Nonrenewal of nontenured teachers, not offering a new contract at the close of the current contract, usually requires no due process.
- A teacher may be suspended temporarily as a disciplinary action or suspended pending a hearing for more severe disciplinary sanctions.
- The procedures for disciplining teachers depend on whether the teacher is tenured or nontentured and on the type of discipline involved (dismissal, suspension, nonrenewal, reprimand, fine).

YOU BE THE JUDGE

*Go to the Companion Website at **http://www.prenhall.com/underwood** select Chapter 4, choose the* You Be the Judge *module and click on the name of the case for more information about the case and the court's decision and rationale.*

Don't Punch Your Boss

Ballard was employed by Colbert School District (OK) as a teacher and baseball coach. In 1998 Ballard was replaced as baseball coach. Shortly thereafter Ballard confronted and threatened to hit Superintendent Dobbs. He also threatened the teacher who had replaced him as baseball coach. Neither threat was witnessed by any student. Dobbs suspended Ballard and brought charges for his dismissal to the school board. After a hearing the board voted to terminate Ballard's teaching contract due to "moral turpitude" (immorality). Ballard brought suit challenging the termination.

Questions for Discussion and Reflection

1. How would the due process rights of a tenured and a nontenured teacher differ in this situation?
2. Is the court likely to uphold this dismissal on the grounds of immorality? Would the district's chances be better if the grounds for the dismissal had been insubordination?
3. What employment rights do teachers have to supplemental employment?

Visit the Companion Website for a more detailed description of the facts in the case **Ballard v. Independent School District of Bryan County.**

* * *

Too Late to Deposit

Winkler was a teacher and eighth-grade class sponsor at Crestview Middle School (TN). When students ordered class rings in the class, the company rebated a portion of the purchase price to the school. When the salesman was making out the rebate check, Winkler told him her name should appear on the check as well as the school's. Ms. Winkler received the check the last day of school before Christmas vacation but never deposited it in the school's account, depositing it in her personal account instead. When she returned from vacation the principal asked her about the money. She told him she had not had time to deposit it in the school account and gave him the money later. As a result of this incident the school board charged her with unprofessional conduct for not depositing the school's funds within 3 days of the receipt of those funds as required by school policy, and for depositing the school's funds into her personal account. Following a hearing, the board voted to suspend her without pay for the remainder of the year. Winkler filed suit.

Questions for Discussion and Reflection

1. What other disciplinary actions might the school district have taken short of suspension for the remainder of the year?
2. What factors should the court consider in making its decision?
3. Was Winkler's suit most likely based on a procedural or a substantive due process claim?

Visit the Companion Website for a more detailed description of the facts in the case **Winkler v. Tipton County Board of Education.**

* * *

Discipline or Reassignment?

In the fall of 2003, a hazing scandal involving the Mepham High School (NY) football team came to light. Three younger players were physically assaulted and sexually abused by four members of the varsity team while the team was attending a summer camp in Pennsylvania. Two of the coaches who attended the camp were teachers at the high school. Although a grand jury found the coaches did not have actual knowledge of the physical assault, it found that the coaches tolerated an atmosphere that encouraged hazing. In the aftermath of criminal charges and civil suits, the school district reassigned the two teachers from classroom duties at the high school to administrative duties at the central administrative office. The teachers sued the school board, claiming that this action violated state law and their federal due process rights because the district had failed to give notice of the charges against them and provide them with a hearing.

Questions for Discussion and Reflection

1. What responsibility does a teacher have to ensure students are in a safe and nonhostile environment?
2. When is the transfer of a school district employee really a form of discipline?
3. What due process should the teachers have been provided?

Visit the Companion Website for a more detailed description of the facts in the case **McElroy v. Board of Education of Bellmore-Merrick Central High School.**

MORE ON THE WEB

*Go to the Companion Website at **http://www.prenhall.com/underwood**, select Chapter 4, choose the More on the Web module to connect to the site mentioned.*

The education statutes of all states can be found at Cornell University's legal information institute, **http://www.law.cornell.edu/topics/state_statutes2.html#education**. Search the education statutes for the state where you plan to teach; list the grounds for dismissal stated in statute. Outline the procedures for dismissal detailed in statute. Are there additional procedures/steps you think should be provided teachers that are not included?

ENDNOTES

1. See *Bd. of Regents of State Colleges v. Roth,* 408 U.S. 564 (1972); *Perry v. Sindermann,* 408 U.S. 593 (1972).
2. *Custis v. Ok. City Public Schools,* 147 F.3d 1200 (10th Cir. 1998).

3. *Bd. of Regents of State Colleges v. Roth*, 408 U.S. 564 (1972); *Perry v. Sindermann*, 408 U.S. 593 (1972).

4. *Cleveland Bd. of Educ. v. Loudermill*, 470 U.S. 532 (1985).

5. 801 N.E.2d 622 (Ind. 2004).

6. 426 U.S. 482 (1976).

7. *Reitmeyer v. Unemployment Compensation Board of Review*, 602 A.D. 505 (Pa. Commonwealth 1992).

8. Imber, M. (2001). Morality and teacher effectiveness. *American School Board Journal, 188*(4), 64–66.

9. See *Zelno v. Lincoln Intermediate Unit No. 12 Bd. of Directors*, 786 A.2d 1022 (Pa. Commonwealth 2001).

10. See, e.g., *Rush v. Bd. of Educ. of Crete-Monee Comty. Sch. Dist.*, 727 N.E.2d 649 (Ill. App. 2000). (Court upheld immediate dismissal of a teacher who offered students the option of receiving a shock from a small engine rather than serving class detention. The school successfully argued that this was a clear violation of the corporal punishment policy.)

11. *Yanzick v. School District No. 23, Lake County Montana*, 641 P.2d 431 (Mont. 1982).

12. *Sherburne v. School Board of Swannee County*, 455 So.2d 1057 (Fla. Dist. Ct. App. 1984).

13. 539 U.S. 558 (2003).

14. 559 P.2d 1340 (Wash. 1977), *cert. denied*, 434 U.S. 379 (1977).

15. 336 F.3d 185 (2d Cir. 2003).

16. 29 F. Supp.2d 1279 (1999).

17. *In re Thomas*, 926 S.W.2d 163 (Mo. App. 1996).

18. *Cope v. Bd. of Educ. of Town of West Hartford*, 495 A.2d 718 (Conn. App. 1985). (Teacher's continual neglect of her overall teaching responsibilities, which involved not supervising her first-grade students to the point that their safety was in jeopardy, despite repeated warnings and admonitions, justified her termination.)

19. *Vukadinovich v. Bd. of Sch. Tr. of North Newton Sch. Corp.*, 47 Fed. App. 417, 2002 WL 31159318 (7th Cir. 2002).

20. Alexander, K., & Alexander, M. D. (2001). *American Public School Law* (5th ed.). Belmont, CA: West/Thompson Learning.

21. *Wingegar v. Des Moines Independent Community School District*, 20 F.3d 895 (8th Cir. 1994).

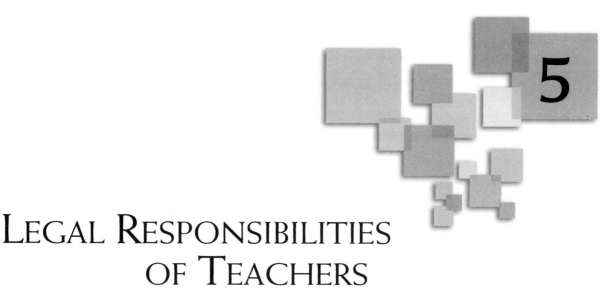

LEGAL RESPONSIBILITIES OF TEACHERS

In addition to the terms and conditions of employment discussed in chapter 2, school districts may make other requirements as conditions of employment so long as they do not violate the constitutional rights of teachers or state or federal laws. Chapter 6 discusses the requirements related to providing reasonable care and maintaining discipline. State and federal legislation imposes a number of job responsibilities on teachers. This chapter addresses several that have become increasingly important to educators in the last decade, including reporting child abuse, use of copyright material, use of the Internet, and acceptable use policies. After reading this chapter you will be able to

- Explain the common forms of child abuse and neglect.
- Identify the common signs of child abuse and neglect.
- Discuss the teacher's responsibility in reporting child abuse.
- Enumerate the criteria for a fair use exemption to the use of copyrighted materials.
- Outline the guidelines for the educational use of copyrighted print material, audiovisual material, and software.
- Distinguish between the permissible and impermissible use of broadcast recordings and commercial videotapes.
- Describe the common elements of an acceptable use policy.

CHILD ABUSE AND NEGLECT

Definition and Incidence

Both federal and state statutes define child abuse. The federal *Child Abuse Prevention and Treatment* Act (CAPTA),[1] as amended by the Keeping Children and Families Safe Act of 2003, defines child abuse and neglect as

> any recent act or failure to act on the part of a parent or caretaker which results in death, serious physical or emotional harm, sexual abuse or exploitation. It includes an act or failure to act which presents an imminent risk of serious harm.

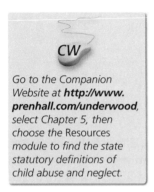

*Go to the Companion Website at **http://www. prenhall.com/underwood**, select Chapter 5, then choose the Resources module to find the state statutory definitions of child abuse and neglect.*

Based on the CAPTA guidelines, each state and U.S. territory has developed its own standard of what constitutes child abuse and neglect and the conditions and acts that will determine the grounds for state intervention. The major forms of child abuse and neglect specified in state statutes include neglect, physical abuse, sexual abuse/sexual exploitation, emotional/mental abuse, and abandonment.[2]

Although any form of child abuse or neglect can occur separately, they most often occur in combination.[3] Emotional abuse is almost always present with other forms of abuse. As shown in Table 5.1, in 2003, an estimated 906,000, or 12 children in every 1,000 in the United States, were victims of child abuse or neglect. Of these, 60% were neglected, almost 20% were physically abused, 10% were sexually abused, and 5% were emotionally abused.[4] Girls were more often victims than boys, and American Indian or Alaska Native children and African American children had higher rates of victimization than other population subgroups.

Child Neglect

Child neglect is a failure to provide for a child's basic needs and can be physical, medical, educational, or emotional in nature. Abandonment, expulsion from home, refusal to allow a runaway to return home, inadequate supervision, and the refusal to provide health care in a timely manner are all forms of *physical neglect*. Failure to provide medical treatment or mental health treatment would constitute medical neglect. Most state statutes provide a religious exception to the standard for parents who do not seek medical care for their children on religious grounds. Failure to attend to a child's special educational needs, failure to enroll a child in school, and the tolerance of chronic truancy are forms of *educational neglect*. *Emotional neglect* includes the failure to provide for the psychological well-being of the child, including being inattentive to a child's needs for affection, and parental permission to use and abuse drugs or alcohol.[5]

Table 5.1   Rates of Child Abuse and Neglect Victimization (victims per 1,000) by Maltreatment Type, Gender, Race, and Ethnicity, 2003

	Number of Victims	Victimization Rate
Maltreatment Type		
Physical abuse	148,877	2.3
Neglect	479,567	7.5
Medical neglect	17,945	0.3
Sexual abuse	78,188	1.2
Psychological maltreatment	38,603	0.6
Other abuse	132,993	3.7
Unknown	1,792	0.3
Gender		
Male	378,374	11.6
Female	405,505	13.1
Race/Ethnicity*		
American Indian/Alaskan Native	13,350	21.3
African American	199,723	20.4
Asian	4,652	2.7
White	419,378	11.0
Multiple Race	11,507	12.8
Hispanic	90,177	9.9

*Not all states reporting
Source: From *Child Maltreatment 2003,* by U.S. Department of Health and Human Services, Administration on Children, Youth and Families, 2005, Washington, DC: U.S. Government Printing Office.

Physical Abuse

Physical abuse includes punching, beating, kicking, biting, burning, shaking, throwing, stabbing, choking, hitting, or otherwise harming a child. The injury is considered abuse whether intentional or not.[6]

Sexual Abuse

Sexual abuse includes the fondling of a child's genitals, penetration, incest, rape, sodomy, indecent exposure, and commercial exploitation through prostitution or the production of pornographic materials by a parent or caretaker.[7] Sexual abuse is considered to be the most underreported form of child maltreatment due to the "conspiracy of silence" often associated with such cases.

Emotional Abuse

Emotional abuse includes acts or omissions by the parents or caregivers that might or could cause serious behavioral, cognitive, emotional, or mental disorders. Examples of emotional abuse include such nonphysical behaviors as constant criticizing, blaming, disparaging, or rejecting the child; habitual scapegoating, belittling, and intimidating; treating siblings unequally; deliberately enforcing isolation such as confinement in a dark closet; and continually withholding love, support, or guidance.[8]

Identifying Child Abuse and Neglect

The National Clearinghouse on Child Abuse and Neglect Information (NCCANI) functions as the gateway for information and resources on child abuse and neglect. It has developed an extensive list of indicators or signs of child abuse and neglect to assist parents, educational personnel, and other caregivers, as well as law enforcement and social service providers in recognizing possible child abuse or neglect. As stressed by the NCCANI, the presence of one of these signs does not prove a child is being abused, but when they occur repeatedly or in combination, they warrant closer examination and possibly reporting. Some of the common signs or indicators of child abuse and neglect that the child may exhibit at school include unexplained injuries, a pattern of accidents, and frequent absences or tardiness. Children who have been subjected to abuse often exhibit a variety of behavior indicators, including aggressive or withdrawn behavior, being overly compliant, passivity, attention-seeking behavior, anxiety, fear, or constant watchfulness, as if expecting something bad to happen.[9] Abused children may engage in self-destructive behaviors and exhibit low self-esteem, depression, and severe emotional problems. They may be socially isolated or repeatedly run away. They may exhibit a sudden decline in school performance, or have a learning problems or difficulty concentrating that cannot be attributed to any specific physical or psychological cause. Abused or neglected children often come to school early, stay late, or do not want to go home.[10]

Parents or caregivers also exhibit behaviors that may be indicators of child abuse or neglect. For example, they may show little concern for the child, provide minimal supervision, see the child as burdensome, or rarely look at or touch the child. They may deny the existence of, or blame the child for, problems the child is having at school or at home. They may see the child as bad or worthless and ask teachers or administrators to use harsh physical discipline if the child misbehaves.[11] There is increasing awareness that abuse of drugs or alcohol by parents and other caretakers may be related to abuse and neglect. Many states have responded by expanding the definition of child abuse or neglect to include exposing children to illegal drugs in the home environment.[12]

Table 5.2 provides some of the signs associated with particular types of child abuse and neglect. However, as the NCCANI reiterates, these forms of abuse are most often found in combination, not isolation. For example, a physically abused child is often emotionally abused, and a sexually abused child may also be neglected.[13]

Table 5.2 Signs of Child Abuse and Neglect

Signs of Physical Abuse

Consider the possibility of physical abuse when the **child**

- has unexplained burns, bites, bruises, broken bones, or black eyes;
- has fading bruises or other marks noticeable after an absence from school;
- seems frightened of the parents and protests or cries when it is time to go home;
- shrinks at the approach of adults;
- reports injury by a parent or another adult caregiver.

Consider the possibility of physical abuse when the **parent or other adult caregiver**

- offers conflicting, unconvincing, or no explanation for the child's injury;
- describes the child as "evil," or in some other very negative way;
- uses harsh physical discipline with the child;
- has a history of abuse as a child.

Signs of Neglect

Consider the possibility of neglect when the **child**

- is frequently absent from school;
- begs or steals food or money;
- lacks needed medical or dental care, immunizations, or glasses;
- is consistently dirty and has severe body odor;
- lacks sufficient clothing for the weather;
- abuses alcohol or other drugs;
- states that there is no one at home to provide care.

Consider the possibility of neglect when the **parent or other adult caregiver**

- appears to be indifferent to the child;
- seems apathethic or depressed;
- behaves irrationally or in a bizarre manner;
- is abusing alcohol or other drugs.

Signs of Sexual Abuse

Consider the possibility of sexual abuse when the **child**

- has difficulty walking or sitting;
- suddenly refuses to change for gym or to participate in physical activities;
- reports nightmares or bedwetting;
- experiences a sudden change in appetite;
- demonstrates bizarre, sophisticated, or unusual sexual knowledge or behavior;
- becomes pregnant or contracts a venereal disease, particularly if under age 14;
- runs away;
- reports sexual abuse by a parent or another adult caregiver.

(continued)

Table 5.2   (Continued)

Consider the possibility of sexual abuse when the **parent or other adult caregiver**

- is unduly protective of the child or severely limits the child's contact with other children, especially of the opposite sex;
- is secretive and isolated;
- is jealous or controlling with family members.

Signs of Emotional Maltreatment

Consider the possibility of emotional maltreatment when the **child**

- shows extremes in behavior, such as overly compliant or demanding behavior, extreme passivity, or aggression;
- is either inappropriately adult (parenting other children, for example) or inappropriately infantile (frequently rocking or head banging, for example);
- is delayed in physical or emotional development;
- has attempted suicide;
- reports a lack of attachment to the parent.

Consider the possibility of emotional maltreatment when **the parent or other adult caregiver**

- constantly blames, belittles, or berates the child;
- is unconcerned about the child and refuses to consider offers of help for the child's problems;
- overtly rejects the child.

Source: From *Recognizing Child Abuse and Neglect: Signs and Symptoms,* by National Clearinghouse on Child and Neglect Information, 2004, Washington, DC: U.S. Government Printing Office. www.nccanch.acf.hhs.gov

Reporting Child Abuse and Neglect

Because child abuse occurs across all socioeconomic classes and ethnic/racial groups, most teachers will likely be confronted with this problem at some point during their teaching careers. In fact, educational personnel made 13% of all reports of abuse and neglect in 2002, including 22% of all physical abuse.[14] Because of frequent contact with children, all states have enacted statutes that include school personnel as among those individuals required to report actual or suspected child abuse or neglect. (Other mandated individuals include health care workers, child care providers, social workers, and law enforcement personnel.) These statutes require mandated reporters such as teachers to make a report immediately upon gaining knowledge or suspicion of the abuse or neglect. Teachers and counselors must report suspected abuse or neglect even though to do so would violate a confidence; they cannot claim privileged communication as a defense for failure to report.

CW

Go to the Companion Website at **http://www. prenhall.com/underwood**, select Chapter 5, then choose the Resources module to find the state-specific child abuse reporting requirements.

Most state reporting statutes detail the procedures to be followed in making the report. In all jurisdictions the initial report may be made orally to either a law enforcement agency, child protective services, or another designated agency. The report will typically require, at a minimum, the name, address, and age of the child, the name of the child's parents or other responsible caregiver, the nature and extent of the child's injuries, and the name and address of the reporter.[15]

State statutes that require teachers to report suspected child abuse do not demand that reporters be certain that the child has been abused, only that there be "reasonable cause to believe" that the child is subject to abuse or neglect. All state statutes provide school employees who report suspected child abuse or neglect with immunity from civil and criminal liability if the report was *made in good faith*. In many states, the law presumes the good faith of the teacher, and the person challenging the reporting teacher would have to prove that the teacher did not act in good faith. Further, most states protect the identity of the reporter from outsiders.

Under most state reporting statutes, mandated reporters who "knew or should have known" of child abuse or neglect and failed to report it are subject to various penalties, including criminal prosecution and/or fines (e.g., in Minnesota, imprisonment of up to 2 years and a fine of up to $4,000[16]). A civil suit claiming negligence may also be brought against the teacher for failure to report child abuse. For example, in a case from New York a music teacher knew his student had had a sexual encounter with an adult during a summer theater program. When the student's mother learned of the sexual encounter she sued the district and the music teacher.[17] The trial court dismissed Mrs. F.'s claim against the school district on the grounds that the district's breach of its statutory duty to report known or suspected child abuse did not create a cause of action for anyone other than the abused child. In addition, school districts may impose disciplinary

---

DEERFIELD REPORTING CHILD ABUSE/CHILD PROTECTION POLICY

It is the policy of the Board of Education that this school district comply with the Child Protection Act.

To that end, any school official or employee who has reasonable cause to know or suspect that a child has been subjected to abuse or neglect or who has observed the child being subjected to circumstances or conditions which would reasonably result in abuse or neglect, as defined by statute, shall immediately upon receiving such information report or cause a report to be made to the appropriate county department of social services or local law enforcement agency. Failure to report promptly may result in civil and/or criminal liability. A person who reports child abuse or neglect in good faith is immune from civil or criminal liability.

measures against employees for failure to follow required reporting statutes. Because of the serious consequences to the child, to the teacher, and possibly to the district for failure to report child abuse, most school boards have adopted policies affirming the responsibility of district employees to report child abuse and detailing the procedures to be followed when abuse is suspected.

Typically school district policies related to reporting abuse and neglect require teachers to report suspected abuse or neglect to the principal, school social worker, or counselor/psychologist. However, if state statutes require the teacher to make a report to a designated state agency, the teacher must also report the suspected abuse or neglect to that agency. Telling the principal or other designated individual does not relieve the teacher of this obligation. An example of a school district policy is the Deerfield Reporting Child Abuse/Child Protection Policy. (See page 85.)

OBSERVING COPYRIGHT

Recognizing the importance of promoting "the Progress of Science and useful Arts," the U.S. Constitution authorized Congress to pass laws "securing for limited Times to Authors and Inventors the exclusive Right to their respective Writings and Discoveries."[18] Beginning with the first federal copyright law in 1790, Congress has enacted a series of laws designed to protect the author or originator of an original work from all forms of unauthorized reproduction or use of the work. Copyright law covers not only written material but also audio and video material and computer programs. Just because a work is "old" or out of print does not mean it is not protected by copyright. Copyrights on works created before 1978 last for 75 years from the date of publication or copyright renewal. Copyrights on works created after January 1, 1978, last for 50 years after the death of the author.

Because of their widespread use of print and nonprint material in the classroom, teachers must be knowledgeable about, and comply with, federal copyright laws and set an example for students in the legal and ethical use of copyrighted materials.

Fair Use of Copyrighted Works

Copyright laws are designed not only to protect the originator of a work from its unauthorized use but also to provide guidelines for its authorized use. These guidelines provide teachers the opportunity to use copyrighted materials under certain conditions, two of which are rather straightforward: (1) They have requested and been granted permission to use the work from the copyright holder and (2) the work is in the public domain. A work is in the public domain if it is over 75 years old or has been created by a governmental agency or an employee of the agency acting in his or her role as an employee. A third condition is if the use is considered "fair use." The *fair use doctrine,* also known as the *face-to-face teaching exemption,* allows the nonprofit reproduction and use of certain materials for classroom use without permission of the copyright owner if the following criteria are met:

- The purpose and character of use criterion requires that the use be for teaching, scholarship, or research.
- The nature of the copyrighted work must permit copying (e.g., textbooks, consumable workbooks, and cable broadcasts cannot be copied unless specifically authorized).
- The amount of the copyrighted material used cannot exceed specified guidelines (see, e.g., Figure 5.1).
- The use of the copyrighted material cannot have a negative effect on the present or future sales or market value of the work.

If the proposed use meets these criteria, a face-to-face teaching exemption is created and the copyrighted materials can be used under stated guidelines related to the use of each form of work. In the case of printed materials, the guidelines state that the proposed use must meet the tests of brevity, spontaneity, and cumulative effect. As detailed in the guidelines provided in Figure 5.1, the *brevity test* places limits on the amount of reproduction that can be made and depends on the type of work. To pass the *spontaneity test* the reproduction must not have been planned in advance and must have been initiated by the teacher, not the principal, or other supervisors, and the time between the decision to use the material and its use must have presented such a time constraint that it was not feasible to request and obtain permission. Last, the *cumulative effect test* states that copying can be for only one course, no more than nine multiple copies per class, per term, and it places limits on how much can be reproduced from the same author, anthology, or journal.

If you are in a distance learning situation, the concepts of fair use are a little less strict. In November 2002, the Technology, Education and Copyright Harmonization (TEACH) Act went into effect. This law is an attempt to somewhat loosen the constraints of copyright law in legitimate distance education programs. As a part of a regular distance learning program, copyrighted material may be stored electronically for students to use at different times and locations. In addition, distance education can digitize and transmit copyrighted work for use in the distance education class.

The Sunshine School District Policy on Copyright Compliance on page 89 presents one district's policy to ensure compliance with federal copyright guidelines.

Broadcast Recording

The increasing use of instructional technology has brought to light a number of issues related to use of copyrighted nonprint materials, namely television programs and videotapes. In 1981 a committee of educators and copyright owners and

Figure 5.1 Guidelines for Classroom Copying

1. A single copy may be made of any of the following for your own scholarly research or use in teaching:
   A. A chapter from a book:
   B. An article from a periodical or newspaper:
   C. A short story, short essay, or short poem:
   D. A chart, graph, diagram, drawing, cartoon or picture from a book, periodical, or newspaper.

2. Multiple copies (not to exceed in any event more than one copy per pupil in a course) may be made for classroom use or discussion, provided that each copy includes a notice of copyright and that the following tests are met:

A. Brevity Test
   (i) Poetry: (a) a complete poem of less than 250 words and if printed on not more than two pages, or (b) from a longer poem, an excerpt of not more than 250 words.
   (ii) Prose: (a) Either a complete article, story, or essay of less than 2,500 words, or (b) an excerpt from any prose work of not more than 1,000 words or 10 percent of the work, whichever is less, but in any event a minimum of 5,000 words.
   (iii) Illustration: One chart, graph, diagram, drawing, cartoon or picture per book or per periodical issue.
   (iv) "Special" works in poetry, prose, or in "poetic prose" that combine language with illustrations and are less than 2,500 words in their entirety may not be reproduced in their entirety: however, an excerpt of not more than two of the published pages of such special work and containing not more than 10 percent of the words may be reproduced.

B. Spontaneity Test
   (i) The copying is at your instance and inspiration, and
   (ii) The inspiration and decision to use the work and the moment of its use for maximum teaching effectiveness are so close in time that it would be unreasonable to expect you would receive a timely reply to a request for permission.

C. Cumulative Effect Test
   (i) The copying of the material is for only one course in the school in which the copies are made.
   (ii) Not more than one short poem, article, story, essay or two excerpts may be copied from the same author, nor more than three from the same collective work or periodical volume during one class term.
   (iii) There cannot be more than nine instances of multiple copying for one course during one class term.

   [These limitations do not apply to current news periodicals and newspapers and current news sections of other periodicals.]

3. Copying cannot be used to create or to replace or substitute for anthologies, compilations, or collective works.

4. There can be no copying of, or from, "consumable" works (e.g., workbooks, exercises, standardized tests and test booklets and answer sheets).

5. Copying cannot substitute for the purchase of books, publishers' reprints, or periodicals.

6. Copying cannot be directed by a higher authority.

7. You cannot copy the same item from term to term.

8. No charge can be made to the student beyond the actual cost of the photocopying.

Source: Excerpt from Report of the House Committee on the Judiciary (House Report No. 94–1476).

SUNSHINE SCHOOL DISTRICT POLICY ON COPYRIGHT COMPLIANCE

The board recognizes that federal law makes it illegal to duplicate copyrighted materials without authorization of the holder of the copyright, except for certain exempt purposes.

Severe penalties may be imposed for unauthorized copying or using of audiovisual or printed materials and computer software, unless the copying or using conforms to the "fair use" doctrine.

Under the fair use doctrine, unauthorized reproduction of copyrighted materials is permissible for such purposes as criticism, comment, news reporting, teaching, scholarship, or research. If duplicating or changing a product is to fall within the bounds of fair use, these four standards must be met for any of the foregoing purposes:

1. *The purpose and character of the use.* The use must be for such purposes as teaching or scholarship.
2. *The nature of the copyrighted work.* Staff may make single copies of book chapters for use in research; instruction or preparation for teaching; articles from periodicals or newspapers; short stories, essays, or poems; and charts, graphs, diagrams, drawings, cartoons, or pictures from books, periodicals, or newspapers in accordance with these guidelines.
3. *The amount and substantiality of the portion used.* Copying the whole of a work cannot be considered fair use; copying a small portion may be if these guidelines are followed.
4. *The effect of the use upon the potential market for or value of the copyrighted work.* If resulting economic loss to the copyright holder can be shown, even making a single copy of certain materials may be an infringement, and making multiple copies presents the danger of greater penalties.

While the district encourages its staff to enrich the learning programs by making proper use of supplementary materials, it is the responsibility of district staff to abide by the district's copying procedures and obey the requirements of the law. In no circumstances shall it be necessary for district staff to violate copyright requirements in order to perform their duties properly. The district cannot be responsible for any violations of the copyright law by its staff.

Any staff member who is uncertain as to whether reproducing or using copyrighted material complies with the district's procedures or is permissible under the law should contact the superintendent or the person designated as the copyright compliance officer. The latter will also assist staff in obtaining proper authorization to copy or use protected material when such authorization is required.

experts developed *Guidelines for Off-the-Air Recording of Broadcast Programming for Educational Purposes.* The guidelines provide that a nonprofit educational institution may tape broadcast television programs for classroom use if requested by an individual teacher. The teacher also may tape programs at home. The program must be recorded in its entirety (but not all must be shown), must include the copyright notice on the program, and cannot be altered in any way. During the 10 days after taping, the individual teacher may show the material once (but to more than one class) in a classroom or other location regularly used for instructional purposes. Its use must be an integral part of the curriculum, not for entertainment. Additional use is limited to viewing for evaluating the program for possible purchase or for obtaining a license. After 45 days, the tape must be erased or destroyed. All other off-the-air recording (except for the purpose of time shifting for personal use) is illegal unless the program is recorded from educational television. The taping of television programs telecast by cable or satellite providers does not fall under these guidelines because they are not free to the public. Before taping any programs carried by cable or satellite, the teacher must contact the particular station or network to determine its taping guidelines.[19]

Fair Use of Audiovisual Material

Generally, teachers cannot duplicate audiovisual materials or convert them from one format to another (e.g., from cassette tape to CD or from 16 mm film to videotape). Use of copyrighted videotapes purchased by the district is, of course, permitted. Other videotapes for which public performance rights in a school setting have been obtained may also be shown if shown as part of a systematic program of instruction and not for entertainment or recreation. Teachers may also make a single copy of a recording of copyrighted music owned by the district or the teacher if the purpose is to construct oral exercises or examinations.

Fair Use of Computer Software

The copying of computer software has become a major area of copyright infringement. The high cost of software, combined with limited school budgets, has resulted in numerous cases of unauthorized copying or loading of software. In 1980 the federal copyright law was amended to include software. According to the amendments, one archival or backup copy can be made of the original computer program for use in the event the original is destroyed or damaged. Making multiple copies, even for educational purposes, violates the fair use principle. In a similar vein, the fair use doctrine also prohibits multiple use of a master program; that is, loading a program on a number of computers for simultaneous use. Student use of the program one at a time is permissible, but not at the same time. However, teachers and school districts can negotiate a network license agreement with a software company that would allow for multiple use of a particular program at a substantial savings over purchasing multiple copies.

> **SUNSHINE SCHOOL BOARD POLICY ON REPRODUCTION OF COPYRIGHTED MATERIALS**
>
> School board employees may reproduce copyrighted materials under the copyrighted provisions of the United States Code, Title XVII. Any reproduction of copyrighted materials shall be done either with the written permission of the copyright holder or within the bounds of the congressional "fair use" guidelines; otherwise the individual responsible for reproduction may be liable for breach of copyright under existing laws.
>
> Willful infringement may result in disciplinary action. In the case of a court action for damages, a finding of willful infringement would preclude the board paying any judgment rendered against the employee or paying any attorney's fees or costs incurred by the employee in conjunction with a lawsuit, and may render the employee liable to the board for any damages the board is deemed liable to pay.
>
> If a question exists as to whether a particular act of copying might be in violation of the copyright law, it is prudent to request permission. A copy of each request must be kept on file in the school and an additional copy forwarded to the appropriate subject area coordinator.

In the use of copyrighted software, as in the use of any copyrighted material, teachers are required to obey both the letter and the spirit of copyright laws and to adhere to any relevant school board policies or guidelines related to the use of copyrighted materials. For example, the Sunshine School Board Policy on Reproduction of Copyrighted Materials (see box above) states that failure to follow established school board policies could result in a teacher charged with copyright infringement not being legally or financially supported by the district.

Use of Internet Materials and File Sharing

The explosion in the use of the Internet and digital technology in curriculum and instruction has created a number of legal issues surrounding their use, many still unresolved. In 1998 the Digital Millennium Copyright Act[20] extended the fair use doctrine to digital technology. In the case of materials found on the Internet or World Wide Web, educators should remember that even if the materials are not registered with the copyright office, copyright laws still protect them and they should not be considered in the public domain unless specifically stated.

Of particular concern to school districts is the practice of file sharing. Not all file sharing is illegal. However, anyone who uploads a copy of a copyrighted song, video, or software with the purpose of making it available to others is violating copyright, as is any person who downloads such a file. The concern of school districts seems justified. A recent poll found that 13% of students 8 to 18

School districts should take note of recent copyright infringement lawsuits filed by the Recording Industry Association of America (RIAA), a trade group representing the five major recording companies. "Are you headed to junior high schools to round up the usual suspects?" asked Senator Dick Durbin (D-Ill.) in a recent hearing. As the RIAA continues its aggressive campaign to sue people who illegally share music online, many schools and colleges are facing increased technical and legal pressures to halt the swapping of music and movie files over campus and school district Internet connections. U.S copyright laws allow for damages of $750 to $150,000 for each song offered illegally on a person's computer. The RIAA has thus far filed 261 federal lawsuits, including a suit against a 12-year-old girl. Additionally, at least 10 universities and colleges have been served with subpoenas demanding that they help the recording industry identify possible targets for such lawsuits. Boston College and the Massachusetts Institute of Technology moved to quash subpoenas that sought the names of students suspected of music piracy because the subpoenas did not allow for adequate time to notify the students as mandated by the Family Educational Rights and Privacy Act (FERPA). Some colleges and universities have initiated campus ads and orientation sessions to educate students on the legal ramifications of illegal file sharing. They also are installing software to block access to the popular file sharing sites. Although there are legitimate reasons for file sharing, most students do not realize that what they are doing could get them into legal trouble.

Source: From "Schools Use Software, Warning to Stop Illegal File-Swapping," October 2003, *eSchool News.* http://www.eschoolnews.com/news/showStory.cfm?ArticleID=4662

years old are most likely to illegally download music, software, videos, or games while at school or the library.[21] (See the In the News feature.)

To address this problem school districts have adopted policies that deal with illegal file sharing, attempted to block access to many sites at which illegal file sharing is known to take place, and disciplined offenders. Teachers have the responsibility to make sure students understand these restrictions and to monitor compliance of school policies. Teachers who knowingly allow students to engage in illegal file sharing could be charged with contributing to the copyright infringement.

Computer and Internet Acceptable Use Policies

Concern about the responsible, ethical, and legal use of computer networks and the Internet, as well as the concern that students may become engaged in inappropriate discussions or receive threats or other dangerous communications through instant messaging services or chatrooms, has led school districts to adopt a number of strategies and technologies designed not only to prevent irresponsible and illegal use but also to protect students from Internet predators.

Congress enacted the Children's Internet Protection Act[22] out of concern that children could access materials through the Internet that may be harmful to them or pornographic. The statute requires school districts and public libraries to use blocking or filtering software to filter out this material as a condition to the receipt of federal funds for technology. The United States Supreme Court upheld this requirement in 2003[23] finding that the requirement to filter material that was pornographic or harmful to children is consistent with libraries' role and not inconsistent with the First Amendment rights to free speech.

In addition to filtering software schools use a variety of methods to protect students from inappropriate content or inappropriate uses. About half use monitoring software that allows teachers or administrators to monitor student Internet activity.[24] Other districts simply ban student use of Internet messaging or chatrooms on school computers. More commonly, student use is allowed, but only in safe chatrooms that the teacher has set up and supervises (and the principal has approved).

The district's so-called acceptable use policies (AUP) typically detail use of these technologies, as well as all other use of computers and the Internet. These policies outline the conditions and establish the guidelines for student and staff use of district computer networks, including the Internet, and transmitting information to classrooms. Most acceptable use policies include the following components:[25]

- A description of the instructional philosophies and strategies to be supported by Internet access in schools;
- A statement on the educational uses and advantages of the Internet in the school;
- A list of the responsibilities of educators, parents, and students in using the Internet;
- A code of conduct governing behavior on the Internet;
- A description of the consequences of violating the AUP;
- A description of what constitutes acceptable and unacceptable use of the Internet;
- A disclaimer absolving the school division, under specific circumstances, from responsibility;
- A statement reminding users that Internet access and the use of computer networks is a privilege;
- A statement that the AUP is in compliance with state and national telecommunication rules and regulations.

Typically AUPs also call for written agreements by teachers, parents, and students that detail access and use that must be signed indicating the signers' intent to abide by the AUP. The Wired School District Acceptable Use Policy for Teachers, shown on the next page, is an example of one.

WIRED SCHOOL DISTRICT ACCEPTABLE USE POLICY FOR TEACHERS

The district provides computers, networks, and Internet access to support the educational mission of the schools and to enhance the curriculum and learning opportunities for students and school staff.

Employees are to use the school's computers, networks, and Internet services for school-related purposes and performance of job duties. Incidental personal use of school computers is permitted as long as such use does not interfere with the employee's job duties and performance, with system operations, or with other system users. *Incidental personal use* is defined as use by an individual employee for occasional personal communications. Employees are reminded that such personal use must comply with this policy and all other applicable policies, procedures, and rules.

Any employee who violates this policy will be subject to disciplinary action, up to and including discharge. Illegal uses of the school unit's computers will also result in referral to law enforcement authorities.

All computers remain under the control, custody, and supervision of the school. The school reserves the right to monitor all computer and Internet activity by employees. Employees have no expectation of privacy in their use of school computers.

Each employee authorized to access the school unit's computers, networks, and Internet services is required to sign an acknowledgment form stating that he or she has read this policy. The acknowledgment form will be retained in the employee's personnel file.

GUIDING LEGAL PRINCIPLES

- All states have child abuse reporting statutes that require teachers to report suspected child abuse to either the police or social service agencies.
- These statutes cover broad forms of child abuse and neglect, including neglect, physical abuse, sexual abuse, sexual exploitation, emotional abuse, and neglect.
- Teachers are not expected to investigate child abuse, but must report once they have a reasonable suspicion of abuse, and leave it to social services or law enforcement to investigate.
- Copyright protections cover not only books and other written materials but also audio material, video material, and software.

- Educators may use copyrighted materials if
  - they have received prior permission from the copyright holder;
  - the work is in the public domain (not held by copyright);
  - the use is considered "fair use," which basically allows a limited number of copies to be made for teaching purposes if the use does not have a negative effect on the market value of the copyright.
- The fair use doctrine applies to other forms of material and prohibits the making of multiple copies of videos, audio recordings, and computer software.
- Anyone who uploads a copy of copyrighted song, video, or game for the purpose of making it available to another or anyone who downloads such a file is violating copyright.
- In most districts computer use is limited to professional uses, allowing only incidental personal use. Districts typically have teachers and students sign an acceptable use agreement outlining the terms and conditions of computer access.

YOU BE THE JUDGE

Go to the Companion Website at ***http://www.prenhall.com/underwood****, select Chapter 5, choose the* You Be the Judge *module and click on the name of the case for more information about the case and the court's decision and rationale.*

Protecting Those Who Report

In accordance with Wisconsin's statute requiring schools to report suspected child abuse to their local department of human services, two Oconto Falls Area School District teachers reported a suspicious mark on a student's forehead. After speaking with the student, a social worker concluded that abuse was unlikely. The student's parents, unhappy with the school making a suspected child abuse report, met with the superintendent, Polashek. Polashek then met with the teachers who made the report. Following that meeting, he sent the parents a letter disclosing the names of the employees and sent copies of the letter to the employees. The teachers filed an action against Polashek for violating Wisconsin's child abuse reporting statute by revealing the names of the persons who had reported suspected abuse.

Questions for Discussion and Reflection

1. Did the teachers fulfill their legal responsibility to report child abuse in this situation, or should they have conducted investigations themselves to make certain their concerns were valid before they reported their suspicions to social services?

2. What protections are afforded teachers in reporting suspected child abuse? Why is it important to protect the confidentiality of teachers when they make reports of suspected child abuse?

3. If the superintendent loses the case, what action should the school board take against him?

Visit the Companion Website for a more detailed description of the facts in the case **State v. Polashek.**

* * *

Icing on the Cake

Marcus taught adult education classes in San Diego. She wrote a booklet entitled "Cake Decorating Made Easy," registered the copyright, and self-published the booklet, which was about 50 pages in length. Marcus sold these booklets to her students. Rowley, a home economics teacher at San Diego Unified School District, enrolled in one of Marcus's cake decorating classes and purchased the booklet. Later, Rowley prepared her own booklet entitled "Cake Decorating Learning Activity Package" for use in her food services class. The learning packet was 24 pages long; she made at least 15 copies of it and made them available to her students for 3 consecutive years. Rowley admits that 11 of the 24 pages in the learning packet were directly from Marcus's booklet. An additional 4 pages of the materials are identical, but contain material from the Consumer Service Department. Marcus learned of Rowley's publication when one of her students accused her of plagiarizing Rowley's work. Marcus filed a copyright infringement action against Rowley.

Questions for Discussion and Reflection

1. Can Rowley justify the duplication of Marcus's material under the concept of fair use? Why or why not?

2. Would your response be the same if Rowley made a profit from the learning packets?

3. Under what conditions can or should teacher-developed materials be copyrighted? Is it important to provide copyright protection for teacher-developed instructional materials?

Visit the Companion Website for a more detailed description of the facts in the case **Marcus v. Rowley.**

* * *

Don't Look

Stueber was a high school art teacher in Citrus County, Florida. A disciplinary complaint was filed against him alleging that he had frequently used his school computer to access pornography on the Internet and that he had reconnected his school computer to access the Internet without authorization. During the hearing on the complaint the school district attorney presented materials documenting the Internet sites Stueber had accessed on his school computer. Stueber admitted accessing inappropriate sites, but claimed they were not teenage pornography, as had been claimed during the hearing.

Questions for Discussion and Reflection

1. Given Stueber's admission, what disciplinary action should the district take?
2. Should it matter if he had never accessed the pornography during school hours?
3. What preventative measures should school districts take to prevent this type of behavior? Should they be the same for teachers and students?

Visit the Companion Website for a more detailed description of the facts in the case **Stueber v. Gallagher.**

MORE ON THE WEB

Go to the Companion Website at ***http://www.prenhall.com/underwood***, select Chapter 5, choose the More on the Web *module to connect to the site mentioned.*

Go to the U.S. Copyright Office website at **http://www.copyright.gov**. Find the directions on how to register written (literary) or performing arts work for copyright protection. What would be the process to copyright an educational game you developed for classroom use? How difficult does this process appear? If you have work you might want to protect, complete the registration process.

ENDNOTES

1. 42 U.S.C. § 5106 (2005).
2. National Clearinghouse on Child Abuse and Neglect Information (NCCANI). (2004). *Statutes-at-a-glance: Definitions of child abuse and neglect.* Retrieved August 24, 2004, from http://www.nccanch.acf.hhs.gov
3. National Clearinghouse on Child Abuse and Neglect Information (NCCANI). (2004). *Recognizing child abuse and neglect: Signs and symptoms.* Retrieved August 15, 2004, from http://www.nccanch.acf.hhs.gov
4. U.S. Department of Health and Human Services, Administration on Children, Youth and Families. (2005). *Child maltreatment 2003: Reports from the states to the national child abuse and neglect data system.* Washington, DC: U.S. Government Printing Office.
5. National Clearinghouse on Child Abuse and Neglect Information (NCCANI). (2002). *HHS reports new child abuse and neglect statistics.* Retrieved August 15, 2004, from http://www.acf.dhhs.gov/news/press/200x/abuse.htm

6. National Clearinghouse on Child Abuse and Neglect Information (NCCANI). (2004). *What is child abuse and neglect?* Retrieved August 15, 2004, from http://www.nccanch.acf.hhs.gov/pubs/factsheets/whatiscan.cfm

7. Ibid.

8. Ibid.

9. NCCANI, *Recognizing child abuse and neglect.*

10. Ibid.

11. Ibid.

12. National Clearinghouse on Child Abuse and Neglect Information (NCCANI). (2004). *Parental drug use as child abuse.* Retrieved August 15, 2004, from http://nccanch.acf.hhs.gov/general/legal/statutes/drugexposed.cfm

13. NCCANI, *Recognizing child abuse and neglect.*

14. NCCANI, *Child maltreatment 2002.*

15. National Clearinghouse on Child Abuse and Neglect Information (NCCANI). (2004). *Statutes-at-a-glance: Reporting procedures.* Retrieved August 15, 2004, from http://www.nccanch.acf.hhs.gov

16. National Clearinghouse on Child Abuse and Neglect Information (NCCANI). (2004). *Statutes-at-a-glance: Reporting penalties.* Retrieved August 15, 2004, from http://www.nccanch.acf.hhs.gov

17. *Lurene F. v. Olsson,* 740 N.Y.2d 797 (N.Y. Sup. 2002).

18. Article I, Section 8, clause 8.

19. Botterbusch, H. R. (1996). *Copyright in the age of new technology.* Bloomington, IN: Phi. Delta Kappa Educational Foundation.

20. Digital Millennium Copyright Act, 17 U.S.C. § 1201 *et seq.* (2004).

21. Soronen, L. E. (2004, August). Stop students from stealing music. *Inquiry and Analysis,* pp. 4–6.

22. 20 U.S.C. § 7001 (2005).

23. *American Library Association v. U.S.,* 539 U.S. 194 (2003).

24. Public schools use many ways to keep Web surfing safe. (2002). *Maintaining Safe Schools,* 8(11), 9.

25. Virginia Department of Education, Division of Technology. (2004). *Acceptable use policies: A handbook.* Retrieved May 3, 2005, from http://www.pen.k12.va.us/go/VDOE/Technology/AUP/home.html

6

NEGLIGENCE AND DEFAMATION IN THE SCHOOL SETTING

A tort is a civil wrong, a violation of a duty, that causes harm. Tort law provides individuals with a way to sue for compensation for harm someone has caused them. In our legal system, an individual injured by a breach of duty can sue the other person to collect compensation for that injury. There are basically two types of torts: intentional torts and unintentional torts. The most common form of intentional torts involving teachers include trespass, assault, battery, and defamation (libel and slander). Unintentional torts include negligence and strict liability (whereby an individual is held responsible for all the results of his or her actions).

Although isolated cases exist of teachers being charged with assault and battery of a student or colleague or unlawful trespass on school property, the most common kinds of tort in the public school context are negligence and defamation. Tort actions may be brought against individuals, such as administrators and school board members, or the district itself. Tort actions may also be brought against teachers: Teachers may be held personally responsible for their own actions that result in an injury. To protect themselves from financial loss resulting from a tort suit, most districts purchase liability insurance as do teachers, often through their professional organizations. After reading this chapter you will be able to

- Explain the elements of negligence.
- Outline the primary duties the school owes students.
- Identify factors to be considered in determining whether a teacher acted as a "reasonable" teacher.

- Discuss the three defenses against negligence.
- Distinguish between educational and professional malpractice.
- Explain the elements of defamation.

ELEMENTS OF NEGLIGENCE

Not all accidents or injuries create liability for negligence. Negligence occurs only when someone acts unreasonably and as a result another is injured. Generally, commonsense notions apply to determine liability. Four elements of negligence must be established for a plaintiff to win in a negligence lawsuit: duty, breach of duty, causation, and injury. All four elements (defined below) must be proven before the plaintiff can recover damages.

Duty

The duty of care is a commonsense notion. A *duty* exists when there is enough of a relationship between two people that a responsibility exists not to expose the other to unreasonable risks. Duties can arise from contracts, common sense, or a special relationship between the parties. Also a duty can arise from an individual's own actions when a person assumes additional responsibilities.

Although teachers have the duty of providing an appropriate standard of care for their students, the standard of care expected is not the same for all teachers and all students. The law holds teachers of younger children to a higher duty of care than teachers of more mature students. The law also requires a higher standard of care of teachers of students with physical or mental disabilities, as well as of physical education and vocational and industrial arts teachers because of the inherent dangers in the activities involved.

In the general workforce, a supervisor, and ultimately the employer, is responsible for the negligent acts of employees under the doctrine of *respondeat superior.* However, in education, generally no one is automatically responsible for the acts of another. School districts and administrators are not automatically

---

ELEMENTS OF NEGLIGENCE

- **Duty:** The defendant had a duty to protect the plaintiff from unreasonable risks.
- **Breach:** The duty was breached by the failure to exercise an appropriate standard of care.
- **Causation:** There was a causal connection between the negligent conduct and the resulting injury.
- **Injury:** An actual injury resulted.

responsible for the negligent acts of teachers. In school situations, usually a plaintiff must find a separate duty on the part of each defendant to find liability. Among the duties schools owe students are the following:

- duty to hire and retain qualified and competent staff;
- duty to adequately supervise students;
- duty to provide adequate and appropriate instruction;
- duty to provide a safe environment;
- duty to provide safe transportation; and
- duty subsequent to injury.

Duty to Hire and Retain Qualified and Competent Staff. Schools have a duty to employ qualified and competent staff. A school district that permits an untrained person to teach physical education or shop classes may have breached this duty. Similarly, hiring someone who has a record of child abuse or assault could lead to a claim of negligent hiring.[1]

Duty to Adequately Supervise Students. Usually a duty to supervise exists while students are in the custody or control of the school (e.g., on school property during the school day, while on field trips, or during extracurricular events). A school may have a duty to supervise students at other times. This duty will depend in part, on whether the student is considered to be in the school's custody or under its control. For example, in an unfortunate but typical case a car struck and injured a seventh-grade student when he ran off school grounds and onto a public street while being chased by another student. The accident occurred prior to the beginning of the school day. The student's family sued the school district for negligent failure to supervise students who are on school property prior to the beginning of the school day. The state supreme court ruled that the school district was not liable for the student's injuries because the school had no duty to supervise or protect a student who was not in the school building and, therefore, not in the school's custody or under its control.[2]

Schools may have a duty to supervise students on school grounds before and after school when they have caused them to be there (e.g., when the bus drops them off). Schools may assume greater duties to supervise when they have, by their previous actions, assumed the duty to supervise at a particular time (e.g., when some staff have consistently supervised students before the official time to arrive).

Clearly schools have a duty to supervise students while they are on school-sponsored field trips. Thomas, a student, visited the National Zoological Park in Washington, DC, while on a field trip with his school. He alleged that during that trip, he was assaulted, kicked, and beaten by five boys who were also students on the field trip. These students attended City Lights, a private, nonprofit school, chartered under District of Columbia law, for at-risk youths. At the time of attack, the students were allegedly unsupervised. The court determined that a school owes a duty to prevent students from being harmed and from harming others while on a field trip; as such the school would be liable as a result of the failure to supervise its students while on the field trip.[3]

Duty to Provide Adequate and Appropriate Instruction. Teachers have a duty to provide proper instruction to students when that is necessary to protect them from known harms. For example, teachers must provide students with proper instructions when they are undertaking dangerous activities (e.g., science lab procedures, working with machinery, or physical education). Instruction must be given on a continual basis if there is an ongoing foreseeable risk of injury.

The following instruction was given to a jury in a negligence case in which a student was injured during a class experiment in a science lab. The jury instruction explains a teacher's duties as follows:

> A teacher occupies a supervisory position in relation to students. A teacher has the duty to instruct and to warn the pupils in his or her custody of any dangers of which the teacher knows, or in the exercise of ordinary care, ought to know are present in the classroom (laboratory, gym, playground) and to instruct them in methods which will protect them from those dangers, whether the dangers arise from equipment, devices, machines or chemicals. A failure to warn students of such danger or instruct them in means of avoiding such danger is negligence.[4]

Duty to Provide a Safe Environment. Schools also have a duty to maintain the school grounds and facilities in a reasonably safe condition. Courts have held schools liable for injuries resulting from unsafe conditions that school officials knew or should have known about and failed to take precautions or provide reasonable warnings (e.g., slippery entranceways, unlighted areas, inadequate handrails, violation of building codes, etc.). Schools cannot guarantee safety, but they do have a duty to act reasonably to provide a safe environment (see the In the News feature). For example, in a case from Indiana the district had hired a private security service to provide exterior security at the high school after experiencing an increase in criminal activity. Even after this four students attacked and brutally beat a student in the school's parking lot just after school was dismissed. The student sued the district for negligence. The Indiana Supreme Court held that the school could be held liable for negligence if it had failed to take reasonable steps to provide adequate security against the criminal acts of third parties. The court concluded that although school districts cannot be sued for failure to prevent crime, they may be held legally responsible for failure to take reasonable safety precautions.[5] This case was sent back to the trial court to determine liability and damages.

Duty to Provide Safe Transportation. If a school district provides transportation to students between school and home, it owes a duty of care with respect to that

IN THE NEWS . . .

Swing sets, "monkey bars," merry-go-rounds, and even slides are disappearing from schoolyard playgrounds and are being replaced with "safer" alternatives due to the risk of school liability for injuries that occur while students use the equipment. Some changes focus on the construction of the playground apparatus, such as favoring rubber-covered metal instead of wooden frames and cushiony wood chips instead of pea gravel for ground covering. But other changes might include complete removal of the most identifiable pieces of a playground, such as slides and swings. Most school districts rely on the U.S. Consumer Product Safety Commission's (CPSC) *Handbook for Public Playground Safety* and directives from insurance carriers when making decisions on playground equipment. But some schools are being influenced by the threat of litigation. Valparaiso, Indiana, schools, for example, are involved in a negligence lawsuit in which a parent claims Hayes Leonard Elementary School is responsible for a child's broken leg after he slid down a wet slide without proper supervision. Such lawsuits are forcing schools to change their playground equipment. "Liability has made us look at it a lot differently," says Don Dean, the maintenance supervisor for Portage Township, Indiana, schools, and fear of lawsuits has forced playground improvements in seven of the eight elementary schools in the township.

Source: From "Playground Safety Left Up to Schools," by Bob Kasarda, September 24, 2004, *Northwest Indiana Times.* http://www.nwitimes.com/articles/2004/09/24/news/porter_county

transportation. This duty could encompass employing qualified and fit bus drivers, supervising loading areas adequately, maintaining buses in safe operating condition, and avoiding dangerous traffic situations related to loading and unloading of schoolchildren from buses.

Duty Subsequent to Injury. When students are injured in the school setting, school personnel have a duty to provide reasonable assistance commensurate with their training and experience. When personnel provide reasonable treatment, no liability will be assessed for the results of treatment even if it is later proven to be inappropriate. Good Samaritan statutes in many states shield individuals who provide treatment in emergency situations from liability.

Breach of Duty

Once a duty has been established, the injured individual must show that the duty was breached. The duty is breached when the individual acts unreasonably in carrying out the duty.

In carrying out a duty, the expectation is to act as an ordinary, prudent, and reasonable person, considering all of the circumstances involved (see list on page 104). The court or jury makes a determination of how a reasonable person would have acted; if the individual did less, he or she is found negligent.

> **FACTORS TO BE CONSIDERED IN DETERMINING REASONABLENESS**
>
> - age and maturity of the parties involved;
> - nature of the risk involved;
> - precautions taken to avoid injury;
> - environment and context, including characteristics of students, location, physical characteristics, and so on;
> - type of activity engaged in; and
> - previous practice and experience.

The reasonableness standard varies for professionals, including teachers and principals. Defendants who are professionals are held to a standard based on the skills or training they should have acquired for those positions. Thus comes this question: What would the reasonable teacher or principal—one with average intelligence and physical attributes, normal perception and memory, and possessing the same special knowledge and skills as others with the same training and experience—have done under the same or similar circumstances? The standard expects teachers to do a better job of protecting students from injury than an average person,[6] but does not expect them to be "super teachers."

A key to determining whether a breach occurred is whether the educator should have foreseen, and thus prevented, the resulting injury. Different school activities pose different sets of dangers and supervision must be adjusted for every situation. Educators should warn students of dangers and teach them proper procedures before students engage in potentially dangerous activities. Supervision and other precautions must increase if past occurrences indicate an increased likelihood of danger. The age, capacity, and past behavior of students are all relevant factors. Each situation gives rise to a unique set of circumstances and the standards are determined on a case-by-case basis.

In determining negligence, children are not held to the same standard of care as adults; instead, their actions must be reasonable for a child of similar age, maturity, intelligence, and experience. Some states further classify children according to a presumption of their capabilities. Those states do not hold children under age 7 responsible for negligence or unreasonable acts. The noted exception, however, is that a child may be held to an adult standard of care when engaged in an adult activity (e.g., driving a car or handling a weapon).

Causation

Even in situations in which the teacher failed in a recognized duty to provide a reasonable standard of care, in order to recover for an injury, the plaintiff must show that the teacher's negligence was the cause of the injury. If the accident would have occurred anyway, there can be no liability. The defendant's negligent act must be a continuous and active force leading up to the actual harm. For example, suppose a high school holds interscholastic meets in an outside track and field arena. Spectators use the old bleachers there, but the school performs no regular inspection or maintenance of the bleachers. Several hours before a meet, the bleachers fall on a passerby. The school could be held liable for the injuries sustained by the passerby.

When there is a lapse of time between the defendant's negligence and the injury, other contributing causes and intervening factors may be the actual cause of the injury. Likewise, when there is a series of events leading up to an injury, the person starting that chain of events may be liable for the resultant injury if it was a foreseeable result of his or her negligence. For example, suppose that during a well-attended track meet at the arena just described, the fans become excited and jump up and down on the bleachers, and they collapse. The court could hold the school responsible for injuries sustained by the spectators under a theory of negligent maintenance of the bleachers by failing to inspect them even though the most immediate cause of the collapse was the fans' behavior.

If the injury at the end of the chain of events was not a logical (foreseeable) result of the negligence, there is no liability. To continue with the example, during the bleacher collapse at the track meet, suppose a spectator's expensive necklace comes loose and is lost. The school could not be held responsible for the loss of the necklace.

When another independent act occurs in between the defendant's negligent act and the plaintiff's injury, it may cut off the liability. In other words, someone else's actions may have been the cause of the injury. For example, suppose one of the spectators at the track meet sprains an ankle due to the collapsing bleachers but decides to drive himself to the hospital. Along the way another vehicle operated by a drunk driver hits his car. The school could not be held responsible for the damages to spectator's car.

Intervening acts will not cut off liability when those intervening acts were foreseeable. For example, the spectators becoming excited and jumping up and down on the rickety bleachers is an intervening act, but the fact that spectators might get excited at a sporting event is foreseeable and therefore their actions do not negate the school's liability.

Many liability cases focus on the consequences of criminal activity. For example, in one case a middle school student was sexually assaulted after she had left campus during school hours. Her parents filed a negligence action against the school district, alleging that the district breached its duty to supervise her. She was allowed to sign out and leave campus in violation of a school district policy that gives only the principal or vice-principal authority to release a student from campus during school hours. The appellate court ruled that the school district was liable for the student's injury because it owed a duty of care to her that it breached when she was allowed to leave campus in violation of district policy.

The court found that given the high crime environment of the surrounding neighborhood, it was foreseeable that the student might be assaulted if she walked through the neighborhood unescorted.[7]

Injury

In order to sustain a claim of negligence, the plaintiff must show an actual loss or real damage (e.g., a physical bodily injury or a real loss). The loss may take many forms (e.g., the medical expenses, lost wages, or damaged or destroyed property). Injuries may be tangible or intangible (e.g., pain and suffering or emotional distress). In some situations an intangible injury is sufficient for recovery. However, some states require at least a physical manifestation of an injury, if there are no tangible injuries. If proven, monetary compensation may be awarded for intangible injuries.

If a child is injured, his or her parents may also have an action to recover their own expenses and compensate their own injuries. Most commonly, these would be the child's medical expenses and the parents' emotional damages.

DEFENSES AGAINST A CLAIM OF NEGLIGENCE

If the basic elements of negligence have been established, the court looks at what defenses may lessen or eliminate the school district's or the teacher's liability. As discussed next, the most common defenses against negligence are

- governmental or sovereign immunity;
- assumption of the risk; and
- contributory or comparative negligence.

Governmental (Sovereign) Immunity

Go to the Companion Website at **http://www. prenhall.com/underwood,** select Chapter 6, then choose the Resources module to find state-specific defenses against negligence.

Sovereign immunity is basically a concept preventing an individual from suing the state. It has its roots in an old British concept that "the king could do no wrong." In those states that still recognize strict sovereign immunity, an individual may not bring legal action against the state. In these states, school districts are often, though not always, treated as the state, and thus cannot be sued for negligence.

In most states, the concept of sovereign immunity has been limited or eroded by court decision or abrogated by statute. In these states, people may sue the state for its proprietary, but not its governmental, actions. Governmental actions are those the state undertakes as a policy maker whereas proprietary actions are not policy related. Thus, these states do not allow an individual to sue the school for an injury caused by a policy decision such as making a curriculum choice or setting the time for school to start. For example, in one case a high school student volunteered at a track and field event for fifth-grade students held at the high school. She was assigned to the discus-throwing venue where there was no adult supervision. While she was measuring a thrower's distance, someone yelled to watch out. When she looked up, she was struck in the face by a discus, causing severe injuries. She filed suit against the school district. The court rejected the school district's contention that it was entitled to immunity from her suit because its decision not to have adult supervision at the discus-throwing venue was within its policy-making or planning powers as a governmental unit. The court found that this decision did not involve the school district's discretionary policy-making powers. According to the court, immunity extended only to the broad type of discretion "involving public policy made with the creative exercise of political judgment."[8]

Some states have abrogated sovereign immunity up to a particular dollar limit or to the extent of insurance coverage. These states usually have strict legal procedural requirements at the outset of a legal action and often require that a written claim be presented by a statutory deadline before a lawsuit can be filed.

Assumption of Risk

The basis of the assumption of risk defense against negligence is the idea that if the plaintiff knowingly and voluntarily accepted the risks of an activity, he or she should not be allowed to recover for injuries caused by those known risks. However, the courts have said that for "knowing" acceptance of risk to occur, it is important that all risks inherent in an activity are apparent or explained and that they are voluntarily assumed.

This is particularly true of students in athletic activities who are asked to assume the risk of playing that sport. In order to use the assumption of risk defense for the injury a student sustains while participating in an athletic activity, the district or teacher must be able to show that the plaintiff understood how the specific activity was dangerous and nonetheless voluntarily engaged in it. For example, students who are playing tennis should be told there is always a risk of falling or twisting an elbow or ankle. If such an injury were to occur during the normal course of a match, the school would not be responsible. However, were the fencing to fall on a student during play, this would not be the kind of risk that would have been assumed, so the school could be held responsible.

The assumption of an unreasonable risk can completely bar the injured person from recovering any damages. Stated another way, if you engage in extreme activities you assume all of the consequences. For example, a student in an Ohio case jumped on the trunk of a car, riding this way down from the school to the baseball field. The student was injured in the course of this "ride" and sued the school and the other student driving the car. The court found no liability on the part of the school or the other student. It held that riding on a car's trunk lid was an inherently dangerous activity, like bungee jumping, and that the risks associated with the activity were assumed by the student.[9]

Contributory and Comparative Negligence

The final defense against negligence sets out that if the injured party caused part of his or her own injuries through negligence, the defendant's liability is reduced and the court should not grant the injured party full monetary recovery. To reduce the damage award state courts use a system of either contributory negligence *or* comparative negligence. Under contributory negligence, if the plaintiff has been negligent and caused any part of his or her own damages, there is no recovery. Recognizing that this all-or-nothing approach often results in drastic consequences, most states have moved to the less severe system of comparative negligence. In practice only a limited number of states still use contributory negligence.

Comparative negligence apportions the damage award among the negligent parties depending on the relative degree of fault or their contributions to the injuries. For example, if the court decides that the injured party's own actions caused 10% of his injuries, this would reduce his damage award by 10%. Various forms of comparative negligence exist as determined by state law.

EDUCATIONAL AND PROFESSIONAL MALPRACTICE

Historically, most educational liability cases have involved student injuries. However, a new topic of concern, *educational malpractice,* has actually popped up in more recent years. As in medical malpractice, the term concerns some alleged negligence on the part of the professional. In general two kinds of educational malpractice suits exist: (1) instructional malpractice cases involving students who have received certificates or diplomas and have actually failed to learn[10] and (2) professional malpractice cases involving misdiagnosis,[11] improper educational placement, or improper advising.

Although a number of the instructional malpractice or failure to learn cases have been litigated, none have been successful. The reasons, according to the courts, are "the absence of an adequate standard of care, uncertainty in determining damages, the burden of proof placed on schools by the potential flood of litigation that would probably result, the deference given to the educational system to carry out its internal operations, and the general reluctance of courts to interfere in an area regulated by legislative standards."[12]

Students have been successful in a limited number of cases when they have alleged *professional malpractice* in education. These claims differ from the instructional malpractice claims in that they do not challenge academic or curriculum decisions or educational standards. Rather, they claim that specific individuals have negligently performed their professional duties. In the first successful suit of its kind in education, **Eisel v. Board of Education of Montgomery County**,[13] the court found two school counselors negligent in failing to communicate to a parent a student's suicidal statements made to other students and to them. The counselors had questioned the student about the statements, but when she denied them, they did nothing further. The court ruled that the counselors had "a duty to use reasonable means to prevent a suicide when they are on notice" of a student's suicide intent.

Another example of professional malpractice is presented when a student is misadvised. Courts have split in deciding whether this malpractice should be recognized. In **Scott v. Savers Property and Casualty Insurance Co.,**[14] the Wisconsin Supreme Court ruled that a school district is not liable for educational malpractice when a guidance counselor's faulty advice regarding NCAA eligibility requirements resulted in a student's losing a college athletic scholarship. The opposite result was reached in **Stain v. Cedar Rapids Comm. School Dist.**[15] The court analogized the incorrect advice given by a high school counselor to negligent misrepresentation that applies to accountants, attorneys, and other professionals who are in the business of supplying information to others who would foreseeably rely upon it. The counselor told a basketball player that the NCAA would approve a particular English course toward its core requirement when, in fact, the course had not been submitted by the school for approval. After graduation the NCAA notified the student that he was one third of a credit short of what was needed to participate in Division I basketball. As a result, he lost his college scholarship. In finding for the student, the court concluded that the high school counselor had a duty "to use reasonable care in providing specific information to a student when (1) the counselor has knowledge of the specific need for the information and provides the information to the student in the course of a counselor–student relationship, and (2) a student reasonably relies upon the information under circumstances in which the counselor knows or should know of the student's reliance."[16]

DEFAMATION

Defamation is the "communication to third parties of false statements about a person that injure the reputation of or deter others from associating with that person."[17] It is a common law tort actionable under the law of most states. Because there is no national law of defamation, except to the extent that there are constitutional limits placed on defamation claims, the laws of each state govern the claims. Generally, defamation refers to a derogatory statement that damages the reputation of a particular individual by casting aspersions on the person's honesty, integrity, virtue, sanity, or other quality of the person's character.

Defamation includes the twin torts of libel (when written) and slander (when spoken). Libelous communication can be conveyed by the written word, video, picture, cartoon, or effigy. The law considers some statements so inexcusable that it judges them to be defamation *per se* even without proof that they caused injury. These include statements that (1) impute a criminal offense punishable by imprisonment, (2) impute guilt of a crime of moral turpitude, (3) impute a loathsome disease (e.g., AIDS), (4) impute lack of chastity, and (5) impute professional incompetence or unprofessional conduct. Teachers and school officials are at risk of defamation actions because they routinely handle personal information and they are often in the public eye. For these precise reasons these individuals must be careful with their statements, especially those regarding students. As discussed in more detail in the following sections, in determining whether a statement is defamation and whether there is liability, the courts will address the following questions:

- Was the communication true or false?
- Was the communication stated as opinion or fact?
- Was the communication privileged?
- Was the subject of the communication a private or public figure?

True or False?

The definition of defamation requires the statements made to be false. The communication of true statements is not defamation. Generally, there can be no recovery in defamation for a statement of fact that is true, although the statement may be made for no good purpose and may be inspired by ill will toward the person about whom it is published and is made solely for the purpose of harming him.[18]

For example, in **Anderson v. Independent School District 97,**[19] a school bus driver was suspended for refusing to undergo a random drug test; that information was made public and the school bus driver sued for defamation. The driver had actually submitted to the test, but failed to provide sufficient urine sample for the test to be conducted. The federal regulations define providing an insufficient sample as refusing to undergo the drug test, punishable by suspension. The court found that the statements made were factually based on the definition provided in the federal regulations.

Opinion or Fact?

Most statements of opinion are not subject to defamation; false statements of fact are subject to defamation. To qualify as an opinion the statement cannot lend itself to being proven true or false and must be communicated to convey a personal perspective. Accordingly, parents may express their opinions about teachers to others, including administrators, school boards, and newspapers, even if those opinions are negative.[20] However, if a parent were to accuse a teacher of stealing club funds, something that could be proven true or false, and an audit found no wrongdoing, the court would consider the statement defamation.

Privilege

A privileged statement cannot be the subject of a defamation action. There are two types of privilege: absolute privilege and qualified privilege.

Statements that are absolutely privileged cannot be the basis of defamation under any circumstance, even if they are false and result in injury. Absolute privilege is very limited and afforded only within the context of official governmental proceedings. Judges, witnesses, legislators, and other public officials have absolute privilege for their statements made in the course of their work, debate, voting, committee meetings, and comments on their proceedings. Very rarely a court will afford absolute privilege to local or state school board proceedings.[21] For example, in **Flynn v. Reichardt**,[22] two students accused a teacher of sexual abuse, harassment, and discrimination. The students conveyed this information to the principal and superintendent directly in a private meeting with them. The teacher sued the students and their parents for defamation. The trial court dismissed the suit on the grounds that the statements were absolutely privileged as protected as a part of the process of investigating alleged abuse. The court of appeals disagreed, finding that an absolute privilege did not exist because the process of accusation and investigation lacked sufficient safeguards against defamation and damages within the school's process itself.

Although school board meetings typically are not afforded absolute privilege, criminal proceedings do have absolute privilege. For example, in **Pitts v. Newark Board of Education**[23] a principal called the police to have a school custodian arrested for trespass after the custodian was ordered to leave the school premises and refused to do so. The custodian filed an action against the principal for defamation. The court held for the principal finding that the filing of a criminal complaint could not constitute defamation because criminal complaints have absolute privilege.

As opposed to communications that have absolute privilege, communications that have qualified privilege can be the subject of defamation only if they are not made in good faith. Courts have generally recognized that statements regarding school matters are qualifiedly privileged if made by those with a common interest and made in good faith.

Teachers are covered by a qualified privilege when acting in their official capacity and in the interest of the school. The courts have recognized that for the necessary exchange of information about students teachers must be given this privilege. Without this privilege teachers would always be subject to legal action and would be reluctant to convey almost any information about students. However, this privilege does not protect teachers whose communication is not in good faith, malicious, knowingly false, or on matters unrelated to the interest of the school.

Because of the potential personal liability that may occur, as well as the potential damage to the student, teachers must be diligent in refraining from making even joking remarks about the student's personal life outside the school (e.g., the student's love life) if it has no relation to the student's conduct at school, and from communicating sensitive information (e.g., the student was sexually abused) to another person who has no need to be informed. By the same token, teachers should take care to include in a student's record or in a letter of recommendation only information that is relevant and, to the best of their knowledge, based on facts, not personal opinions.

Parents and members of the community may also have a qualified privilege when discussing information at official school meetings if the discussion relates to issues of public concern. For example, the statement of a parent who made disparaging remarks about the fitness to teach or the teaching practices of one of his or her children's teachers is considered privilege. If, however, the statement were false and made with malice, the privilege might be destroyed.

Public Figure

The law affords private individuals a great deal more protection in defamation than public figures. To win in a defamation action a private individual need only prove that a false communication was made about him or her, was understood by others, and that he or she was injured as a result of the false communication. A public figure, however, must show that the communication was made with either malice and knowledge that the statement was false or with reckless disregard for the truth. The U.S. Supreme Court made this distinction in **New York Times v. Sullivan**[24] when it found a publisher had a constitutional right to criticize or question the actions of public officials. The Court found that the First Amendment protects the publisher's right to speak and prohibits a public official from recovering damages in defamation for a false statement relating to official conduct unless actual malice or reckless disregard of the truth is proven. Statements made about a public official that are not related to the individual's official conduct may not be protected. For example, a newspaper may be protected in publishing an article naming teachers who had their license revoked, but publishing a list of divorced teachers would not be protected.

Public figures are those individuals who have achieved such a significant place in public life that they themselves are subjects of interest to the general public (e.g., sports figures, musicians, actors), public officials, or those who have voluntarily injected themselves into the public eye over particular controversies or issues of importance to the general public.[25] School administrators and board members are generally considered to be public figures.[26]

Most jurisdictions do not consider teachers to be public figures; however, there are exceptions. For example, the Connecticut Supreme Court found that a teacher was a public official for purposes of his defamation action against the school. In that case, a social studies teacher being investigated for improperly touching female students decided to retire in lieu of being fired. Although the superintendent did not disclose the findings of her investigation, the public demanded more information and eventually the state commission on teacher certification began an investigation. The teacher sued school officials. The court held that the teacher was a public official because teachers "exercise almost unfettered control over the classroom" and the public has an intense interest in their qualifications. According to the court, "robust and wide open debate concerning the conduct of the teachers in the schools of this state is a matter of great public importance."[27]

The distinction between being considered a public figure or a private figure is important to teachers who as public figures would have to prove malice to support a charge of defamation, but as private persons would not. It is more likely that a court will find a teacher a public figure if the teacher plays an additional role in the school, for example, as coach or athletic director, or if the teacher puts him- or herself in the midst of public discussion.

GUIDING LEGAL PRINCIPLES

- Negligence is the failure to exercise due care or reasonably fulfill one's duty of care, which results in injury or loss to another person. Either the failure to act (omission) or the commission of an improper act can be negligence.
- Four elements must be established for a plaintiff to prevail in a negligence lawsuit:

    Duty: The defendant had a duty to protect the plaintiff from unreasonable risks.

    Breach: The duty was breached by the failure to exercise an appropriate standard of care.

    Causation: There was a causal connection between the negligent conduct and the resulting injury.

    Injury: An actual injury resulted.

- Although all teachers have the duty to provide a standard of care for their students, it is not the same for all teachers and all students; the younger the child and the more dangerous the activity, the higher the standard of care required.
- In carrying out their duties, teachers are expected to act as a reasonable teacher would have done in the same situations.
- Several defenses are available in negligence suits such as sovereign immunity, assumption of risk, and contributory and comparative negligence.
- Contributory and comparative negligence are the most common defenses (states have either one or the other); this takes into account the injured person's part (or contribution) to the injury. In comparative negligence the "blame" of both parties is weighed and liability is apportioned out according to each degree of fault.
- Students have not yet been successful in winning educational malpractice cases for failure to learn, but they have been when claiming other types of malpractice, such as misadvisement.
- Defamation is the communication of false information or a derogatory statement that causes damage.

- There is no recovery in defamation for a statement of fact that is true.
- Most statements of opinion, statements that cannot easily be proved true or false, are not subject to defamation.
- Statements that are absolutely privileged cannot be the basis of defamation under any circumstance; statements of qualified privilege can be the subject of defamation only if they are not made in good faith.
- School administrators and school board members are generally considered public figures; teachers generally are not.

YOU BE THE JUDGE

Go to the Companion Website at **http://www.prenhall.com/underwood**, *select Chapter 6, choose the You Be the Judge module, and click on the name of the case for more information about the case and the court's decision and rationale.*

Out to Lunch

Zachary Thomason, a student at Westview High School (AZ), caused a multiple car accident that injured several motorists while driving back to campus after going off campus for lunch. Zachary's presence off campus during school hours was in violation of school policy, which required students to sign out and have prior parental permission before they could leave campus. The motorists filed a negligence suit in state court against both Zachary and the school district. They claimed the school district, by virtue of its policy of allowing students to leave campus for lunch, should have forseen that given the limited time allotted for lunch students would speed and had a duty to protect the public from the negligent driving of students.

Questions for Discussion and Reflection

1. Did the district have a duty to protect other motorists? What duty did it have to the students?
2. Which of the defenses against negligence might the school district use in this situation?
3. Are the motorists likely to win their suit against Zachary? the district?

Visit the Companion Website for a more detailed description of the facts in the case **Collette v. Tolleson Unified School District.**

* * *

An Experiment Gone Up in Smoke

Sean Tackett was enrolled in Brenda Vrable's advanced chemistry class at Pine Richland High School in Allegheny County, Pennsylvania. Sean sustained severe burns when two classmates ignited ethyl alcohol while conducting an experiment. Although the classroom was equipped with a fume hood to exhaust flammable vapors, Ms. Vrable did not instruct the students to conduct the experiment under the hood. Sean filed suit against the school district and Ms. Vrable. He alleged that the defendants were negligent for failing to have adequate safety equipment on the premises, failing to properly inspect the premises, and permitting a dangerous condition to exist on the premises.

Questions for Discussion and Reflection

1. What standards would be used by the court to judge the teacher's conduct?
2. Are the defenses against negligence the same for teachers as for school districts?
3. What was the proximate cause of Sean's injuries? Explain.

Visit the Companion Website for a more detailed description of the facts in the case **Tackett v. Pine Richland School District.**

* * *

Better to Be Seen to Avoid a Bean

Rosamaria Bonamico was a student at Woodrow Wilson Middle School (CT). While walking down a corridor in the school, she was struck in the eye with a bean that was thrown in her direction by fellow student Asa Black. Black had just come from a home economics class in which he, along with the other students, learned how to make beanbags. Black failed to return some of the beans in his possession and instead took them with him out of the classroom and into the corridor. The school had a policy that required all teachers to be physically present and visible in the hallway to supervise the students as they changed class periods. Black's home economics teacher, Mary Ann Vinci, was not in the hallway when Black threw the bean, contrary to school policy. Bonamico suffered injury to her eye and sued the school district and Vinci, the home economics teacher.

Questions for Discussion and Reflection

1. How would a court take the school policy into consideration in determining whether Vinci was responsible for Bonamico's injuries?
2. Should Vinci's choice of activities be considered in part a contribution to the injuries?
3. What, if any, responsibility does the district have for Bonamico's injuries?

Visit the Companion Website for a more detailed description of the facts in the case **Bonamico v. City of Middletown.**

MORE ON THE WEB

Go to the Companion Website at ***http://www.prenhall.com/underwood***, *select Chapter 6, choose the* More on the Web *module to connect to the sites mentioned.*

For a look at some of the more unusual lawsuits a teacher or district may encounter, go to the schools section of Overlawyered.com website, **http://www. overlawyered.com/archives/cat_schools.html**. Briefly describe three of what you consider to be the most trivial cases.

ENDNOTES

1. See, e.g., *Di Cosala v. Kay,* 450 A.2d 508 (N.J. 1982); *Garcia v. Duffy,* 492 So.2d 35 (Fla. Ct. App. 1986).

2. *Glaser v. Emporia Unified School District No. 253,* 21 P.3d 573 (Kan. 2001).

3. *Thomas v. City Lights School, Inc.,* 124 F. Supp.2d 707 (D.D.C. 2000).

4. *Kimps v. Hill,* 546 N.W.2d 151, 156 (Wis. 1996).

5. *King v. Northeast Security, Inc.,* 790 N.E.2d 474 (Ind. 2003).

6. Some states set this standard at a different level by statute; e.g., Illinois teachers are liable only for willful and wanton misconduct; e.g., *Albers v. Community Consolidated School,* 508 N.E.2d 1252 (Ill. App. 1987).

7. *D.C. v. St. Landry Parish School Board,* 802 So.2d 19 (La. App. 2001).

8. *Spaid v. Bucyrus City Schools,* 760 N.E.2d 67 (Ohio App. 2001).

9. *Cave v. Burt,* 2004 WL 1465730 (Ohio App. 2004).

10. See, e.g., *Peter W. v. San Francisco Unified School District,* 131 Cal.Rptr. 854 (Cal. App. 1976). See also *Denver Parents Ass'n v. Denver Bd. of Educ.,* 10 P.3d 662 (Colo. Ct. App. 2000); *Vogel v. Maimonides Acad.,* 754 A.2d 824 (Conn. App. Ct. 2000).

11. See, e.g., *Hoffman v. Board of Education of the City of New York,* 400 N.E.2d 317 (1979). The court in *Sellers v. School Board of the City of Manassas,* 141 F.3d 524 (4th Cir. 1998) did not recognize a claim of educational malpractice for failure to correctly diagnose a student's disabilities.

12. *Stain v. Cedar Rapids Comm. School Dist.,* 626 N.W.2d 115, 119 (Iowa 2001).

13. 597 A.2d 447 (Md. 1991).

14. 663 N.W.2d 715 (Wis. 2003).

15. Ibid.

16. Ibid. at 125.

17. *Merriam-Webster's Dictionary of Law* (2000).

18. Restatement (Second) of Torts Section 581A.

19. 357 F.3d 806 (8th Cir. 2004).

20. See, e.g., *Nodar v. Galbreath*, 462 So.2d 803 (Fla. 1984); *Ansorian v. Zimmerman*, 627 N.Y.S.2d 706 (App. Div. 1995).

21. See, e.g., *Matthews v. Holland*, 912 S.W.2d 459 (Ky. App. 1995); *DeBolt v. McBrien*, 96 Neb. 237, 147 N.W. 462 (1914).

22. 749 A.2d 143 (Md. App. 2000).

23. 766 A.2d 1206 (N.J. Super. App. Div. 2001).

24. 376 U.S. 254 (1964).

25. *Gertz v. Robert Welch, Inc.*, 418 U.S. 323 (1974).

26. See, e.g., *Garcia v. Bd. of Education*, 777 F.2d 1403 (10th Cir. 1985); *Jordan v. World Publishing*, 872 P.2d 946 (OK. App. 1994).

27. *Kelley v. Bonney*, 606 A.2d 693, 710 (Conn. 1992).

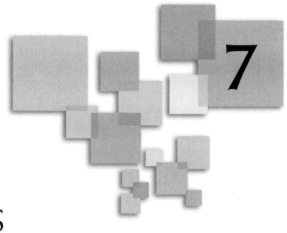

STUDENTS' RIGHTS

The Supreme Court has repeatedly stated that the U.S. Constitution applies to children as well as adults. Students' constitutional rights include the right to free speech, the right to be free from unreasonable search and seizure, due process, equal protection, and certain privacy rights. Various federal and state statutes also protect students' rights. The challenge to the schools has been to maintain a balance between the rights of students, the rights of others within the school community, and the responsibility of educating students in a safe and orderly environment. This chapter discusses student constitutional rights of freedom of speech/expression, freedom of association, and freedom from unreasonable search and seizure, along with federal statutory rights regarding educational records. After reading this chapter you will be able to

- Summarize the conditions under which student speech can be restricted.
- Outline the time, place, manner, and prior restrictions that can be placed on student expression.
- Explain the restraints that can be placed on student personal experience.
- Distinguish between the probable cause and reasonable suspicion standards as applied to student searches by school officers and police officers.
- Compare the reasonableness standard as it applies to search of lockers, purses and bookbags, and persons.
- Discuss how the Family Educational Rights and Privacy Act protects parents' and student rights.

FREEDOM OF SPEECH/EXPRESSION

Free speech is one of our most highly treasured and protected constitutional liberties. This is especially true within the public schools. The Supreme Court has noted that First Amendment rights must receive scrupulous protection in schools "if we are not to strangle the free mind at its source and teach youth to discount important principles of our government as mere platitudes."[1] However, the Court has recognized that even the right to free speech must be balanced within the public schools to ensure student safety and learning. The Supreme Court has recognized that students have constitutional rights (see the boxed case summary), although they are not as broad as the rights of adults in other settings."[2]

What Is Speech?

The First Amendment protects all forms of expression, not only verbal communication. Protected expression may also be written or symbolic. Symbolic speech is defined as an action intended to convey a message (e.g., dance or art). If it is a symbolic act, it is protected as speech. Even some forms of dress can be symbolic speech. For example, a student wears gang colors as a symbol in order to express his or her gang affiliation.

Restrictions on Student Speech

Forum Restrictions. The extent to which schools can restrict the content of a student's speech usually depends on where the expression is taking place, or the *forum* involved. There are basically three types of forums: open, limited, and closed. An *open forum* is a public place traditionally used as a place for speech and public discourse (e.g., a "speakers' corner" in a public park). A *limited forum* is generally a public area that has other purposes but has been made available for speech too. This is the most typical forum in schools. Often schools create a limited forum by designating a bulletin board for announcements or creating a speakers' series.

A *closed forum* is a place not open for an exchange of ideas, and the purpose of the place would be lost if the free exchange of ideas were allowed. A closed forum occurs in schools when the time is not appropriate or the place is not intended for an open exchange of views. Expression in such a forum can be limited to those forms of expression compatible with the intended purpose of the forum, provided that the restrictions are reasonable and do not constitute viewpoint discrimination (i.e., are not an attempt to limit the expression of a certain opinion or perspective). Examples of closed forums include class time, school events, and school-sponsored activities. Schools have the greatest ability to restrict speech in the closed forum and the least ability to restrict speech in the open forum.

The landmark case in student expression is **Tinker v. Des Moines Independent School District.**[3]

TINKER v. DES MOINES INDEPENDENT SCHOOL DISTRICT

Students were suspended for wearing black armbands to protest the Vietnam War. The Supreme Court said that "It can hardly be argued that either students or teachers shed their constitutional right to freedom of speech or expression at the school house gate." The Court found that the suspensions were unconstitutional.

*Go to the Companion Website at **http://www. prenhall.com/underwood**, select Chapter 7, choose Cases module, and click on **Tinker v. Des Moines Independent School District** to read the entire opinion of the court.*

The case involved three students who were suspended for wearing black armbands in protest of the Vietnam War. The Supreme Court found that students did have rights to free speech, but that they could be limited if the school had facts that reasonably led it to believe that the speech would substantially disrupt school activities. However, the school must show more than a desire to avoid the discomfort and unpleasantness that accompany unpopular viewpoints. The Court in *Tinker* recognized students' constitutional rights, but reinforced the schools' authority to regulate those rights if the exercise of the rights might be reasonably predicted to cause a material and substantial disruption or invasion of the rights of others.

The standard set out in *Tinker,* proof of a reasonable forecast of a material and substantial disruption, does not apply to school-sponsored speech or speech within the curriculum. Student expression that appears to be sponsored by the school or is part of the curriculum can be more directly restricted as long as the restrictions are reasonably related to legitimate pedagogical concerns and as long as viewpoint discrimination does not occur (see the boxed case summary of **Hazelwood School District v. Kuhlmeier**[4] and the flowchart in Figure 7.1).

HAZELWOOD SCHOOL DISTRICT v. KUHLMEIER

A high school principal removed two pages from the school paper because articles talked about student pregnancy, birth control, and the impact of divorce on students. The Court upheld the school's actions by finding that the newspaper was part of the school curriculum.

Even if student speech does not cause disruption, it may be restricted if it is harmful to students or pervasively vulgar. At a high school assembly Matthew Fraser nominated a classmate for a student council office using what the Court described as "an elaborate, graphic, and explicit sexual metaphor." Fraser was suspended for 2 days. Lower courts found his suspension to be a violation of his rights to free speech and that his speech was not disruptive under the *Tinker* guidelines. The Supreme Court, however, went beyond *Tinker*'s concern with the effect

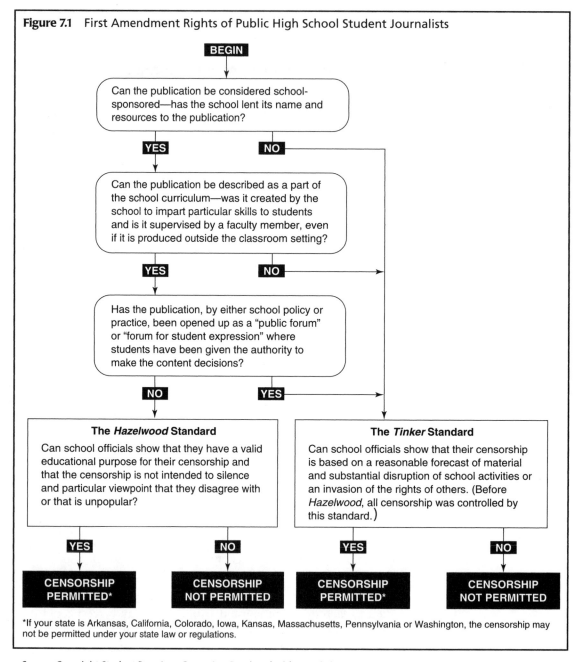

Figure 7.1 First Amendment Rights of Public High School Student Journalists

BEGIN

Can the publication be considered school-sponsored—has the school lent its name and resources to the publication?

YES NO

Can the publication be described as a part of the school curriculum—was it created by the school to impart particular skills to students and is it supervised by a faculty member, even if it is produced outside the classroom setting?

YES NO

Has the publication, by either school policy or practice, been opened up as a "public forum" or "forum for student expression" where students have been given the authority to make the content decisions?

NO YES

The *Hazelwood* Standard

Can school officials show that they have a valid educational purpose for their censorship and that the censorship is not intended to silence and particular viewpoint that they disagree with or that is unpopular?

The *Tinker* Standard

Can school officials show that their censorship is based on a reasonable forecast of material and substantial disruption of school activities or an invasion of the rights of others. (Before *Hazelwood*, all censorship was controlled by this standard.)

YES — **CENSORSHIP PERMITTED***

NO — **CENSORSHIP NOT PERMITTED**

YES — **CENSORSHIP PERMITTED***

NO — **CENSORSHIP NOT PERMITTED**

*If your state is Arkansas, California, Colorado, Iowa, Kansas, Massachusetts, Pennsylvania or Washington, the censorship may not be permitted under your state law or regulations.

Source: Copyright Student Press Law Center Inc. Reprinted with permission.

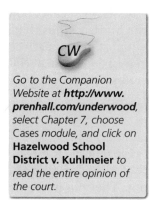

Go to the Companion Website at *http://www. prenhall.com/underwood*, select Chapter 7, choose Cases *module, and click on* **Hazelwood School District v. Kuhlmeier** *to read the entire opinion of the court.*

of the student's speech to the content of the speech and concluded that the school board has the authority to prohibit vulgar or offensive speech or conduct that is inconsistent with the educational mission of the school. In fact, the court said that schools must teach by example the "shared values of a civilized social order."[5]

The summary of judicial opinion is that restrictions can be placed on student speech if the speech is (1) materially and substantially disruptive to the school, (2) harmful to students, or (3) pervasively vulgar.

Time, Place, and Manner Restrictions. Reasonable time, place, and manner restrictions on expression are allowed even in open forums. The courts have concluded that reasonable restrictions are justified to ensure that student expression and the distribution of student publications do not hinder the learning environment or endanger the safety of students and employees. The restrictions, however, must be reasonable, must not treat speech differently based on viewpoint, and must be consistently applied to all expression. Schools must provide students with specific guidelines as to when and where they can express their ideas and distribute materials.

Website Restrictions. Whether the school has control over a website depends on whether it is a school website or an individual's website. If it is a school website, then the next question is, as in other expression situations, whether there is an open, closed, or limited forum. School websites maintained as closed forums may be regulated in the same manner as other school-sponsored expression such as school newspapers. Student expression on a school website that has been established as a limited open forum is subject to the *Tinker* standard, the *Hazelwood* standard, and viewpoint-neutral time, place, and manner restrictions.

Whether schools can discipline students for the content of websites created off school property that have the potential for causing on-campus disruption or that criticize the school or some members of the school community has been a frequently litigated question in recent years. As with any off-campus behavior, the key is whether there is a connection between the school and the behavior and whether the speech has been disruptive under the *Tinker* standard. For example, in **Mahaffey v. Aldrich** (2002)[6] the court ruled that a student could not be suspended for creating a website listing people the student wished would die and encouraging readers, in a section entitled "SATAN'S MISSION FOR YOU THIS WEEK," to commit acts of violence and murder because the school district failed to establish that the website was produced on school grounds or that it disrupted the school's educational process. However, in **J.S. v. Bethlehem Area Sch. Dist.** (2002)[7] the court reached the opposite conclusion under similar facts, upholding a student's expulsion. In the latter case the teacher featured in the website was so upset by the student's online solicitation for money to hire a hit man to kill her that she was unable to continue teaching for the remainder of the year or the next year.

Prior Restraint. In their effort to regulate student speech schools often enact policies that limit expression before it occurs. Schools bear the burden of justifying such prior restraint policies. Nonetheless, courts tend to support disciplinary action *after* the expression has occurred. Students can be punished and materials confiscated if the expression materially and substantially disrupted the educational process, or was pervasively vulgar, harmful, or defamatory.[8]

Dress Codes

Thus far the U.S. Supreme Court has refused to accept a case that deals directly with student appearance. As a result, some circuit courts of appeals have ruled that dress is an expressive activity, whereas others have not. The split in the circuits can be seen by the map in Figure 7.2. Where dress is considered protected speech, then attire (possibly including hairstyles, tattoos, and piercings) can be restricted only if it is materially and substantially disruptive, pervasively vulgar, or harmful. For example, in **Boroff v. Van Wert City Board of Educ.**[9] the court agreed that the school could prohibit a student from wearing a Marilyn Manson T-shirt it considered offensive based on the band's promotion of values contrary to the school's educational mission. But in **Doe v. Brockton School Comm.**[10] the court ruled in favor of a student's cross-dressing because the school did not show any disruption.

Students also have a First Amendment free exercise right to wear prescribed religious garb. For example, a policy against hats could not be enforced against

Figure 7.2 Dress as a Form of Expression. Where Does Your State Fall?

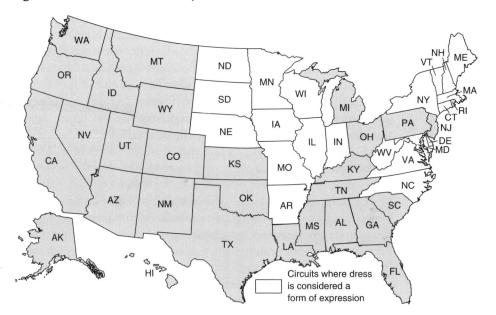

a student wearing a yarmulke[11] or other headgear for religious reasons. In another case, a Muslim student in the Muskogee Public School District was ordered to remove her headscarf (*hijab*) and she refused, for which she was suspended. She sued the district and was backed by the U.S. Department of Justice, the American Jewish Congress, and the Council on American-Islamic Relations. The district settled the lawsuit by agreeing to let her wear the headscarf and agreeing to revise its dress code to provide religious exceptions.[12]

In jurisdictions in which dress is not considered protected speech, it can be restricted for any legitimate reason. For example, schools have been successful in prohibiting dirty, scant, or revealing clothing, loose clothing in shop areas, clothing bearing obscene pictures, or various other dress that they deemed inconsistent with the mission of the school. However, schools must be cautious. Policies should be written to ensure they reasonably relate to their asserted purpose and are not vague. For example, in response to an increase in gang-related activity, one school adopted a policy intended to prohibit dress related to gangs. But, in court the school could not prove that it had accurately described the gang attire it sought to restrict: That the dress code prohibited the wearing of clothing identifying any college or professional sports teams, but testimony showed that gang members were, in fact, wearing Pendleton shirts, Nike shoes, white T-shirts, and baggy or black pants. Absent a rational relationship between the dress code and the activity it aimed to curtail, the court did not uphold the dress code.[13]

A growing number of schools have also adopted school uniforms policies as a strategy to reduce gang activity. Advocates of school uniforms also argue that the policies reduce school violence and improve school climate. The growing popularity of uniforms is evidenced by a 2000 National Association of Elementary School Principals' survey of 755 principals nationwide that showed that one in five (21%) public schools had uniform policies. About one quarter (23%) of all public, private, and parochial school principals either had uniform policies in place, were currently writing such policies, or were considering them.[14]

While the number of schools and school districts adopting school uniform policies has grown, in several school districts students have challenged the policies, alleging a violation of their First Amendment rights to self-expression. Also alleged in some cases is a violation of the right to free exercise of religion. To date, the courts have been unanimous in holding that uniform policies do not violate the First Amendment rights of students, that the policies were content neutral in regard to religion, and that the policies furthered a compelling state interest. Important to the court's decision in these cases is that the policy contained an "opt out" provision whereby students, with parental permission, could request an exemption from the requirement. Accordingly, and to sidestep the legal issues involved, most schools that have adopted a uniform policy have made wearing uniforms voluntary.

Hopefully it is obvious by now how difficult and delicate balancing student rights and student freedoms often is. Many times not only do the students' and

IN THE NEWS . . .

The Pinellas County School Board (FL) is considering whether to prohibit the display of the Confederate flag in the county's schools. The board met to discuss a possible ban after recent student displays of the flag at county schools led to conflicts among students. Pinellas County's current dress code prohibits "clothes or tattoos that show profanity, violence, sexually suggestive phrases or pictures," but does not specifically ban the Confederate flag or any other symbol. Opinions among members of the community and board fall on both sides of the issue. Many African American residents support amending the dress code to ban display of the symbol. They view the Confederate flag as a symbol of slavery and racism. Mary Brown, the first African American board member, supports revising the dress code to prohibit display of the flag. She said, "To allow symbols onto our school grounds that hold historically negative sensitivity to any group of people shows disrespect. I am asking this board to deal with what type of environment is best for all students and what type of attire will support an environment of respect for all." But Charles Pedrick, a member of the Sons of Confederate Veterans, opposes the ban. He believes that if the board bans the Confederate flag, it should ban all symbols, including the Christian cross and the Star of David. Pinellas County School Superintendent Howard Hinesley believes the decision to ban Confederate flag displays should be left to individual school principals, who are best placed to decide whether such displays are disruptive. He said the ban could raise serious questions about students' rights.

Source: From "Pinellas Delays Vote on Rebel Flag," by Candace Rondeaux, February 11, 2004, *St. Petersburg Times.* http://www.sptimes.com/2004/02/11/Tampabay/Pinellas_delays_vote_.shtml

the schools' interests conflict, but also the students' interests conflict. In fact, sometimes the purpose of the schools' attempt at restricting speech is to protect other students. The In the News feature details such a concern.

FREEDOM OF ASSOCIATION

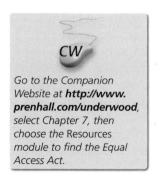

Go to the Companion Website at **http://www. prenhall.com/underwood**, select Chapter 7, then choose the Resources module to find the Equal Access Act.

The First Amendment protects the freedom of association as well as the freedom of speech. Freedom of association issues in the school setting usually involve membership in organizations. Generally, the rules governing the restricting of membership rights are the same as those for speech. That is, schools may place time, place, and manner restrictions on these rights only by general rules that apply to all organizations. In addition, schools can limit student groups just as they would student speech, if they create a substantial disruption or present harm to students.

In addition to the constitutional protections, a federal statute, the Equal Access Act (EAA),[15] protects student organizations. The statute relates to secondary schools that receive federal funds and allows student-initiated groups that are classified as non-curriculum related to meet during noninstructional time (e.g., during the lunch hour or before and after school) under certain conditions. The Supreme Court has upheld this statute against an Establishment Clause challenge.[16] (See the *Mergens* boxed case summary.)

> ### BOARD OF EDUCATION OF WESTSIDE COMMUNITY SCHOOLS v. MERGENS
>
> A high school student requested that his Christian student club be allowed to meet in the school after hours. The school denied the request even though it had given several other groups permission to meet. The school based its refusal on Establishment Clause concerns. The student filed suit, claiming the school had violated his rights under the Equal Access Act. The U.S. Supreme Court held that (1) the school had created a limited open forum as set forth in **Widmar v. Vincent,** 454 U.S. 263 (1981); (2) denial of the student's request based on the religious content of his group's speech violated the Equal Access Act; and (3) based on application of the *Lemon* test to the Equal Access Act, it did not violate the Establishment Clause.

*Go to the Companion Website at **http://www. prenhall.com/underwood**, select Chapter 7, choose Cases module, and click on **Board of Education of Westside Community Schools v. Mergens** to read the entire opinion of the court.*

The courts have defined the term *non-curriculum-related student group* as any student group that does not directly relate to the body of courses offered by the school. A student group is curriculum related if its purpose directly relates to a subject matter that is actually taught or will soon be taught. Once the school allows *any* non-curriculum-related group to meet, it must allow other non-curriculum-related groups to meet, regardless of their views. In other words, schools cannot prohibit student groups from meeting based on the religious, political, philosophical, or other content of the groups' activities. However, schools can still prohibit meetings of groups that may be harmful or may threaten a material and substantial disruption (e.g., the Aryan Nation). Schools can also avoid the issue of controversial student groups by not allowing any student group to meet on campus, though few are likely to do so.

Although the Supreme Court has held that allowing student religious groups to meet in the school is not a violation of the Establishment Clause,[17] educators still need to be cautious not to cross the line created by the Establishment Clause and appear to endorse the religious mission or message presented in the student religious club. To be cautious educators should ensure

- The meeting is voluntary and student initiated;
- There is no sponsorship of the meeting by the school;
- Employees of the school are present at religious meetings only in a non-participatory capacity;

- The meeting does not materially and substantially interfere with the orderly conduct of educational activities within the school;
- Nonschool persons do not direct, conduct, control, or regularly attend activities of student groups; and
- Groups are not excluded solely on the basis of the religious, political, or philosophical speech at their meetings.

Not only religious groups but also other student groups have used the Equal Access Act to gain access to the schools. For example, many gay student groups have been successful in asserting their right to access on the same terms as other non-curriculum-related student groups.[18]

FREEDOM FROM UNREASONABLE SEARCH AND SEIZURE

The Fourth Amendment protects an individual's rights to privacy against government intrusion. However, like their First Amendment rights, students' privacy rights in school are not equivalent to those of adults. The school has more leeway in searching students than the police do in searching citizens. Police can search citizens only when they have "probable cause" or have sufficient exigent circumstances to reduce this requirement. However, the courts have said that the school's obligation to teach and protect students permits the "probable cause" standard to be relaxed to one of "reasonable under the circumstances."

Under this standard, schools may conduct a reasonable search of a student or a student's belongings if they have reason to believe the student was violating the law or school rules. However, the search must be reasonable both at its inception and in its scope. Some of the things the courts consider in determining the reasonableness of the search are the

- child's age, history, and record in the school;
- prevalence and seriousness of the problem in the school;
- exigency to make the search without delay;
- probative value and reliability of the information used to justify the search;
- school's experience with the student and the type of problem; and
- type of search.

"The right of the people to be secure . . . against unreasonable searches and seizures, shall not be violated, and no Warrants shall issue, but upon probable cause."

U.S. CONST. AMEND. IV

The reasonableness of a search depends on the degree of certainty that a student has violated a school rule or the law, as well as the extent to which the search will infringe on the student's expectation of privacy. The lower the expectation of privacy, the less certainty required to make a search reasonable. Reasonableness also depends on the purpose of the search. Imminent danger may justify an intrusive search based on reasonable suspicion. Reasonableness also requires a search of only those places where the item sought could actually exist.

Anything found during a reasonable search is fair game. For example, evidence of drug use found during a search for cigarettes in a purse would justify a more intrusive search. Any evidence of wrongdoing found during a reasonable search also can be used in a student disciplinary hearing.

What Is a Search?

A search is an invasion of someone's reasonable expectation of privacy. It does not matter if the individual owns or borrows the property searched, only that he or she has a reasonable expectation of privacy in it. For example, students have an expectation of privacy in their bookbags, their personal items, their clothes, and their bodies. Students also have a limited expectation of privacy in their school lockers—even though they are school owned. That expectation of privacy may be extremely low, but it still exists. However, if items are in "plain view," no search has taken place because no one intruded on a reasonable expectation of privacy.

*Go to the Companion Website at **http://www. prenhall.com/underwood**, select Chapter 7, then choose the Resources module to find additional state law limitations on school searches.*

Types of School Searches

The general rules regarding school searches are derived from federal constitutional law. Some states have provided students greater protection than that provided by federal law (e.g., limited the school's ability to search). The current position of the courts in regard to the various types of searches in the school environment follows.

Consensual Searches. An individual may waive his or her constitutional right to privacy and freedom from unreasonable searches. However, the person must give the consent or waiver knowingly and voluntarily. The question always exists of whether a student really voluntarily consents to a search or whether the student feels compelled to consent. Because consent is not necessary for a reasonable search, and it is thin protection for an unreasonable search, generally it is better not to rely on consent alone.

Locker Searches. Schools often state in their student codes that students have no expectation of privacy in their student lockers. Nonetheless, many courts have found that students may have a minimal expectation of privacy in their lockers. Still, courts usually uphold even general or random searches of lockers based on a minimal suspicion.[19]

Although not required to make a locker search legal, it is good practice to attempt to notify the student and let him or her be present for the search. However, when school authorities have a reasonable suspicion that the locker contains materials that pose a threat to the health, welfare, and safety of students, a locker may be searched without prior warning.

Purses and Bookbags. Students have a greater expectation of privacy in their personal property and effects than they do in their lockers. The U.S. Supreme Court has stated that, "schoolchildren may find it necessary to carry with them a variety of legitimate, non-contraband items, and there is no reason to conclude that they have necessarily waived all rights to privacy in such items merely by bringing them onto school grounds."[20] For searches of personal property schools need only a reasonable suspicion to justify a search. One difference between searches of personal possessions and locker searches is that courts generally require individualized suspicion (a reason to suspect *that* particular person) to justify possession searches but not for locker searches.[21]

Canine Searches. The Supreme Court has held that the use of dogs to sniff objects is not a search because it is not a violation of someone's reasonable expectation of privacy. The dogs merely sniff the air surrounding the object, that is, they explore only that which is within "plain smell."[22] This holds true in schools as well, but there are limitations. Schools may use dogs to sniff lockers, possessions, and bookbags. However, canine searches of students have been more limited, and because the dogs may touch the children and individually sniff them, a greater expectation of privacy is involved. Thus, most schools limit canine searches to unpopulated areas. Some schools employ private companies or local law enforcement with dogs to regularly sniff hallways and parking lots.

Body Searches. It is well established that people have an expectation of privacy in their own body. But the degree of intrusion into that expectation of privacy that the courts will allow varies significantly depending on what type of a search is being conducted.

For example, pat-down searches are relatively unintrusive so they are generally accepted with only an individualized reasonable suspicion. However, once the search is more intrusive than a simple pat down, it must, at a minimum, be based on reasonable cause.

The most extreme search is a strip search. Because strip searches are very invasive, they require a very *high* degree of certainty to be justified.[23] In the vast majority of cases they have been disallowed. As stated by one court: "It does not require a constitutional scholar to conclude that a nude search of a thirteen-year-old child is an invasion of constitutional rights of some magnitude. More than that: it is a violation of any known principle of human decency."[24] A number of states (e.g. California, Iowa, New Jersey, Oklahoma, Washington, and Wisconsin) prohibit strip searches of students by state law.

Drug Testing. The Supreme Court has found that urinalysis (the most common form of drug testing) is a search under the Fourth Amendment.[25] In one of the lead cases, **Doe v. Renfrow** (1981),[26] the Supreme Court upheld a school's drug policy that authorized random urinalysis drug testing for students in athletic activities. The Court's rationale hinged on three factors:

- The policy was adopted out of concern for student safety.
- Students have a diminished expectation of privacy when they are involved in athletics, particularly in locker rooms.
- The school was concerned over the drastic increase in drug use by students (particularly athletes).[27]

The Supreme Court later broadened the *Doe* ruling and held that schools may require students who want to participate in "competitive" extracurricular activities to submit to random urinalysis.[28] The Court found the required urinalysis to be only a negligible intrusion on the student's privacy, a privacy that is limited in the school environment in which the school district bears responsibility for maintaining a safe and orderly environment. Also important to the court's decision was the fact that the school did not turn over the results of the urinalysis to law enforcement or use them to discipline the students.

While allowing the drug testing of students who participate in competitive extracurricular activities, the courts have been unanimous in invalidating the blanket drug testing of the general student population. In addition, some state supreme courts have ruled that their state constitutions provide students more search and seizure protection from drug testing than the federal Constitution and have limited the drug testing of students. For example, in **Trinidad School District No. 1 v. Lopez**[29] the Colorado Supreme Court blocked mandatory drug testing of members of a school marching band.

Searches by School Security Officers and Police Liaison Officers. Most courts have held that the reasonableness standard applies to searches conducted by school security officers or liaison officers (also referred to as school resource officers) when they are acting under the direction of the school rather than the law enforcement agency. However, when outside police officers initiate a search, when school employees, including security officers and liaison officers, act at the behest of law enforcement agencies, or when there is significant involvement by outside police officers, the higher standard of probable cause usually applies.[30] In these cases the police must have a warrant or obtain the permission of the student before they conduct the search.

STUDENT RECORDS AND PRIVACY

Family Educational Rights and Privacy Act

School authorities keep various records for every student who attends the public schools. The Family Educational Rights and Privacy Act (FERPA)[31] addresses questions about the contents of these records and who has access to them. FERPA

> "The interest of the student must supersede all other purposes to which records might be put."
>
> THE NATIONAL EDUCATION ASSOCIATION (NEA) CODE OF STUDENT RIGHTS AND RESPONSIBILITIES

is a federal statute that sets out students' and parents' rights to access students' "educational records," protects the privacy of those records from disclosure to others, and requires that school districts establish procedures for providing parents, guardians, and eligible students (over age 18) access to student records. Such procedures identify staff members with access to the records and include a log of those who access the records. FERPA applies to all educational institutions that receive federal funds. Although the statute sets out "rights," it does not allow parents or students actually to bring a lawsuit for damages against a school for violating FERPA.[32] The only remedy a parent or student has is through the Family Policy Compliance of the Department of Education, which investigates and will enforce school district compliance if a FERPA violation is found.

What Is an Educational Record? The definition of an *educational record* is "those records, files, documents, and other materials which—contain information directly related to a student; and are maintained by an educational agency or institution or by a person acting for such agency or institution."[33] To be an educational record the information must be "maintained" by school, whether it be in administrative offices, the nurse's office, or the teacher's desk or file. For example, the Supreme Court found that a student's score on an assignment is not an educational record. In the **Owasso Indep. Sch. Dist. v. Falvo**[34] case (see the boxed case summary) the court ruled that peer grading does not violate FERPA because the student's grade is not being "maintained" but only handled while a student grades another student's papers or when a student calls out his or her grades. Also, information a teacher has, such as what is referred to as "sole possession records," personal knowledge or personal notes, or information disclosed to no one else, is not considered a student record under FERPA.

OWASSO INDEP. SCH. DIST. v. FALVO

Several teachers had students grade each other's assignments and tests and then call out the grades to the teacher in class. A parent alleged that the grading practice violated her children's right to privacy under the Fourteenth Amendment and FERPA. The Supreme Court disagreed. Pursuant to FERPA, grades must be "maintained . . . by a person acting for [an educational] agency or institution." According to the Court, this suggests that grades kept in a record room file or secure database would be covered, but in this case the student grades were not "maintained" but only handled for a few moments before being recorded by the teacher. The Court also stated that student graders were not "acting for" the educational institution when they graded papers; but rather, they were merely assisting the teacher.

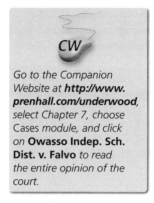

Go to the Companion Website at **http://www. prenhall.com/underwood**, select Chapter 7, choose Cases module, and click on **Owasso Indep. Sch. Dist. v. Falvo** to read the entire opinion of the court.

Release of Educational Records. The school may not release the educational records or any personally identifiable information of a student to any individual, agency, or organization without the prior written consent of a parent or guardian. The exceptions to this rule include release of student information to

- other school officials or teachers who have a legitimate educational interest;
- officials of another school or school system in which the student seeks or intends to enroll;
- authorized federal representatives for purposes of auditing and evaluating federally supported education programs or for enforcement of federal requirements related to these programs;
- state and local officials to assist the juvenile justice system to effectively serve the student whose records are released;
- organizations conducting studies for educational agencies to develop, validate, or administer predictive tests, to administer student aid programs, and to improve instruction;
- accrediting organizations in order to carry out their accrediting functions;
- parents of a dependent student;
- emergency care providers if necessary to protect the health or safety of the student or other persons;
- comply with a judicial order or lawfully issued subpoena; or
- the attorney general or his or her designee in response to an *ex parte* order in connection with the investigation or prosecution of terrorism crimes.

The school may release directory information—simple information such as names, addresses, telephone numbers—regularly without prior written consent. However, the school must give parents an opportunity to "opt out" of the release of directory information. Secondary schools receiving Elementary and Secondary Schools Act (ESEA) funds *must* disclose students' directory information to military recruiters, unless parents have opted out of providing this information.

Although FERPA guarantees parents and eligible students access to records, this does not mean that records must be produced anytime or anywhere on demand. School officials can adopt rules that specify reasonable time, place, and notice requirements for reviewing. After reviewing the record, if the parents or eligible student believes that information contained in the record is inaccurate, misleading, or in violation of the rights of the student, the parents or student can request that the information be amended. If school officials believe the information is accurate and refuse, they must advise the parents or eligible student of the

*Go to the Companion Website at **http://www. prenhall.com/underwood**, select Chapter 7, then choose the Resources module to find the Protection of Pupil Rights Amendment.*

student's right to a hearing. If the hearing officer also agrees that the record should be amended, the parent or student is entitled to place a statement of explanation or objection in the record.

Protection of Pupil Rights Amendment

Another federal statute that outlines rights of parents and students is the Protection of Pupil Rights Amendment.[35] The statute deals with the rights of parents to inspect all instructional materials used in connection with any Department of Education–funded survey, analysis, or evaluation. According to the terms of the act, schools must get prior written parental consent before they require students to take a survey, analysis, or evaluation that reveals information regarding:

- political affiliations;
- potentially embarrassing mental and psychological problems;
- sexual behavior and attitudes;
- illegal, antisocial, self-incriminating, and demeaning behavior;
- critical appraisals of other individuals with whom the student has close family relationships;
- legally recognized privileged or analogous relationships;
- religious practices, affiliations, or beliefs; or
- income other than required by law to determine eligibility for certain programs.

The Protection of Pupil Rights Amendment also requires schools to adopt policies regarding the right of parents to inspect surveys created by third parties before they are administered to students, surveys used in the educational curriculum, or any instrument used to collect this information. It also requires additional policies be adopted that address arrangements to protect student privacy, including parental inspection, if a survey includes the topics just outlined; administration of physical exams performed by the school; and collection, disclosure, or use of personal student information for marketing or selling purposes.

The amendment also provides that schools must allow parents to opt students out of (1) collection, disclosure, or use of personal student information for marketing or selling purposes; (2) administration of any non–Department of Education–funded survey regarding the eight items listed; and (3) nonemergency, invasive physical examinations that are a condition of attendance, administered by the school in advance, and not necessary to protect the immediate health and safety of students.

GUIDING LEGAL PRINCIPLES

- The Supreme Court has repeatedly stated that the United States Constitution applies to children as well as adults.
- In evaluating student freedoms, the courts have basically used the standard of reasonableness to assess the constitutionality of schools' conduct. The courts have used the reasonableness standard for both student expression and student search–related cases.
- Schools can limit student speech when they reasonably believe the speech may cause a substantial disruption to school activities.
- If student speech is within a school-sponsored activity or within the curricular context, schools have greater latitude in controlling student speech. Even if not potentially disruptive, student speech may be curtailed if it is harmful to students or pervasively vulgar.
- Distribution of literature may be similarly regulated but any prior review policy must be clearly communicated and provide reasonable time lines.
- Some jurisdictions consider student dress expressive and schools can regulate it only for reasons of potential disruption or harm.
- Student groups are protected by the Equal Access Act and the First Amendment freedom of association. Groups must be treated similarly; that is, they may not receive harsher or more favorable treatment based on their views or purposes. However, schools can still prohibit meetings of groups that may be harmful or disruptive.
- Students have the protections of constitutional rights of privacy. Yet these rights, like others, are not absolute. Schools may conduct reasonable searches of students, of both their person and their possessions.
- The Family Educational Rights and Privacy Act protects students' educational records from disclosure without prior parental permission with certain exceptions.

YOU BE THE JUDGE

Go to the Companion Website at **http://www.prenhall.com/underwood**, *select Chapter 7, choose the* You Be the Judge *module and click on the name of the case for more information about the case and the court's decision and rationale.*

The NRA and the Dress Code Challenge

A middle school student wore to school a T-shirt bearing the initials *NRA* and depicting three gunmen. The school's dress code prohibited any clothing associated with weapons and violence. Although Newsom was never suspended, the school instructed him to turn the shirt inside out. Represented by the National Riffle Association, he filed suit in federal district court, challenging the dress code on First Amendment grounds.

Questions for Discussion and Reflection

1. In your opinion, does the school board's action represent a reasonable attempt to balance the student's right to expression and the school's interest in maintaining an orderly learning environment? Explain.
2. What argument and evidence would the school need to present to support its dress code and its application to this situation?
3. Should the fact that Newsom was not disciplined for wearing the T-shirt be a factor in the court's decision? Why or why not?

Visit the Companion Website for a more detailed description of the facts in the case **Newsom v. Albemarle County School Board.**

* * *

Denying Access to the Gay–Straight Alliance Club

Pursuant to school district policy, a group of students submitted an application to form a Gay–Straight Alliance Club (GSA). Although the principal usually reviewed and approved applications to form clubs, the gay-alliance application was passed on to the superintendent, who in turn presented it to the school board. After several months, the board voted to deny the club approval on the grounds that (1) the club would be discussing subject matter that was part of the school's sex education curriculum; and (2) it considered the unrestricted and unsupervised student-led discussion of sexually related topics age inappropriate and likely to interfere with the legitimate educational concerns regarding sex education. The board further stated that it would reconsider the club's application if it changed its name and revised its mission statement to indicate that sex, sexuality, and sex education would not be discussed in club meetings. The students filed suit, alleging violation of their rights under the Equal Access Act and the First Amendment.

Questions for Discussion and Reflection

1. Under what conditions may a school board constitutionally prohibit student groups from meeting on campus? Were they present in this case?
2. How would a review of the process used for review and approval of other groups and the health and family life curriculum affect the arguments and potential outcome of this case?
3. Did the conditions for reconsideration presented by the school board represent a "reasonable accommodation" of the GSA? Why or why not?

Visit the Companion Website for a more detailed description of the facts in the case **Colin v. Orange Unified School District.**

* * *

How Far Is Too Far to Search?

An elementary school teacher discovered $10 was missing from her desk. She stopped four students who were in the classroom at the time the money went missing. She searched their bookbags and had them turn their pants pockets inside out. She then had the students turn the waistbands of their pants out so she could check their waistlines. She let two of the students go and had two accompany her to the supply closet, where she looked down one student's pants for the money, which she did not find. The students' parents sued the teacher.

Questions for Discussion and Reflection

1. What are some of the things the court will consider in determining whether this search was reasonable under the circumstances?
2. What expectations of privacy did the students have in regard to their bookbags? their clothing?
3. Would a past history of missing items in the class possibly affect the outcome of this case?

Visit the Companion Website for a more detailed description of the facts in the case **Watkins v. Millennium School.**

MORE ON THE WEB

Go to the Companion Website at **http://www.prenhall.com/underwood**, *select Chapter 7, choose the* More on the Web *module to connect to the site mentioned.*

Go to the American Civil Liberties Student Rights website at **http://www.aclu.org/ StudentsRights/StudentsRightsMain.cfm.** What are the topics of the "Latest News"? Pick one topic (e.g., discrimination or drug testing) and describe the involvement of the ACLU in the cases/incidents described. Scroll to the end of "Press Releases" to the "Legal Documents" section, and summarize the arguments made by the ACLU in support of student rights as described in the Amicus Brief for one of the cases listed.

ENDNOTES

1. *West Virginia State Bd. of Educ. v. Barnette*, 319 U.S. 624, 637 (1943).
2. *Bethel School District No. 403 v. Fraser*, 478 U.S. 675, 682 (1986).

3. 393 U.S. 503, 506 (1969).

4. 484 U.S. 261 (1988).

5. *Bethel School District No. 403 v. Fraser,* 478 U.S. 675 (1986).

6. *Mahaffey v. Aldrich,* 236 F. Supp.2d 779 (E.D. Mich. 2002).

7. *J. S. V. Bethlehem Area Sch. Dist.,* 807 A.2d 847 (Pa. 2002).

8. See, e.g., *West v. Derby Unified School Dist.,* 206 F.3d 1358 (10th Cir.), *cert. denied,* 53 U.S. 825 (2000). (School properly suspended student for drawing Confederate flag in class; school had a policy that prohibited racial harassment or intimidation.)

9. *Botoff v. Van Wert City Board of Education* 220 F.3d 465 (6th Cir. 2000), *cert. denied,* 532 U.S. 920 (2001).

10. *Doe v. Brockton School Committee,* 2000 WL 33342399 (Mass. App. 2000).

11. See, e.g., *Menora v. Illinois High School Association,* 683 F. 2d 1030 (7th Cir. 1982), *cert. denied,* 459 U.S. 1156 (1983).

12. *Hearn v. Muskogee Public School District,* 2004 WL 80465249 (E.D. OK. 2004).

13. *Stephenson v. Davenport Community School District,* 110 F.3d 1303 (8th Cir. 1997); *Chalifoux v. New Caney Independent School Dist.,* 976 F. Supp. 659 (S.D. Tex. 1997).

14. NAESP Principal Online. (2004). *Information and resources: School uniforms.* Retrieved May 3, 2005, from www.naesp.org/misc/uniforms.htm

15. 20 U.S.C. § 4071 *et seq.*

16. *Board of Educ. of Westside Comm. Schools v. Mergens,* 496 U.S. 226 (1990).

17. Ibid.

18. See, e.g., *Colin v. Orange Unified School Dist.,* 83 F. Supp.2d 1135 (C.D. Cal. 2000); *Franklin Cent. Gay/Straight Alliance v. Franklin Tp. Comty. Sch. Corp.,* 2002 WL 31921332 (S.D. Ind. 2002); *Boyd County High Sch. Gay/Straight Alliance v. Bd. of Educ. of Boyd County, Ky.,* 258 F. Supp.2d 667 (E.D. Ky. 2003).

19. See, e.g., *S.C. v. State,* 583 So.2d 188 (Miss. 1991); *In re Isiah B.,* 500 N.W.2d 637 (Wis. 1993), *cert. denied,* 510 U.S. 883 (1993); *State v. Jones,* 666 N.W.2d 142 (Iowa 2003).

20. *New Jersey v. T.L.O.,* 469 U.S. 325, 339 (1985).

21. See, e.g., *Desroches v. Caprio,* 156 F.3d 571 (4th Cir. 1998); *In re Murray,* 525 S.E.2d 496 (N.C. Ct. App. 2000).

22. *United States. v. Place,* 462 U.S. 696 (1983).

23. See, e.g., *Jenkins v. Talladega City Bd. of Educ.,* 95 F.3d 1036 (11th Cir. 1996); *Konop v. Northwestern School Dist.,* 26 F. Supp.2d 1189 (D. S.D. 1998).

24. *Doe v. Renfrow,* 631 F.2d 91, 92–93 (7th Cir. 1980), *cert. denied,* 451 U.S. 1022 (1981).

25. *Skinner v. Railway Labor Executives' Ass'n,* 489 U.S. 602 (1989); *National Treasury Employees Union v. Von Raab,* 489 U.S. 656 (1989).

26. 631 F.2d 91, 92–93 (7th Cir. 1980), *cert. denied,* 451 U.S. 1022 (1981).

27. *Vernonia School District 47J v. Acton,* 515 U.S. 646 (1995).

28. *Board of Education of Independent School District No. 92 of Pottawatomie v. Earls,* 536 U.S. 822 (2002).

29. 963 P.2d 1095 (Col. 1998).

30. See, e.g., *People v. Dilworth,* 661 N.E.2d 310, 317 (Ill. 1996), *cert. denied,* 517 U.S. 1197 (1996).

31. 20 U.S.C. § 1232g (2000); 34 C.F.R. Part 99.

32. *Gongaza Univ. v. Doe,* 536 U.S. 273 (2002).

33. Family Educational Rights and Privacy Act, 20 U.S.C. § 1232g (2005).

34. 534 U.S. 426 (2002).

35. 20 U.S.C. § 1232h (2005).

8

EDUCATION OF STUDENTS WITH DISABILITIES

Special education is one of the most dynamic and fastest growing educational programs in America's public schools. In the 2001–2002 school year the 6.4 million students with disabilities made up approximately 13% of the students in the public schools.[1] The number of students with disabilities has almost doubled since the 1970s when the federal government began mandating special education programming (see Table 8.1). Before that time, most states' laws either allowed the expulsion from school or failed to provide education for children who were deemed uneducable, untrainable, or otherwise unable to benefit from the regular education program. When children with disabilities were admitted, many of them received an ineffective or inappropriate education. Two important court decisions in the early 1970s (**Pennsylvania Association of Retarded Citizens v. Commonwealth of Pennsylvania**[2] and **Mills v. Washington DC Board of Education**[3]) sparked the trend that led states and school districts to recognize the right of children with disabilities to a public education.

These decisions, combined with intense lobbying by special education professionals, interest groups, and parents of children with disabilities, prompted Congress to pass the Education for All Handicapped Children Act of 1975 (EHA)[4] and Section 504 of the Rehabilitation Act of 1973.[5] The EHA has been amended several times since 1975, extending the ages of covered children, broadening the categories of disabilities covered, and expanding the services provided. In 1990 the EHA was reauthorized and renamed the Individuals With Disabilities Education Act (IDEA). That same year Congress further expanded the legal protection available to individuals with disabilities with the passage of the Americans With Disabilities Act (ADA).[6] In 2004, Congress again reauthorized the statute as the Individuals With Disabilities Improvement Act

Table 8.1   Children 3 to 21 Years Old Served in Federally Supported Programs for the Disabled, by Type of Disability: Selected Years, 1976–1977 to 2001–2002

Type of Disability	(numbers in thousands)							
	1976–1977	1980–1981	1990–1991	1995–1996	1997–1998	1999–2000	2000–2001	2001–2002
All Disabilities	3,694	4,144	4,710	5,573	5,903	6,190	6,296	6,407
Specific learning disabilities	796	1,462	2,129	2,579	2,725	2,830	2,843	2,846
Speech or language impairments	1,302	1,168	985	1,022	1,056	1,078	1,084	1,084
Mental retardation	961	830	535	570	589	600	599	592
Emotional disturbance	283	347	390	438	453	468	473	476
Hearing impairments	88	79	58	67	69	70	70	70
Orthopedic impairments	87	58	49	63	67	71	72	73
Other health impairments	141	98	55	133	190	254	292	337
Visual impairments	38	31	23	25	25	26	25	25
Multiple disabilities	—	68	96	93	106	111	121	127
Deaf-blindness	—	3	1	1	1	2	1	2
Autism and traumatic brain injury	—	—	—	39	54	80	94	118
Developmental delay	—	—	—	—	4	19	28	45
Preschool disabled	—	—	390	544	564	582	592	612

Source. From *Digest of Education Statistics, 2003,* by U.S. Department of Education, National Center for Education Statistics, 2004, Washington DC: NCES.

(IDEA). The IDEA, Section 504, and the ADA together establish the procedures that schools must follow to ensure the rights of students with disabilities are protected.

The EHA introduced a number of principles that have had a major impact on American education. Summaries of these educational principles, expanded through the IDEA and subsequent legislation and litigation, follow. Also discussed are the provisions and protections provided under Section 504 and the ADA. After reading this chapter you will be able to

- Explain the major considerations in determining whether the school has met its obligation to provide a free and appropriate education.
- Outline the requirements in conducting a nondiscriminatory evaluation to determine eligibility and related services.
- List the components of an Individualized Education Program (IEP) required by the IDEA.
- Discuss the major factors the courts consider in determining the least restrictive environment.

- Describe the procedural due process protections afforded parents under the IDEA.
- Compare the eligibility requirements of the IDEA with those of Section 504.
- Distinguish between the requirements placed on school districts under the ADA and those under Section 504.

INDIVIDUALS WITH DISABILITIES EDUCATION ACT

The Individuals With Disabilities Education Improvement Act (IDEA) stands as the most specific of the statutes addressing the rights of students with disabilities. The IDEA applies to all children with disabilities between the ages of 3 and 21 and includes preschool, elementary school, secondary school, and vocational education. The statute defines children with disabilities as those with mental retardation, hearing impairments, speech or language impairments, visual impairments, emotional disturbance, orthopedic impairments, autism, traumatic brain injury, multiple disabilities, or specific learning disabilities.[7]

In order to receive services under the IDEA a student must not only have a disability, but the condition must also have an impact on the student's education to an extent that requires the delivery of special education programs and related services (i.e., services necessary for the student to benefit from the special education). The major principles included in the IDEA are (1) the right to a free and appropriate education, (2) identification and nondiscriminatory evaluation, (3) an individualized education program, (4) least restrictive environment, and (5) procedural due process.

Free and Appropriate Education

Perhaps the most fundamental and important principle of the IDEA is that all children aged 3 to 21 years with disabilities, regardless of the nature or severity of their disabilities, must have available to them a free and appropriate education and related services designed to meet their unique needs. The IDEA does not specify what programs or services must be provided to satisfy the guarantee of an appropriate education. Rather, this must be decided on a case-by-case basis through the decision-making process required for developing the student's IEP. The question of what should be included in the IEP has been the subject of considerable litigation. The U.S. Supreme Court in 1982 provided some guidance in **Board of Education v. Rowley**[8] (see the boxed case summary), in which it stated that a free appropriate public education did not mean "an opportunity to achieve full potential commensurate with the opportunity provided to other children," but rather "access to specialized instruction and related services which are designed to provide educational benefit to the handicapped child." From this landmark case came the two-prong test used to determine whether school districts have met their obligation to provide a free and appropriate public education:

BOARD OF EDUC. OF HENDRICK HUDSON CENTRAL SCHOOL DISTRICT v. ROWLEY

Amy Rowley was a deaf student attending regular classes. During her kindergarten year she received an FM hearing aid that amplified words spoken by teachers and students. She successfully completed the year. The following year Amy received the FM hearing aid as well as instruction from a tutor for the deaf for 1 hour a day and from a speech therapist 3 hours a week. Her parents wanted the school also to provide her with a sign language interpreter and filed an action against the school district. The Supreme Court held that the school did not have to provide the best education, but one reasonably calculated to confer educational benefits.

- Has the district complied with all the procedural requirements? If it has not, did the violations lead to an inappropriate placement?
- Is the IEP reasonably calculated to confer educational benefit? (Parents do not have the right to determine methodology in the IEP as long as it is an appropriate one.)

Since *Rowley,* while the courts have supported parents in their attempts to secure an appropriate education and expanded services for their children with disabilities, they tend to accept the most reasonable program rather than to require the best possible program. In other words, the courts have said that the word *appropriate* means that the child who is eligible for services under the IDEA is being provided at least the minimum level of services that will provide a reasonable chance of the student making progress toward meeting the goals and objectives detailed in the Individualized Education Program (IEP) for that child. For example, in **LT v. Warwick School Committee**[9] the district had offered a self-contained classroom that used a modified version of educational techniques known as Treatment and Education of Autistic and Communication-Handicapped Children; the parent rejected this offer, preferring the use of a different technique known as Discrete Trial Training. The First Circuit Court of Appeals found that an autistic student was not entitled to the particular program preferred by the parent, stating "IDEA does not require a public school to provide what is best for a special needs child, only that it provide an IEP that is 'reasonably calculate' to provide an 'appropriate' education as defined in federal and state law."[10]

Nor does IDEA require schools to provide the most services and programs available. For example, in **Dale M. v. Board of Educ. of Bradley Bourbonnais High School**[11] the student had been a serious disciplinary problem for some time and was placed in a therapeutic day school. The student was jailed and then released. His parent then placed him in a residential placement and sought

CW

Go to the Companion Website at **http://www.prenhall.com/underwood**, select Chapter 8, choose Cases module, and click on **Board of Educ. of Hendrick Hudson Central District v. Rowley** *to read the entire opinion of the court.*

reimbursement alleging that only a residential placement was appropriate. The Seventh Circuit Court of Appeals found that the residential placement was not educationally necessary, only custodial, and upheld the school district's offer of services as appropriate.

Identification and Evaluation

The first obligation the IDEA imposes on the schools is to take affirmative steps to identify children with disabilities who may be entitled to special education. This "child find" responsibility extends to all children within the community, even those in private schools. A teacher or other educator who has reason to believe a student has a disability and is in need of special education services may refer the student for an evaluation. The evaluation's intent is to describe the child's functioning and determine whether the child has a disability under IDEA. (See Figure 8.1 for a sample referral form.) It is important for teachers to understand their responsibility to students in this evaluation process; teachers, especially regular education teachers, provide a great service to students by calling attention to a student's potential disability.

Informed parental consent for evaluation must be obtained before the evaluation can take place. This parental consent is for the purpose of conducting evaluation and cannot be construed as consent for the delivery of a special education program. The IDEA gives schools 60 days from the receipt of parental consent to the determination of the eligibility and educational needs of the child.

A multidisciplinary team must carry out the evaluation, which should assess all areas related to the suspected disability, and provide information that directly assists in determining the educational needs of the child. The team uses a variety of formal and informal assessment tools and strategies (including teacher observations and information provided by the parent) to gather relevant functional and developmental information about the child. This information can assist in determining (1) whether the child qualifies for services and (2) what special education and related services the child needs. The assessment should "assess all areas related to the suspected disability, including health, vision, hearing, social and emotional status, general intelligence, academic performance, communicative status, and motor disabilities."[12]

The tests and other evaluation methods used to conduct the evaluation must be selected and administered so as not to be racially or culturally discriminatory and must be given in the child's native language or other mode of communication (e.g., Braille or sign language). They must also "measure the extent to which the child who has limited English proficiency has a disability and needs special education rather than measure the child's English language skills."[13] Any standardized test given must be (1) validated for the specific purpose for which it is used; (2) administered by trained and knowledgeable personnel; and (3) administered in accordance with any instructions provided by the producer of such

Figure 8.1 Sample Referral Form to Evaluate a Child's Need for Special Education Services

---

Washington Elementary School District – Special Services
8610 N. 19th Avenue – Phoenix, AZ 85021   **Team Approach Process Request – Part I**

Date Given to Referring Agent_____

Student_____Gender_____ DOB_____ School_____ Gr____ ID#_____

Name of Person Making Referral_____ Relationship to Child_____

Parent/Guardian Name(s)_____ Phone # [wk]_____[hm]_____

_____   _____   _____

Primary Language [Home]_____Primary Language [Child]_____Racial/Ethnic Background_____

Screening Procedures	Y/N	Date Completed	Result
45 Day Screening	___	_____	_____
Home/Language Survey	___	_____	_____
Oral Home Lang./English Proficiency	___	_____	_____
Reading Home Lang./English Proficiency	___	_____	_____
Writing Home Lang./English Proficiency	___	_____	_____

Area(s) of concern: [ ] Academics Part II, III [ ] Behavior Part II, III, IV [ ] Speech/Language Part II, III, V
[ ] Delayed Development Part II, III [ ] Hearing Part II, III [ ] Vision Part II, III [ ] Gross/Fine Motor Part II, III, VI

Reason for Referral [Describe reasons or situations that make you feel or suspect the child has a disability.]

Summarize the efforts that have been made to date, to educate the child in the regular classroom. Specify the modifications used with the student, the date initiated, frequency, duration, date ended and results.

Form completed by_____ Title_____ Date_____

Principal's Signature_____ Date_____ Disposition_____

Source: Washington Elementary School District, Phoenix, Arizona.

tests. Last, a school district may not use any single procedure or test as the criterion for determining whether a child is eligible for services under the IDEA and for determining the appropriate educational program. If an assessment determines the child to be eligible for services under IDEA, reevaluations must be done at least every 3 years.

Upon completion of the evaluation the IDEA requires that parents be given a copy of the evaluation report. As discussed in a later section, if the parents disagree with the results of the evaluation they can request a due process hearing. Parents also have the right to seek an independent educational evaluation, at their own expense, which then must be considered in addition to the school's evaluation as a part of the eligibility determination.

If the evaluation determines that the student is not eligible for services under the IDEA, he or she may still be eligible for services to accommodate a disability under Section 504. On the other hand, if as a result of evaluation the team decides that the student requires special education services, an Individualized Education Program must be prepared.

Individualized Education Program

The IDEA requires that an individualized education program (IEP) be prepared for each child who is to receive special education services. The IEP is a written document that provides the plan for implementation of the special education program and any related services to the eligible student. As illustrated in the excerpt of an IEP in Figure 8.2, the IEP identifies the specialized needs of the student and outlines appropriate learning goals and objectives or benchmarks that will guide the student to achieve academic progress.

The IEP is developed at a meeting that, under the requirements of the IDEA, must include parents, the student's teachers (special education and regular education), special education specialists, others who may contribute to the individually tailored learning plan, and, when appropriate, the student as well. The law requires the IEP to include the following components:

1. A statement of the student's current levels of educational performance in terms of academic, socialization, behavioral, and communication skills. This statement also should address how the disability affects the student's involvement and progress in the general education curriculum. In developing the IEP, the team also should assess and address the strengths of the child and the child's family's concerns for enhancing their child's education.

2. A list of annual goals including benchmarks and short-term objectives relating to student's progress in the general education curriculum, as well as other educational needs.

3. A statement of the special education and related services as well as supplementary aids and services and other supports to help the student reach the annual goals, be involved and progress in the general education

(*continues on page 152*)

Figure 8.2 An Excerpt of an Individualized Education Program

Washington Elementary School District—Special Services
8610 N. 19th Avenue, Phoenix, Arizona 85021
Phone: (602)347-2632

Individualized Education Program
The IEP and educational placement will be reviewed and, if necessary, revised at least annually.

Student Data   Page   of   Date

Name John Reyes	DOB 5/20/1992	Gender M	Grade 3	Student ID# 12345

Address 2641 W. Butler	City Phoenix	Zip 85021

Phone ☐ Home ☐Cell ☐ Pager 602-347-8999	Work Phone	Parent/Guardian Maria Reyes	Primary Language of Home Spanish

Limited English Proficient ☒ Yes ☐ No	Language of Instruction English w/clarification	School of Residence Washington Elem School	School of Attendance Washington Elem School

Meeting Notice Documentation

Describe records of telephone calls, attempted or completed, and the results of calls. Attach copies of correspondence sent to the parents and any responses received. Describe visits made to the parent's home or place of employment and the results of those visits.

Date of Meeting Notice August 27, 2001	Date of IEP Meeting September 5, 2001	Type ☒ Initial ☐ Annual Review & Revision ☐ Other:

Consideration of Other Factors

	Needed	Not Needed
Language needs (if student is identified as limited English Proficient)	☒	☐
Braille instruction (if student is blind or visually impaired)	☐	☒
Communication needs of the student (if hearing impaired, mode of communication with peers/school staff)	☐	☒
Assistive devices and service needs of the student	☐	☒
Statement of transition services	☐	☒
Positive behavior interventions and supports if behavior impedes learning or understanding/ following school rules. Documentation of behavior intervention plan can be found: ☐ goals ☐ adaptations section ☐ attachment	☐	☐

Documentation of Participants

Position/Relationship to Student	Name	Attended (A) Consulted (C)	A or C
Parent(s)	Maria Reyes		
Regular Education Teacher			
Special Education Teacher			
District Representative			
Psychologist			
Therapist/Pathologist			
Other at discretion of parent/district			
Principal			
Student, if appropriate			

Census Data

Census Code:
Special Education & Related Services Codes:
Evaluation Codes:
Date of last Vision Screening: _____   Date of last Hearing Screening: _____

PS3408A SE9 (11-2000) IEP Form 1   1st: Special Services; 2nd: Parent; 3rd: School

Source: Washington Elementary School District, Phoenix, Arizona.

Figure 8.2 Continued

Washington Elementary School District - Special Services
8610 N. 19th Avenue, Phoenix, Arizona 85021
Phone: (602) 347-2632

Name John Reyes _____ ID# _____ 12345 _____ Page ___ of ___ Date _____

Present Level of Educational Performance

Describe the student's current functional performance to include the parents' perspective and insights. Describe how the student's disability affects his/her involvement and progress in the general curriculum based on the Arizona Academic Standards. For a preschool child describe how the disability affects the child's participation in appropriate activities.

English Language Acquisition

Sample Statement   1

According to the SELP test, John's English oral proficiency level is at an emergent level meaning John's speech contained numerous errors in grammar, syntax and vocabulary. John has been observed to use English speaking with his classmates and tends to avoid initiating conservation in the classroom. John's writing and reading skills were assessed at a preproduction level in both English and in Spanish. The learning of English for John will be slow and should not be expected to be at the same rate for similar LEP students given John's identified learning disability. While some of John's English language learning difficulties are external factors highlighted in the evaluation report, John also exhibits significant delays in short term memory, auditory processing and long term memory as a primary cause to his learning difficulties. John would benefit from sheltered English instructional strategies and he should be reassessed on the SELP at annually.

Sample Statement 2

The team was unable to determine the present status of John's English and native language proficiency due to John's profound cognitive delays. John is a recent refugee from Sudan and according to his parents was not allowed to attend school. Parents are native language speakers and they live in an area that share the family's customs and language. John's verbal communication is limited to vocalizations and gestures express happiness and displeasure. John will require a highly specialized setting to address his sensory needs. The extent of John's cognitive delays suggest a poor prognosis in acquiring basic functional English skills. John will benefit from a picture communication system.

Figure 8.2 Continued

Washington Elementary School District - Special Services
8610 N. 19th Avenue, Phoenix, Arizona 85021
Phone: (602) 347-2632

Name John Reyes   ID#   12345   Page   of   Date _____

Instructional and Assessment Adaptations

The student will participate in the accountability system and, to the extent possible, in the regular assessment, taking into account the child's instructional goals, current level of functioning,and learning characteristics. Adaptations are changes made to the environment, curriculum, and instruction and/or assessment practices consisting of **accommodations** or **modifications.**

Accommodations are provisions made in how the student accesses and demonstrates learning. **Modifications** are substantial changes in what the student is expected to learn and demonstrate.

Instructional

Alter Assignments by Providing:	**Manage Behavior by Providing:**
Adapt Instruction by Providing: Opportunity to Repeat and Explain Instructions Visual Aids (cues, tapes, etc.)/Auditory Aids (cues, tapes, etc.) Sheltered English instruction Basic interpersonal communication skills Language acquisition strategies	**Equipment/Assistive Technology Devices:**
Adapt Materials by Providing:	**Grading:** Anecdotal notes Portfolios

Assessment

		AIMS	WESD
The student will participate in the testing program under standardized conditions.	☐	☐	☐
The student will participate in the testing program with the adaptations listed above.	☐	☐	☐
The student's grade level is not scheduled to participate. (AIMS-A /AIMS grades 3,5, and 8 or ages 9,11, and 14)	☐	☐	☐
This student qualifies for an alternate assessment in ☐ Reading ☐ Writing ☐ Mathematics	☐	☐	

Explain why each academic area of alternate assessment is appropriate for student

How will the student be assessed?

Reporting Progress

Describe how the parents will be **regularly** informed of their child's progress toward annual goals. The report must be provided at least as often as parents are informed of nondisabled student's progress.

Figure 8.2 Continued

Washington Elementary School District - Special Services
8610 N. 19th Avenue, Phoenix, Arizona 85021
Phone: (602) 347-2632

Name John Reyes   ID#   12345   Page   of   Date

Special Education, Supplementary Aids, Related Services, and Program Supports

Provisions to enable this student to: advance appropriately toward attaining the annual goals; be involved and progress in the general curriculum as appropriate; participate in extracurricular and other nonacademic activities; be educated and participate with disabled and nondisabled children in nonacademic settings. Describe special education instruction, supplementary aids and related services to be provided to the child or on behalf of the child. Describe any program supports (information, consultation, training, material or staffing) for school personnel on behalf of the child.

☐ Supplementary aids and Related Services not needed.   ☐ Program supports for school personnel not needed.

Services	Initiation Date	Frequency/ Amount	Duration	Location
Sample Statements				
Consultation with the ELL Specialist as a program support to the IEP Team for technical assistance.	m/d/y	weekly/30 minutes	m/d/y	classroom
ELL strategies integrated into the child's special education instruction.	m/d/y	daily	m/d/y	classroom
Native Language Clarification–bilingual aide for academic support integrated with ELL strategies.	m/d/y	daily/instructional activities	m/d/y	classroom

General Statement of Student's Transportation Needs   (if needed, complete Transportation Plan)   ☐ None Needed

☐ Student requires transportation only to access program location without any adaptation, special equipment or additional assistance.

Student requires: ☐ special seating arrangement   ☐ special equipment, aids or mobility assistance

☐ medications during an emergency   ☐ medical considerations:

☐ behavioral management plan   Student may be left at stop unattended ☐ Yes ☐ No ☐ other:

Explanation of non-participation. Describe the extent the child will not participate in regular class, extracurricular and other nonacademic activities with nondisabled students.

Extended School Year Consideration

This service is provided to prevent irreparable harm to the child's ability to maintain identified skills/behavior or accommodate critical learning periods if the child is unlikely to receive another opportunity to learn or generalize targeted skills or behaviors.

☐ Insufficient data. Data collection activities to include the following considerations: regression-recoupment factors, critical stages, data-based student observations, least restrictive environment considerations, teacher and parent interviews and recommendations, past history and parental skills/abilities. The IEP meeting will be conducted when data collection is complete.

☐ **ESY services not required.**

☐ **Student is ESY eligible.**   ☐ ESY IEP Addendum attached.   ☐ Future IEP meeting.

PS3413A SE12 (11-2000) IEP Form 5   1st: Special Services; 2nd: Parent; 3rd: School curriculum, and participate in extracurricular and nonacademic activities with other students. . . . This statement also should address the program modifications and support for school personnel, such as general educators receiving consultation services or training related to specific issues.

4. An explanation of the extent, if any, to which the student will *not* participate in the general education classroom and in other activities with students without disabilities.

5. A statement of any testing accommodations that the student will need to participate in state or district-wide assessments. If the IEP team determines that a student will not participate in a particular assessment, the IEP must include an explanation of why the test is not appropriate and state what alternative methods will be used to assess the student's learning and progress.

6. A statement describing how the student's progress toward the goals in the IEP will be measured and how the student's family will be regularly informed of their child's progress. Student's progress reports must be as frequent as the progress reports sent to families of general education students. This statement also should state what the student must do to achieve the goals in the IEP by the end of the school year.

7. A projected date for the initiation of services and modifications, as well as their anticipated frequency, location, and duration.[14]

The child's teachers (regular education and special education teacher) play an important role in the development of the IEP and at the IEP meeting. For example, in **Shapiro v. Paradise Valley Unified School District**,[15] the court found a violation of IDEA when the district failed to include a teacher from the student's school in the IEP process. The multidisciplinary team should use the teacher's observations to establish progress and assess whether a proposed service or strategy may be appropriate.

Related Services

One of the most expensive and possibly most controversial aspects of the IDEA is its mandate that schools provide students with all related services necessary for the child to benefit from special education. Many services fall into this category, including bus transportation and various psychological and health services. The IDEA defines related services as

Transportation, and such developmental, corrective, and other supportive services (including speech-language pathology and audiology services, psychological services, physical and occupational therapy, recreation, including therapeutic recreation, social work services, counseling services, including rehabilitation counseling, orientation and mobility services, and medical services, except that such medical services shall be for diagnostic and evaluation purposes only) as may be required to assist a child with a disability to benefit from special education.[16]

Assistive technology devices and transition services were later added to the statutory list.

What, if any, related service(s) a child should receive has been the subject of a growing number of cases, most often brought by parents seeking to obtain expanded services for their children. In **Irving Independent School District v. Tatro**[17] (see the boxed case summary), the Supreme Court devised a three-part test to determine whether the school district is required to provide a particular service to a student as a related service:

- The child must have a disability so as to require special education under IDEA;
- The proposed service must be necessary for the child to benefit from his or her special education; and
- The service must not fall within a specific exclusion, such as the physicians' services or individually prescribed equipment.

In *Tatro* the Supreme Court emphasized that the child must have a disability under IDEA before he or she can be eligible for related services. The Court said: "In the absence of a handicap that requires special education, the need for what otherwise might qualify as a related service does not create an obligation under the Act." Thus a student who may need some counseling services but is not eligible for special education services does not qualify for related services.

IRVING INDEPENDENT SCHOOL DISTRICT v. TATRO

A student with spina bifida required Clean Intermittent Catheterization (CIC) services in order to attend special education classes. The student's IEP made no provision for school personnel to administer the CIC services. After exhausting their administrative remedies in an attempt to obtain their services, the student's parents filed suit against the school district. They alleged that CIC was a "related service" that the school district was required to provide under the EHA. The court agreed, reasoning that without the procedure being made available during the school day the student could not attend classes and benefit from special education instruction.

Therefore, the Court concluded that CIC was related to the effort to educate because it was a service necessary in order to allow the student to remain in the classroom.

One of the points of frequent contention between parents and the school is whether a particular service is actually necessary for the student to receive educational benefits. In resolving these disputes the courts address the following questions:

- Is the service necessary for the student to gain access to or remain in the special education program?

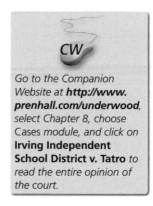

Go to the Companion Website at **http://www. prenhall.com/underwood**, select Chapter 8, choose Cases module, and click on **Irving Independent School District v. Tatro** *to read the entire opinion of the court.*

- Is the service necessary to resolve other needs for the student before educational efforts will be successful?
- Is the service necessary for the student to make meaningful progress on the identified goals?

In some situations the related service provided may in fact deal with the student's needs inside and outside of the classroom (e.g., counseling, physical therapy). In **Stratham School v. Beth and David P.**[18] the question was whether the district should have to pay for the mapping of a student's cochlear implant (but not for the cochlear implant itself) and for the transportation of the student and his parents to the specialist doing the mapping and customization of the implant. The mapping of the implant involves using a computer to determine the proper level of electrical current needed to stimulate electrodes implanted in the ear. The court found that the mapping and the travel expenses were necessary for the implant to work correctly, which was necessary to improve the student's ability to communicate.

The U.S. Supreme Court provided clarification as to the specific exception of medical services in **Cedar Rapids Independent School District v. Garrett F.** (see the boxed case summary).[19] The case raised the issue of whether continuous nursing care needed by a quadriplegic student during school constitutes a related service for which the school is obligated to pay or a medical service excluded from the school's statutory responsibility. The Supreme Court concluded that the only services that are medical for purposes of IDEA are those that must be rendered only by a physician. All other supportive health services that can be provided by someone other than a physician, the Court reasoned, can be considered related services that the school district must pay for and provide if deemed necessary for the student to benefit from special education under IDEA.

CEDAR RAPIDS INDEPENDENT SCHOOL DISTRICT v. GARRETT F.

A quadriplegic student, who was ventilator dependent, required continuous one-on-one nursing services. The parents provided the nursing services at school until the student entered fifth grade. They then requested the school district to provide the services. The school district refused, and the parents requested a due process hearing under IDEA. After an administrative law judge ruled that the school district was required to provide the services under IDEA as a "related service," the school district appealed to the district court. The district court granted the parents' summary judgment on the ground that the nursing services were "related services" rather than excluded "medical services."

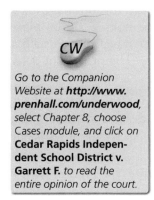

Go to the Companion Website at **http://www. prenhall.com/underwood**, select Chapter 8, choose Cases module, and click on **Cedar Rapids Independent School District v. Garrett F.** to read the entire opinion of the court.

Least Restrictive Environment

Not only must a child be provided with a free and appropriate education through an IEP, the IDEA requires that these special education services must be provided to the student in the least restrictive environment (LRE). The least restrictive environment principle does not require all children with disabilities be educated in the regular classroom. However, the language of the IDEA establishes a clear preference for educating all children within that setting when possible: "To the maximum extent appropriate, children with disabilities . . . are educated with children who are nondisabled."[20] The courts have interpreted the LRE provision to mean that children with disabilities should not be removed from the regular educational setting unless the nature or severity of the disability is such that education in the regular classroom, even with the use of supplemental aids and services, cannot be satisfactorily achieved.

The law has required schools to provide supplemental services in the regular classroom before moving the child to a more restrictive environment. This does not mean, however, that all students are entitled to a placement in their neighborhood school. For example, in **McLaughlin v. Holt Public Schools**[21] the Sixth Circuit Court of Appeals specifically found that a student could be served outside of the neighborhood school if another school in the district, rather than the neighborhood school, offered the program the student needed. Similarly, in **Beth B. v. Clay**[22] the student had a cognitive ability ranging from a 1-year-old to a 6-year-old. In addition, she could not walk unassisted and communicated primarily by eye gaze. Beth began school in 1994 in a regular classroom and remained there until 1997. In 1997 the school district—over her parents' objections—developed an IEP that placed Beth in a self-contained program. The Seventh Circuit deferred to the knowledge of the school, saying, "the school officials' decision about how to best educate Beth is based on expertise that we cannot match."

The courts have considered several factors in addressing the issue of LRE. In **Sacramento City Unified School Dist. v. Holland**[23] the Ninth Circuit adopted, and a number of other courts have cited, the following factors in determining the least restrictive environment:

- the educational benefits available in a regular classroom supplemented with appropriate aids and services as compared with the educational benefits available to the child if placed in a special education classroom;
- the nonacademic benefits of interaction with children who do not have disabilities;
- the effect of the child's presence on the teacher and other children in the classroom; and
- the cost of mainstreaming the child into the regular classroom.

The least restrictive environment principle calls for a careful consideration of all possible placement alternatives for each child before making a final placement. Schools must ensure that a continuum of alternative placements such as those detailed in Figure 8.3 is made available if necessary. The process of determining placement in the LRE involves three steps:

1. development of the appropriate goals and objectives/benchmarks as outlined within the IEP and determination of necessary related services;
2. identification of alternative programs and settings in which the IEP can be implemented; and
3. determination of the program option that maximizes interaction with peers without disabilities in a regular education setting.

Figure 8.3 Continuum of Educational Placements for Students With Disabilities

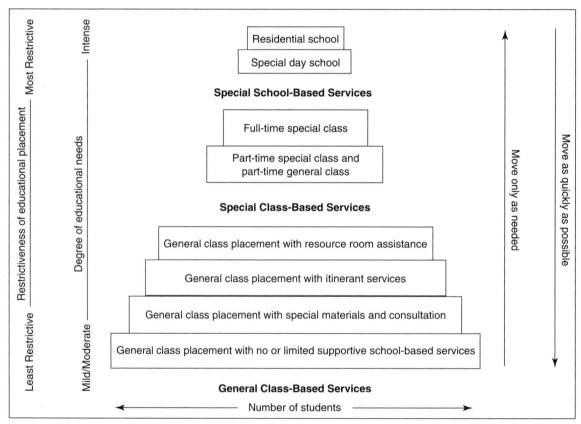

Source: Mercer, Cecil D.; Pullen, Paige C., *Students with Learning Disabilities,* 6th Edition, © 2005. Reprinted by permission of Pearson Education, Inc., Upper Saddle River, NJ.

In the end, it may be necessary to place the child in a segregated setting in order to provide the most appropriate education or to prevent the disruption of the educational process for other students. Students may also be placed in private schools at public expense if the district is not able to provide an appropriate placement.

Procedural Due Process

The extensive procedural requirements of the IDEA are designed to ensure children with disabilities receive a free and appropriate education and to protect them from improper evaluation, classification, and placement. Under the IDEA, parents have many procedural safeguards, including these rights:

- to be notified in writing or in a format understandable by them of a referral;
- to grant or deny permission to evaluate;
- to be notified of and be present at IEP meetings regarding their child;
- to participate in decision making, including specific program and/or placement decisions;
- to bring an advocate to any meeting;
- to examine all records pertaining to their children; and
- to be notified of parental rights and procedural safeguards under the IDEA.

When the parents and school disagree on a decision, each has the right to request a due process hearing. The request can be filed at almost any point in the process. For example, the parents may disagree with the eligibility determination, the evaluation, or the IEP. Likewise, the district has the right to request a due process hearing if the parents deny permission for the district to evaluate the child. (Whenever a due process hearing is conducted, the IDEA also requires that voluntary mediation be made available to the parties.) Impartial hearing officers, whose qualifications are determined by state statues and regulations, conduct due process hearings.

If disagreement continues after the due process hearing, appeal may be made to the courts. Parents must go through the due process hearing step before they file in court; this is referred to as "exhausting administrative remedies." This may not be true though when the question involves a claim of systemic violations of IDEA as in the case of **J.S. v. Attica Central Schools**,[24] which was brought by a group of parents claiming that the district's procedures violated IDEA.

The appeal to the due process decision is usually filed in federal district court, although it can be filed in state trial court because states have state legislation similar to the IDEA. While any proceedings are occurring, the child must "stay put." In other words, the child remains in the current—or last agreed-upon placement—pending the outcome of the proceedings. This does not require that the student stay in the precise physical placement, but that the agreed-upon program be provided.

SECTION 504 OF THE REHABILITATION ACT

Section 504 of the Rehabilitation Act is a civil rights law that prohibits educational institutions that receive federal financial assistance from discriminating in the delivery of programs and activities, employment, and access to facilities. Section 504 is broader than the IDEA and is intended to prevent discrimination against, rather than just provide services to, students with disabilities. Although the emphasis in the IDEA analysis is on the individualized need of the student, in Section 504 the thrust is comparing the services and treatment provided students with disabilities to those provided to students without disabilities. Section 504 seeks to remove physical and programmatic barriers to participation in schools. Under Section 504 schools must make reasonable accommodations for student disabilities.

Section 504 applies to any student with a physical or mental impairment that substantially limits any major life activity, or who is regarded as having, or has a history of, such impairment. Included could be students with communicable diseases, diabetes, attention deficit hyperactivity disorder (if the student is not in need of special education and related services under IDEA), or students with life-long health conditions such as epilepsy, diabetes, asthma, arthritis, or allergies.

Students who qualify for services under IDEA are also afforded the protections under Section 504. In addition, Section 504 may protect some children who do not qualify for special education under IDEA because they are over 21 (Section 504 covers the entire life span) or do not have a condition serious enough to qualify for IDEA services. For example, a student with a physical disability who is not entitled to special education under IDEA may be entitled under Section 504 to accommodations that would permit him or her to participate in field trips, physical education, or extracurricular activities on a nondiscriminatory basis.[25] The U.S. Supreme Court has said that an otherwise qualified individual who merits protection under Section 504 is one who, with *reasonable* accommodation or modification can meet all the program's requirements despite his or her disability (i.e., unreasonable or discriminatory accommodation is not required).[26]

> "No otherwise individual with a disability in the United States . . . shall solely by reason of his or her disability, be excluded from participation in, be denied the benefits of, or be subjected to discrimination under any person or activity receiving Federal financial assistance."
>
> 20 U.S.C. §794

Like the IDEA, Section 504 requires that schools provide a free and appropriate education and that the child learn in a setting that constitutes the least restrictive environment. Both also require notifying the parents of the evaluation and placement of the child. Although Section 504 does not require the development of an IEP, it does require the development of a Section 504 Accommodation Plan such as that presented in Figure 8.4. Many districts follow many of the same procedures in developing the accommodation plan as they do in developing the IEP.

Figure 8.4 Section 504 Student Accommodation Plan

MESA PUBLIC SCHOOLS

SECTION 504 STUDENT ACCOMMODATION PLAN

Student Name: _____   School: _____

Student #: _____   Date of Birth: _____   Age: _____   Grade: _____   Year: _____

Date 504 Plan Initiated: _____   Date 504 Plan will be reviewed: _____

Area(s) of Need	Accommodation(s)	Person Responsible

Describe location of services, if other than the classroom setting and the reason(s) necessary, or any other relevant information:

Participation of Eligible 504 Student in AIMS/Stanford 9 Standardized Testing:
AIMS for 3rd, 5th, 8th and 9th-12th Graders:

_____ The student should take AIMS under routine conditions, without any accommodations.

_____ The student should NOT take AIMS under routine conditions and is eligible for the following Standard Accommodations (as outlined by the Arizona Department of Education and reprinted on the Addendum) that are consistent with the instructional accommodations used in the student's educational program.

If the second line is checked, please identify which standard accommodations on the MPS Addendum to Section 504 Student Accommodation Plan the team has selected and attach.

Stanford 9 Testing:

_____ The student should take the Stanford 9 under routine conditions, without any accommodations.

_____ The student should NOT take the Stanford 9 under routine conditions and is eligible for the following Stanford 9 Standard Accommodations (as outlined by the Arizona Department of Education and reprinted on the Addendum) that are consistent with the instructional accommodations used in the student's educational program.

If the second line is checked, please identify which standard accommodations on the MPS Addendum to Section 504 Student Accommodation Plan the team has selected and attach.

My signature indicates that I have been informed and received notice of this Accommodation Plan and further acknowledge I am familiar with my responsibilities pursuant to Section 504 of the Rehabilitation Act of 1973.

Participant Signature	Position/Title	Date

Source: Mesa Public Schools, Mesa, Arizona.

The team that prepares the Section 504 Accommodation Plan is familiar with the student, the assessment data, and the placement and accommodations options. As with the IDEA, parents have a right to participate in any identification and placement decisions as well as to a hearing by an impartial party if they disagree with the identification, education, or placement of their child. Figure 8.5 provides a comparison of the eligibility, evaluation, free appropriate public education, and procedural due process requirements of the IDEA and Section 504.

Figure 8.5 A Comparison of the Individuals With Disabilities Education Act (IDEA) and Section 504

IDEA	SECTION 504
Type/Purpose/Funding/Enforcement	
• A federal law guaranteeing and guiding the delivery of special education services to eligible children with disabilities. • Monitored and enforced by the Office of Special Education Programs of the U.S. Department of Education. • Provides some federal monies to states and school districts.	• A civil rights law forbidding discrimination against individuals with disabilities who are otherwise qualified by programs that receive federal funds. • Monitored and enforced by the Office of Civil Rights of the U.S. Department of Education. • Provides no additional federal monies to states and local school districts, and does not allow IDEA funds to be used to provide service to individuals covered only by 504.
Eligibility	
• Covers individuals up to age 21. • Defines *disability* categorically as having one or more of the 13 disability classifications that have an adverse effect on educational performance.	• Covers individuals throughout their lives. • Defines *disability* functionally as having a physiological or mental impairment that substantially limits one or more major life activities.
Evaluation	
• A multifactored and nondiscriminatory evaluation in all areas related to suspected disability must be conducted to determine eligibility. • Eligibility decision is made by a multidisciplinary team of professionals, family members, and the child when appropriate.	• A multiple source and nondiscriminatory evaluation in the area(s) of suspected need(s) must be conducted to determine eligibility. • Eligibility decision is made by a group of individuals who are knowledgeable with respect to the child, the assessment procedures, and the placement options.

Figure 8.5 Continued

Free Appropriate Public Education	
• Defines appropriate education in terms of its educational benefits. • An individualized education program (IEP) is required. • Related aids and services are required to be delivered to help students benefit from special education. • Requires that students be educated in the least restrictive environment.	• Defines an appropriate education in terms of its comparability to the education offered to students without disabilities. • An individualized accommodation plan (often called a 504 accommodation plan) is required. • Related aids and services are delivered if they are needed to help students access appropriate educational programs. • Requires that students be educated in the least restrictive environment including having equal access to nonacademic and extracurricular activities.
Due Process Procedure	
• Informed and written consent from parents/guardian is required. • Establishes specific due process procedures for notification and impartial hearings. • Families who disagree with the identification, education or placement of their child have a right to an impartial hearing. • Families have the right to participate in the hearing and to be represented by counsel.	• Notice must be given, but consent is not required. • Leaves due process procedures up to the discretion of school districts. • Families who disagree with the identification, education or placement of their child have a right to an impartial hearing. • Families have the right to participate in the hearing and to be represented by counsel.

Source: Salend, Spencer J., *Creating Inclusive Classrooms: Effective and Reflective Practices for All Students,* 5th Edition, © 2005. Reprinted by permission of Pearson Education, Inc., Upper Saddle River, NJ.

AMERICANS WITH DISABILITIES ACT

The Americans With Disabilities Act (ADA) of 1990 prohibits discrimination against persons with disabilities in services, programs, and activities provided by state and local governments or any of their agencies. This prohibition applies to educational services provided students and, unlike the IDEA, applies to all school districts whether or not they receive any federal funds. Under the ADA school districts must make all facilities accessible to students, employees, and patrons. Moreover, school districts must make programs available and accessible to all individuals with disabilities who are "otherwise qualified" to participate in the program. The ADA prohibits school districts from denying a student with a disability the opportunity to participate in a program or from providing different or separate programs or services for students with disabilities unless to do so is necessary to provide a benefit or service as effectively as those provided students without disabilities. The ADA also prohibits providing inequitable opportunities to participate in or benefit from programs or services as well as adopting program eligibility criteria or methods of program administration that are discriminatory. (See the In the News feature.)

As with Section 504, the requirements under the ADA are not absolute. That is, access or participation of a student with a disability is not required if participation would pose a significant risk to health or safety of the individual(s) or others or would require a modification that would fundamentally alter the program, services, or activities being offered or result in undue financial or administrative burden. In addition, the ADA does not require the school district to provide personal devices (e.g., eyeglasses or hearing aids) or personal services (e.g., assistance in eating) in order to facilitate participation.

IN THE NEWS . . .

Special-education students who pass their high school classes should still be able to graduate even if they do not pass the AIMS test, Arizona Attorney General Terry Goddard said in a legal opinion Wednesday. State Superintendent of Public Instruction Tom Horne said he will abide by the opinion, meaning that special-education students, who make up an estimated 10 percent of Arizona's school population, will be able to graduate with regular diplomas. Horne asked Goddard several months ago whether it was legal for special-education students who had met their Individual Education Plan goals but had not passed AIMS to receive a diploma.

About 6,000 special-education juniors took the test last spring as sophomores. Only 6 percent, or about 360, who were tested passed math; 17 percent met reading requirements; and 20 percent passed writing. A passing score on all three portions of the test, also known as Arizona's Instrument to Measure Standards, is required for all high school students starting with the Class of 2006.

Many special-education students have learning disabilities, often not obvious, that make it difficult to process information in traditional ways. Their learning levels are above 3rd grade but below 10th grade. Although many of the learning-disabled students receive accommodations, such as being allowed to take the test in a room by themselves or use calculators on the math portion, parents argued that their children aren't being taught the material on the test.

Goddard's opinion means local districts can develop graduation requirements for students enrolled in special-education programs. The requirements would take into consideration a student's Individual Education Program, which is different for each student, and would be consistent with the federal Individuals With Disabilities Education Act.

Source: From "Special Education Gets AIMS Break," by O. Madrid, February 10, 2005, *Arizona Republic.* http://www.arizonacentral.com/12news/news/articles

GUIDING LEGAL PRINCIPLES

- The IDEA mandates that school districts make a free and appropriate public education available to all children with disabilities between the ages of 3 and 21.
- In order to receive services (i.e., special education programs and related services), a student must have a qualifying disability and the condition must have an impact on education to an extent that requires special education.
- An Individualized Education Program (or plan) (IEP) is a written document that provides the plan for implementation of the special education program and related services.
- The IEP meeting, at which the plan is developed, must include parents, teachers, special education specialists, a school representative, and the student, when appropriate.
- To be appropriate the IEP must be reasonably calculated to confer educational benefits for the student.
- The IDEA requires that the student receive the special education services in the least restrictive environment, based on his or her individual specialized needs.
- Parents have a number of procedural rights under the IDEA including the right to notice, consent, and ability to challenge decisions through an administrative hearing process.
- Section 504 prohibits discrimination against individuals with disabilities. It is broader than IDEA and is intended to prevent discrimination rather than require the delivery of services.
- The Americans With Disabilities Act prohibits discrimination against individuals with disabilities in services, programs, and activities.

YOU BE THE JUDGE

*Go to the Companion Website at **http:www.prenhall.com/underwood**, select Chapter 8, choose the You Be the Judge module and click on the name of the case for more information about the case and the court's decison and rationale.*

Words Can hurt

M. L. attended kindergarten at Mark Twain Elementary School. He had autism and was receiving special education services under IDEA. His mother alleged that M. L. was subjected to constant vicious teasing by the other children from the first day of school, with other children mimicking his attempts to speak and making fun of him. She said that she called the teacher's attention to the problem, but nothing was done. After 1 week in this placement she withdrew M. L. from the placement and initiated due process alleging that the district's failure to stop the teasing prevented M. L. from receiving an appropriate education under the IDEA.

Questions for Discussion and Reflection

1. What were the teacher's responsibilities to M. L. in this placement?
2. Can teasing be serious enough to make a placement inappropriate?
3. Should other students' actions be taken into consideration when determining what placement might be the least restrictive environment?

Visit the Companion Website for a more detailed description of the facts in the case **M. L. v. Federal Way School District.**

* * *

Declining Performance

Throughout elementary school, S. Costell received special education services. However, when she entered middle school the school determined she no longer needed these services. School staff informally monitored her performance during her first semester of the seventh grade. Several weeks into the semester her parents became aware that she was no longer receiving special education services. S. Costell's grades were average during the first quarter, but started to slide downward starting the second quarter. By the end of the semester she was failing band and was diagnosed as having depression with suicidal ideations. Her parents pulled her out of school and began homeschooling her. Her parents challenged the district's actions in ending special education services.

Questions for Discussion and Reflection

1. What procedural steps did the school district fail to follow in the placement of the student?
2. What should the parents have done before taking the student out of school?
3. What process should be used to determine whether the student is still receiving an appropriate education?

Visit the Companion Website for a more detailed description of the facts in the case **Costello v. Mitchell Public School District 79.**

* * *

How Much Is Enough

J. Popson suffers from autism and speech apraxia. Autism is a generic term for a range of neurological disorders that affect individual children differently. One treatment program that has shown promise for treating autistic children is the Applied Behavior Analysis (ABA) method advanced by Dr. O. Ivar Lovaas. Popson's parents believe that the ABA/Discret Trial Training (DTT) program is far superior to other programs in teaching autistic children like J. Popson. The school disagrees, preferring to use a variety of techniques that, it argues, have proven to be successful in treating autistic children. While the school's program includes some ABA/DTT training, it also includes other features such as a structured classroom, which, the school argues, provides a more meaningful context for the development of functional communication, a greater opportunity for the development of social skills, and an easier transition to a regular classroom. The school and the Popsons disagree about J.'s placement and services and have taken their challenge to court. They argue that the program has been designed primarily to keep costs to a minimum, has not given J. Popson anything more than trivial educational benefits, and is inappropriate.

Questions for Discussion and Reflection

1. What is the process under the IDEA for determining an appropriate program for J. Popson?
2. When do you think there could be only one type of instructional approach for a student? Does requiring only one approach run counter to the notion of individualized programs under IDEA?
3. What is the process for parental appeal under the IDEA?

Visit the Companion Website for a more detailed description of the facts in the case **J.P. ex rel. Popson v. West Clark Community.**

MORE ON THE WEB

Go to the Companion Website at **http://www.prenhall.com/underwood**, *select Chapter 8, choose the* More on the Web *module to connect to the site mentioned.*

Go to the Department of Education, Office of Special Education and Rehabilitative Services website at http://www.ed.gov.about/offices/list/osers/osep/index.html. Where is the parent training and information center(s) in your state located? Visit that center's website and list the major programs and services it provides.

ENDNOTES

1. U.S. Department of Education, Office of Special Education and Rehabilitative Service. (2004). *National Center for Education Statistics, Statistics of Public Elementary and Secondary School Systems.* Retrieved August 17, 2004, from http://nces.ed.gov/programs/digest/d03/tables/pdf/table52.pdf
2. 343 F. Supp. 179 (E.D. Pa. 1972).
3. 348 F. Supp. 866 (D.D.C. 1972).
4. Education for All Handicapped Children Act of 1975, Pub. L. No. 94-142, 89 Stat. 773 (1975).

5. 29 U.S.C. § 794 (2005).

6. 42 U.S.C. §§ 12101–12213 (2005).

7. 20 U.S.C. §1401 (2005).

8. 458 U.S. 175 (1982).

9. 361 F.3d 80 (1st Cir. 2004).

10. Ibid. at 4.

11. 237 F.3d 813 (7th Cir. 2001).

12. 45 C.F.R. 1308.6 (2005).

13. Ibid.

14. Salend, S. J. (2005). *Creating inclusive classrooms: Effective and reflective practices for all students* (5th ed., pp. 51–54). Upper Saddle River, NJ: Merrill/Prentice Hall.

15. 317 F.3d 1072 (9th Cir. 2003).

16. 20 U.S.C. §1401(22) (2005).

17. 468 U.S. 883 (1984).

18. 2003 WL 260728 (D. N.H. 2003).

19. 526 U.S. 66 (1999).

20. 20 U.S.C. §1412a(5)(A) (1997).

21. 320 F.3d 663 (6th Cir. 2003).

22. 282 F.3d 493 (7th Cir.), *cert. denied,* 537 U.S. 948 (2002).

23. 14 F.3d 1398 (9th Cir. 1994).

24. 386 F.3d 107 (2d Cir. 2004), *cert. denied,* 125 S. Ct. 1727 (2005).

25. *Lyons v. Smith,* 829 F. Supp. 414 (D.D.C. 1993).

26. *Southeastern Community College v. Davis,* 442 U.S. 397 (1979).

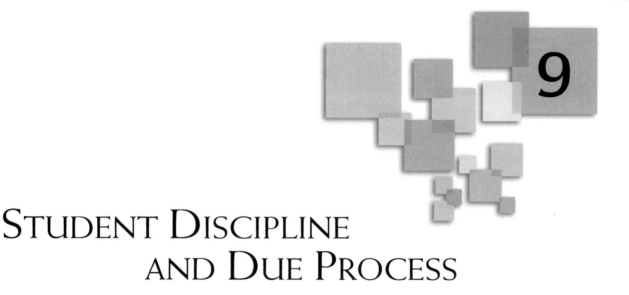

STUDENT DISCIPLINE AND DUE PROCESS

The traditional doctrine of *in loco parentis* (in the place of the parent) is usually cited as the basis for the school's authority over students. The courts have affirmed that school officials have not only the authority but also the duty to establish reasonable rules of student conduct designed to protect students and employees, as well as the rules necessary to establish and maintain a climate conducive to learning. However, the authority and the duty of the school to regulate student behavior must be exercised within the context of students' constitutional and statutory rights. This chapter discusses the constitutional rights of students in disciplinary actions, along with the position of the courts in regard to the application of various forms of discipline. The chapter concludes with an overview of the procedures required in the disciplining of special education students. After reading this chapter you will be able to

- Distinguish between substantive and procedural due process.
- List the major forms of permissible and impermissible discipline in the schools.
- Compare the due process required for suspensions and expulsions.
- Outline the standards under which corporal punishment will be upheld.
- Describe the conditions under which students can be disciplined for off-campus conduct.
- Outline the steps in the special education discipline process.

DUE PROCESS IN STUDENT DISCIPLINE

The authority and responsibility to establish rules of conduct carries with it the authority to discipline students for violations of these rules. The severity of the violation will determine the nature of the discipline and the due process required. Due process is afforded under the Fourteenth Amendment to the U.S. Constitution, which requires due process before the state can deny a person of life, liberty, or property. Although education is not a right protected by the federal Constitution, a student does have a property interest in education by virtue of the right to an education provided under a state constitution or state law. In addition, some student sanctions may implicate a liberty interest. (Review the discussion of property and liberty interests in chapter 4.) Because a property or liberty interest may be involved, the due process clause is often applied in student disciplinary situations.

As explained in chapter 4, the concept of constitutional due process contains two components: *substantive due process* and *procedural due process*. Substantive due process deals with ensuring that government actions are reasonably related to a legitimate state purpose and are not arbitrary or capricious. The state's interest in disciplinary situations is to maintain order in the school and to protect students. Thus, to pass the substantive due process test, a school must show its rules are reasonably related to these purposes. However, when the school's actions are related to a legitimate state interest, substantive due process can be violated if the school's actions are unreasonable or unreasonably severe. The bottom line on substantive due process is fundamental fairness.

Procedural due process is designed to ensure the process by which students are disciplined is fair and equitable. In the lead case in student due process, **Goss v. Lopez**[1] (see the boxed case summary), the Supreme Court applied the concepts of procedural due process to disciplinary measures. The Court concluded that due process applies to school discipline because education is a property right under state law. The Court held that due process requires that students be given (1) oral or written notice of the charges, (2) an explanation of the evidence the authorities have, and (3) an opportunity to present their side of the story. In essence the *Goss* decision means that before taking away a student's liberty or property interest, a school must use fair procedures.

> "No State shall . . . deprive any person of life, liberty, or property, without due process of law."
>
> U.S. Const. Amend. XIV, Section 1

GOSS v. LOPEZ

Nine students were suspended for misconduct. The state statute provided that parents must be notified within 24 hours and that the principal state the reason for his action. The students filed suit, alleging violation of their due process rights. The Supreme Court found that the students' due process rights had been violated because they were not given a hearing prior to or within a reasonable time after being suspended.

Go to the Companion Website at *http://www. prenhall.com/underwood*, select Chapter 9, choose Cases *module, and click on* **Gross v. Lopez** *to read the entire opinion of the court.*

Go to the Companion Website at *http://www. prenhall.com/underwood*, select Chapter 9, then choose the Resources module to find the state-specific student disciplinary statutes.

The extent of the due process required depends on the nature of the interest being taken away; that is, the greater the potential deprivation, the more procedural protections that must be provided. Typically, if the maximum penalty that could be imposed is relatively small (e.g., a 1-day detention), only a minimal amount of procedural due process is required. Even within this constitutional framework, the laws governing student discipline vary significantly from state to state.

TYPES OF DISCIPLINE

The forms of discipline imposed vary from school district to school district and depend upon the nature of the infraction, the disciplinary record of the student, and other circumstances. Potential discipline measures span the continuum from a simple verbal reprimand to permanent expulsion from the district. The ones most often the subject of legal challenges follow.

Grade Reduction and Academic Sanctions

Academic decisions (e.g., promotion or entry to programs) are most often considered nondisciplinary questions of educational policy. Courts generally defer to schools on matters of educational policy, unless the policy is arbitrary, malicious, or capricious. Students and parents who contend that a grade was given unfairly, or that the student simply deserved a better grade, have often asked the courts to review the situations. The courts, however, have routinely denied these requests. To have a grade changed, it must be shown that the teacher acted in a manner deemed arbitrary, capricious, or malicious, or that there is a basis for the grade change established by statute. For example, in **Las Virgenes Educators Ass'n v. Las Virgenes Unified Sch. Dist.,**[2] a California appellate court held that even the marks given for citizenship were grades and could not be changed absent incompetence, fraud, mistake, or bad faith.

The courts have generally ruled that the schools should not lower a student's grade as a form of discipline. Grades should be based upon a standard of acceptable classroom performance. For example, in **Smith v. School Dist. of Hobart,**[3] the federal court held that a high school's rule that grades would be reduced 4% for each day of a suspension for alcohol-related misconduct violated substantive due process. The court did not believe that the school district could articulate a reasonable relationship between the use of alcohol and a reduction of grades. On the other hand the courts have upheld the inclusion of class attendance as a portion of a teacher's regular evaluation for students' grades. Courts have upheld grade reductions imposed for absenteeism or truancy on the theory that grades can reflect a student's effort, including class attendance and performance.[4]

Withholding Diplomas

The position of the courts with regard to withholding diplomas as a form of student discipline is similar to that regarding grades: standards for grading–academic recognition, including the awarding of diplomas, should reflect academic accomplishment. If a student has earned a diploma, the diploma may not be withheld, even if the student has engaged in misconduct that would justify discipline. Conversely, when a student has not fulfilled all the requirements for a diploma, the district is under no obligation to issue one. It is important to note that this means the student has "graduated," not that the student is eligible to participate in the graduation ceremony. Actual participation in the graduation ceremony can be withheld for disciplinary purposes.[5]

Suspension or Expulsion From Extracurricular Activities

Suspension or expulsion from extracurricular activities is a common student disciplinary sanction. Students have challenged their removal from extracurricular activities either for failure to meet eligibility requirements or as a penalty for inappropriate behavior. Courts have found that due process protections do not apply to suspension or expulsion from extracurricular activities, because students have no property interest or right in participation in extracurricular activities. As such, the courts typically uphold school district actions in suspending or expelling students from extracurricular activities.

In some states the state athletic association rules may dictate the procedures that a school must follow before imposing an athletic suspension or expulsion. In these situations the athletic association imposes the rules and sanctions. These rules are similarly upheld.

Corporal Punishment

Corporal punishment is defined as the use of physical force as a form of discipline. As noted in chapter 1, the U.S. Supreme Court in **Ingraham v. Wright**[6] found that reasonable corporal punishment was not unconstitutional as "cruel and unusual punishment" under the Eighth Amendment. However, over half the states have banned corporal punishment by state statute (see Figure 9.1 to see where your state falls). In a number of others, local school board policy prohibits corporal punishment. Where not prohibited by statute or policy, the common law notion that reasonable corporal punishment in schools is permissible still prevails.

As opposed to permissible and reasonable corporal punishment, many courts have found it to be a violation of a student's substantive due process rights if the student is subjected to unreasonable or severe corporal punishment. As in police brutality cases, the substantive due process inquiry in school corporal punishment cases varies considerably by jurisdiction. Generally the courts look to see whether the punishment was so out of line that it has shocked one's conscience.

Go to the Companion Website at *http://www. prenhall.com/underwood*, select Chapter 9, then choose the Resources module to find state-specific corporal punishment provision.

Figure 9.1 The State of Corporal Punishment

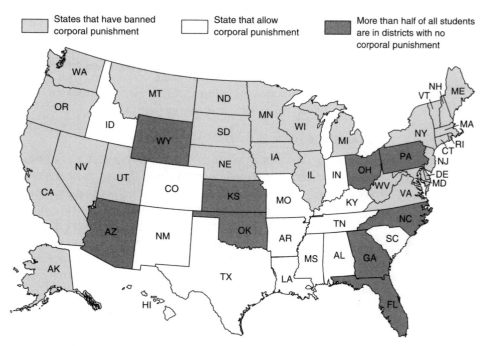

States that have banned corporal punishment	State that allow corporal punishment	More than half of all students are in districts with no corporal punishment

For example, in **Doe v. State of Hawaii Dep't. of Educ.,**[7] the Circuit Court of Appeals found a district violated a student's rights when an elementary school principal taped a student's head to a tree. Among the other things that the courts consider in determining reasonableness are those listed below.

REQUIREMENTS OF CORPORAL PUNISHMENT

To be upheld, corporal punishment must

- be allowed by state law;
- be permitted or at least not prohibited by district policy;
- be implemented consistent with state and district requirements;
- be used as a method of correction;
- be suitable for the age, sex, and physical and mental condition of the child;
- be appropriate for the offense;
- be consistent with the terms of any applicable IEP;
- not be motivated by anger or malice; and
- not be cruel or excessive.

If a school employee administers corporal punishment where it has been banned or engages in unreasonable corporal punishment, the employee may be subject to criminal action for battery or to a civil action for any injuries the student sustains. Further, the employee administering the corporal punishment may also be subjected to disciplinary action from the school board. For example, in **Rush v. Bd. of Educ. of Crete-Monee Comm. Sch. Unit Dist. No. 201-U,**[8] a shop teacher was dismissed for administering electric shocks as a disciplinary measure. (See also the In the News feature on page 172.)

Suspensions

Suspension, whether in school or out of school, is a common form of school discipline. The U.S. Supreme Court has held that exclusion from educational services may require some form of due process. The precise parameters, or what process is due, depends upon the length and nature of the exclusion.

*Go to the Companion Website at **http://www. prenhall.com/underwood**, select Chapter 9, then choose the Resources module to find state-specific suspension statutes.*

In **Goss v. Lopez**[9] the Supreme Court decided that for an out-of-school suspension of fewer than 10 days, sufficient due process is afforded if the hearing is conducted spontaneously and informally as long as the student is given (1) oral or written notice of the charges; (2) an opportunity to explain, deny, or admit the charges or evidence; and (3) a decision based on the merits of the situation. However, the Court did recognize that there might be situations that would require more detailed procedures, such as those in which the facts are disputed and are not easily resolved, as well as emergency situations in which the safety of persons or property is threatened, where no due process is required prior to disciplinary action. Even in the latter situations due process must be followed as soon as possible after the danger of harm has passed. In addition to the minimal constitutional standards required by *Goss*, most states have statutes that address school suspension and may require additional procedures.

IN THE NEWS . . .

The Indianapolis Public School Board (IN) voted to eliminate corporal punishment as a form of discipline in its schools. Although most schools in the district already had abandoned its use, the issue resurfaced when two teachers were suspended for 5 weeks for paddling students. Both teachers were cleared of wrongdoing and have been reinstated. While the superintendent applauds the board's action, some in the community oppose the decision as depriving teachers and school administrators of a legitimate disciplinary tool. The president of the Indianapolis Education Association believes the practice is fading. While acknowledging that there is no research supporting her assertion, she argues that the threat of lawsuits against educators and the lack of familiarity on the part of younger teachers with how and when to use corporal punishment are important factors discouraging its use.

Source: From "School Board Eliminates Corporal Punishment as a Form of Discipline," by Theodore Kim, June 2004, *Indianapolis Star.* http://www.indystar.com/articles/06/04

Alternative Educational Assignments or Disciplinary Transfers

Recognizing that removing students entirely from the school environment may provide them with reinforcement rather than negative consequences for inappropriate behavior, many schools have turned to the practice of in-school suspensions, alternative assignments, or disciplinary transfers. The question then becomes whether the due process guarantees apply to this disciplinary sanction and, if so, what due process must a student be provided before an in-school suspension can be imposed. The Supreme Court has not addressed this question, but most courts that have held that an in-school suspension, alternative assignment, or transfer warrants some minimal due process because a student's liberty interests may be implicated.

Expulsions

In contrast to the minimal due process required for a suspension, an expulsion—long-term removal from school (greater than 10 days)—requires greater procedural due process because the property interest being taken away from the student is greater. Although a teacher or administrator may initiate an expulsion proceeding, normally only the school board can expel the student. Because of the severity of expulsion, state statutes and school board regulations usually detail the grounds for expulsion, as well as the procedures that must be followed. Grounds for expulsion typically include theft or vandalism of school property, possession of weapons (may be mandated by "zero tolerance" policies), possession or use of alcohol or drugs, causing or attempting to cause injury to another, and engaging in any behavior forbidden by law. In addition, the Gun Free Schools Act of 1994[10] requires as a condition of the receipt of federal funds that schools expel any student who brings a weapon to school.

Go to the Companion Website at **http://www. prenhall.com/underwood**, select Chapter 9, then choose the Resources module to find the state-specific school expulsion statutes.

Procedures for Expulsion. As previously stated, state statutes commonly specify expulsion procedures. In many states students are entitled to full evidentiary hearings before the school board with representation, presentation of witnesses, and subpoena power. In others the statute provides for a more informal hearing. Whatever the state requirements, to meet constitutional due process requirements students facing expulsion must be provided

- written notice of the charges, with sufficient specificity so the student can mount a defense;
- sufficient time between the notice and the hearing to allow the student to prepare a defense;
- a hearing by an impartial party or body;
- the right to present evidence and cross-examine witnesses at the hearing; and

- a written statement of the findings/recommendations of the hearing body that demonstrates the decision was based on the evidence presented.

In addition to statutory or state department of education guidelines, the courts have provided some useful guidance on various procedural issues related to student expulsion. Among those issues that have most often been brought into question are the following:

Adequate warning. School disciplinary rules must provide students with adequate warning of prohibited conduct, but need not be as detailed as a criminal code.

Cross-examination of witnesses. In the absence of state statute, whether a student has the right to cross-examine witnesses depends on several factors (e.g., the existence of an essential disputed fact, the identity of the witness, the burden to the process, and the burden to the witness). In some situations, student witnesses can remain anonymous to the student charged if there is a substantial likelihood of reprisal or harm to the student witnesses.

Rules of evidence. Because an expulsion hearing is an administrative proceeding, formal rules of evidence do not apply. Generally, any relevant evidence can be admitted.

Self-incrimination. Because the Fifth Amendment right against self-incrimination applies *only* to criminal proceedings, a student's refusal to testify may be used against him or her in the disciplinary hearing.

Right to counsel. Courts have generally applied a rule of fundamental fairness, that students have the right to use counsel to the same extent that the school district uses counsel, especially when the proceedings may be complex and the potential penalty severe.

Right to review. The constitutional notions of due process do not require an internal appeal. In expulsion situations, most states provide a right of appeal to the state department of education, an intermediate-level educational agency such as the county board of education, and/or the courts.

Historically schools have not continued to provide regular education students educational services once they have been expelled. Expelled students can be barred from all educational and extracurricular activities. Expelled students continue to be subject to compulsory school attendance laws; thus parents typically have to enroll their children in a private school or otherwise meet the requirements of the compulsory attendance during the term of the expulsion. However, some states require districts to provide some educational services for expelled students.

DISCIPLINE FOR OFF-CAMPUS CONDUCT

Disciplining students for off-campus behavior has been recognized by some courts as reasonable when the student's action has a direct and immediate effect on school discipline or the safety and welfare of students and staff. School policy must inform students that they are subject to discipline for such actions even though away from school grounds. While on a school bus, on a field trip, athletic trip, band trip, or other off-site activity, there must be some connection between the student's behavior and the school. For example, in **Sherrell v. Northern Community School Corp.,**[11] a high school student told two of his friends while off campus that he was going to "get his dad's gun in Indianapolis, bring it to school, start with seventh grade, and work his way up." The school board expelled him, relying on a state statute that allowed schools to suspend or expel a student for engaging in unlawful activity on or off school grounds if (1) the unlawful activity reasonably may be considered an interference with school purposes or an educational function, or (2) the student's removal is necessary to restore order or protect persons on school property. The court upheld the expulsion of the student for his off-campus threat to carry out a mass shooting at school, even though law enforcement officials refused to charge him with a crime.

Typically, cases involving discipline for off-campus conduct involve such conduct as

- improper behavior at school functions or on school buses;
- fighting, physically intimidating, or threatening the safety of other students;
- harassing or threatening speech, including harassment of teachers;
- posting offensive, harassing, or threatening content on personal websites;
- off-campus use or possession of alcohol or drugs;
- possession of weapons; and
- dangerous or criminal behavior.

DISCIPLINE OF STUDENTS WITH DISABILITIES

As discussed in chapter 8 students with disabilities must be provided with special education services and may not be discriminated against on the basis of their disability. These rights substantially affect the manner in which students with disabilities may be disciplined.[12] The flowchart in Figure 9.2 provides an overview of the procedures that must be followed in disciplining a special education student.

Does the Student Have an IEP?

The first question that must be asked is whether the student has an IEP. If the answer is yes, a determination must be made as to whether the IEP includes a behavior intervention plan. If so, the procedures detailed in the IEP must be followed.

Figure 9.2 Special Education Discipline Flowchart

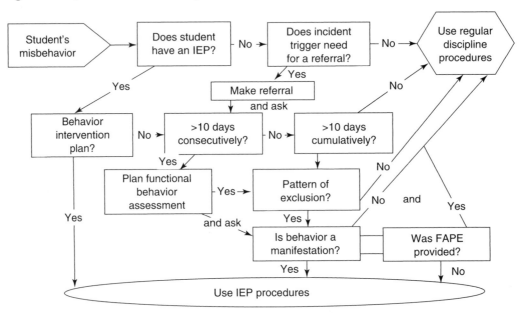

Source: From "The Implications of IDEA's Discipline Section for Administrative and Legal Practice," by Julie F. Mead, 2000. Presentation Materials for the Winter Seminar of the Education Law Association, Lake Tahoe, California, March 16–19. Reprinted with permission.

Does the Incident Trigger Need for a Referral?

Even if a student does not have an IEP, all of the procedural protections of the IDEA are available to a student who has not been found eligible for special education if the school knew or should have known that the student was eligible for services under IDEA. A school may have "knowledge" of a disability if

- The parent has expressed concern or requested an evaluation;
- The behavior or the performance of the child clearly demonstrates the need for services; or
- The teacher has expressed a concern to the special education staff.

Short-Term versus Long-Term Suspensions

The school district may suspend a child and discontinue all educational services for a period of up to 10 days (to the extent the district would apply such alternative to children without disabilities). Short-term suspensions are not considered "changes in placement" and do not require that a "manifestation" hearing be conducted. However, the suspension of a child with a disability for a cumulative period exceeding 10 days during any school year may be considered a "change in placement" (1) if the series of removals constitutes a pattern, and (2) because of factors such as the length of each suspension, the total amount of time the child is removed, and the proximity of the removals to one another.

Is the Behavior a Manifestation of the Disability?

Any discussion of discipline of a child with a disability should involve a consideration of whether the misbehavior is a manifestation of the child's disability. In other words, is the disability causing the child to act out? If the conduct is a manifestation of the child's disability, the consequences for the behavior should be dealt with through the IEP process rather than the disciplinary process.

According to the 2004 reauthorization of the IDEA, a hearing to determine whether the behavior is a manifestation of the disability must be held within 10 school days of any decision to change a placement for disciplinary reasons. A disciplinary violation is considered a manifestation of the student's disability only if the conduct

- was caused by the child's disability;
- had a direct and substantial relationship to the student's disability; or
- was the direct result of the school's failure to implement the IEP.

If the student's conduct is not a manifestation of his or her disability, the school system may discipline the student in the same manner as a child without a disability.

Interim Alternative Educational Settings

A school system may remove a student to an interim alternative educational setting for not more than 45 school days without regard to whether the behavior is determined to be a manifestation of the student's disability, in cases in which a student

- carries or possesses a weapon to or at school or a school function;
- knowingly possesses or uses illegal drugs, or sells or solicits the sale of a controlled substance while at school, on school premises, or at a school function; or
- has inflicted serious bodily injury upon another person while at school, on school premises, or at a school function.

"Stay Put" Placements

Students who have been identified as having disabilities may not have their placements changed without IDEA procedures. Removing a child for more than 10 days is typically considered a change in placement triggering a need for a new IEP. During the time it takes to do this, the student needs to remain in the previously agreed-upon placement. This is often referred to as the "stay put" provision, which essentially means that if the school district seeks to expel a child with a disability, it may not change the child's educational placement without the consent of the parents. However, as previously stated the IDEA allows schools to remove students with disabilities to an interim placement of up to 45 school days should the behavior involve drugs, weapons, or the infliction of bodily injury. In addition, the school district may request permission from a hearing officer to have the student removed from school if there is substantial evidence that the student is a danger to himself or others.

Parents and the school have the right to a hearing regarding the interim alternative educational setting or a manifestation determination. However, the student must remain in the interim setting pending the decision of the hearing officer or up to 45 days, whichever occurs first, unless the parent and school agree otherwise. In such cases, the school must arrange for an expedited hearing, which must be held within 20 school days of the date of the hearing request.

GUIDING LEGAL PRINCIPLES

- School districts have the right to adopt reasonable rules and regulations to control student conduct. Such rules are necessary to ensure order and safety and to set the parameters of appropriate behavior.
- The cornerstone of due process is the concept of reasonableness. The rule and punishment must be reasonable in terms of content, severity, and procedures.
- Academic sanctions and the withholding of diplomas should only reflect academic performance and should not be used as a form of discipline for nonacademic conduct.
- Students are not entitled to due process protections when suspended or expelled from extracurricular activities.
- Corporal punishment, the use of physical force as a means of discipline, has been banned in over half the states. But where not prohibited by statute or policy, when corporal punishment is inflicted it must be reasonable.
- The amount of procedural due process needed is dependent on the extent of the discipline sought—from minimal as in a short-term suspension to significant as in an expulsion. The greater the punishment sought, the greater the procedures that must be afforded to the student. At a minimum, students must receive notice, an opportunity to be heard, and a decision based on the merits of the situation.
- Students may be disciplined for off-campus conduct that has a direct and immediate effect on school discipline or on the safety and welfare of students and staff.
- Students with disabilities have rights that substantially affect the procedures used in discipline. Schools cannot expel students with IEPs through

the traditional due process procedures; they must go through special education procedures.

YOU BE THE JUDGE

*Go to the Companion Website at **http://www.prenhall.com/underwood**, select Chapter 9, choose the You Be the Judge module and click on the name of the case for more information about the case and the court's decision and rationale.*

Unfairly Spiked?

Wooten was a senior at Pleasant Hope High School (MO). She was expelled from the softball team after being absent from a game without permission. The next Monday she and her mother met with the superintendent, principal, and softball coach about the expulsion. Even after the meeting the principal was unwilling to overturn the expulsion. She filed suit against the district alleging that her due process rights had been violated.

Questions for Discussion and Reflection

1. What due process rights does Wooten have as a member of the softball team?
2. Was the discipline imposed (expulsion from the team) reasonable for the violation? Justify your response.
3. How likely is the court to reinstate Wooten to the softball team? Are there other facts that might affect the court's decision?

Visit the Companion Website for a more detailed description of the facts in the case **Wooten v. Pleasant Hope R-VI.**

* * *

Carrying a Torch

On January 24, 2002, the Olympic torch passed through Juneau on its way to the Winter Olympics in Salt Lake City, Utah. Students at Juneau-Douglas High School (JDHS) were given permission to watch the torch pass in front of the school. As the torch relay and the national TV camera crew passed by, Frederick, a JDHS student, held up a banner with the words "Bong Hits 4 Jesus" on it. His principal told him to take down the sign. He refused. Frederick was suspended as a result of the incident.

Questions for Discussion and Reflection

1. Under what conditions can students be disciplined for off-campus conduct?
2. Would the school's response be different if the incident had occurred on the weekend or after the school day?

3. What procedures should Frederick have been given before being expelled?

Visit the Companion Website for a more detailed description of the facts in the case **Frederick v. Morse.**

* * *

I Want My Mom!

On the Wednesday afternoon before Thanksgiving, several students at Colonial Elementary School reported to their teacher that M. D., a 10-year-old classmate, had brought a gun to school. The student was found and brought to the principal's office. Her desk was searched, but no weapon was found. The student was released to go home on the bus. The next Monday the principal again brought the student in for questioning. The student asked that her parents be called. The student was held for questioning by administrators and by a school police officer. The parents were not called until the questioning ended. The student and her parents sued the school district, asserting that the detention and the failure to call her parents violated her right to due process under the Fourteenth Amendment.

Questions for Discussion and Reflection

1. Was this detention a form of punishment subject to due process procedures?
2. What due process should have been provided the student before she was detained?
3. What arguments would you make on behalf of the student?

Visit the Companion Website for a more detailed description of the facts in the case **Wofford v. Evans.**

MORE ON THE WEB

*Go to the Companion Website at **http://www.prenhall.com/underwood**, select Chapter 9, choose the More on the Web module to connect to the sites mentioned.*

Every state department of education has provided guidance to school districts and teachers in disciplining students. One that is particularly informative comes from the Massachusetts Department of Education, http://www.doe.mass.ed/lawsregs/advisory/discipline/AOSD1.html. It not only discusses Massachusetts state law but also provides guidance on federal law as well as state and federal court decisions that govern discipline in our schools. According to the interpretation of the Massachusetts Department of Education, Goss and other court decisions, what six steps are required for a long-term suspension? Go to http://www.law.cornell.edu/topics/state_statutes2.html#education and compare these requirements for student suspensions with those provided in your state statutes.

ENDNOTES

1. 419 U.S. 565 (1975).

2. 149 Ed. Law Rep. 852 (Cal. Ct. App. 2001).

3. 811 F. Supp. 391 (N.D. Ind. 1993).

4. *Williams v. Bd. of Educ. of Marranna Sch. Dist.*, 626 S.W.2d 361 (Ark. 1982); *Campbell v. Bd. of Educ. of New Milford*, 475 A.2d 289 (Conn. 1984).

5. *Appeal of Clarion-Limestone School District*, 782/A.2d/1069 (Pa. Commonwealth 2001).

6. 430 U.S. 651 (1977).

7. 334 F.3d 906 (9th Cir. 2003).

8. 727 N.E.2d 649 (Ill. App. 2000).

9. 419 U.S. 565 (1975).

10. 20 U.S.C. § 8921 (2002).

11. 801 N.E.2d 693 (Ind. App. 2004).

12. 20 U.S.C. § 1415 (2005).

Discrimination and Harassment in the School Environment

Provisions within the U.S. and state constitutions, federal and state statutes, and local government and school district policies prohibit discrimination. Discrimination occurs when a pubic institution, through its policies or employees, treats an individual differently solely or predominantly because of a certain personal characteristic, including race, gender, religion, age, disability, and heritage. These antidiscrimination rules protect various categories of people—teachers, students, and community members—anyone affected by the school's actions. The major legal principles discussed in this chapter focus on the most important federal constitutional and statutory protections against discrimination. There are *many* more protections both within federal and state law which have not been included. Rather than outlining all protections and possible forms of discrimination, this chapter covers the basic principles that apply to all forms of discrimination. After reading this chapter you will be able to

- Distinguish between the three levels of judicial review used to evaluate claims of discrimination.
- Identify the major federal antidiscrimination statutes.
- Discuss the history of desegregation since **Brown v. Board of Education.**

- Describe the design of an affirmative action plan that will pass judicial muster.
- Compare the requirements for employment discrimination claims brought under disparate treatment and under disparate impact.
- Define what is meant by a "person with a disability" and "reasonable accommodation" under Section 504 and the Americans With Disabilities Act.
- Compare *quid pro quo* sexual harassment and hostile environment sexual harassment.
- List the major factors the courts look at to determine whether hostile environment sexual harassment has occurred.
- Describe the conditions under which a school district may be liable for the sexual harassment of a student by an employee or by another student.
- Give the arguments for and against single-sex instruction.

CONSTITUTIONAL PROTECTIONS AGAINST DISCRIMINATION

The constitutional principle underlying nondiscrimination rules is the Equal Protection Clause of the Fourteenth Amendment. The original intent of the Fourteenth Amendment was to ensure fair and equal treatment of ex-slaves. Basically, the Equal Protection Clause requires the government to treat people who are similarly situated the same. The Equal Protection Clause comes into play when the government classifies individuals for protection,

> "No State shall make or enforce any law which shall . . . deny to any person within its jurisdiction the equal protection of the laws."
> U.S. Const. Amend. XIV, Section 1

LEVELS OF REVIEW

- **Strict scrutiny.** If the government classification is based on race or national origin or materially impacts a fundamental right (voting, criminal appeals, interstate travel), courts apply strict scrutiny. This means the law will be validated only if it is necessary to achieve a compelling governmental interest.
- **Intermediate scrutiny.** Courts apply middle-level scrutiny to classifications based on gender and alienage. This type of review requires that the governmental objective be "important" and that the means chosen be "substantially related" to achieving that objective.
- **Rational basis review.** All other challenged classifications are subjected to a deferential level of review in which a court will determine whether the classification bears a rational relationship to a legitimate governmental purpose.

benefits, or services. The courts have developed a three-tier approach to evaluating government actions under the Equal Protection Clause. (See the box below for an overview of three levels of review.)

STATUTORY PROTECTIONS AGAINST DISCRIMINATION

In addition to constitutional protections, various federal and state statutes prohibit discrimination. Plaintiffs who file an action under one statute, often bring claims under the other statutes too. Here is an overview list of major federal statutes providing protections against discrimination.

Title VI of the Civil Rights Act of 1964, 42 U.S.C. § 2000d, prohibits discrimination on the basis of race, color, or national origin in federally assisted programs and activities.

Title VII of the Civil Rights Act of 1964, 42 U.S.C. § 2000e, prohibits employers, including political subdivisions of a state, with 15 or more employees from discriminating on the basis of race, color, religion, gender, or national origin.

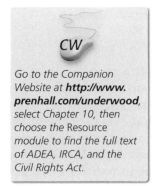

Go to the Companion Website at **http://www. prenhall.com/underwood**, select Chapter 10, then choose the Resource module to find the full text of ADEA, IRCA, and the Civil Rights Act.

Title IX of the Education Amendments of 1972, 20 U.S.C. §§ 1681–86, prohibits discrimination on the basis of sex in any education program or activity receiving federal financial assistance.

The Equal Pay Act of 1963, 29 U.S.C. § 206(D), prohibits gender-based wage discrimination; men and women must be provided equal pay and benefits for the same job or for jobs that require equal skill, effort, and responsibility.

The Pregnancy Discrimination Act (PDA) prohibits employers from discriminating on the basis of pregnancy, childbirth, or related medical conditions. The PDA acts as a floor of protection; although employers may not treat pregnant employees less favorably than other employees, employers may treat them more favorably by granting special leave and other benefits.

The Equal Educational Opportunities Act of 1974, 20 U.S.C. § 1703, prohibits discrimination on the basis of sex, as well as race, color, and national origin, in public elementary and secondary schools, requiring equal educational opportunities.

Section 504 of the Rehabilitation Act of 1973, 29 U.S.C. § 794, prohibits discrimination against any "otherwise qualified" person with a disability in federally assisted programs and activities.

The Americans With Disabilities Act of 1990, 42 U.S.C. § 12101 *et seq.,* prohibits discrimination on the basis of disability in employment, public services, public accommodations, telecommunications, and public transportation services.

The Age Discrimination in Employment Act (ADEA) of 1967, 29 U.S.C. § 621 *et seq.,* prohibits employers from discriminating against individuals on the basis of age in hiring, discharge, compensation, terms, and conditions or privileges of employment. The ADEA applies to most employers with 20 or more employees. Employees must be at least 40 years old to assert a claim under the ADEA.

The Immigration Reform and Control Act (IRCA), 8 U.S.C. § 1324a, not only prohibits employers from knowingly hiring unauthorized aliens but also prohibits discrimination on the basis of national origin or the citizenship status of an "intending citizen." 8 U.S.C. § 1324b. IRCA does not apply to undocumented aliens. Employers may discriminate when citizenship is required to comply with law, regulation, or government contract and when the qualifications of competing job applicants are otherwise equal. 8 U.S.C. § 1324b(2).

Section 1981 of the Civil Rights Act, 42 U.S.C. § 1981, prohibits discrimination on the basis of race or alienage in the making, performance, modification, or termination of a contract or the enjoying of benefits, privileges, terms, and conditions of a contractual relationship.

DISCRIMINATION ON THE BASIS OF RACE OR ETHNICITY

Racial and Ethnic Segregation

As noted in chapter 1, in the landmark case dealing with segregation of the public schools, the U.S. Supreme Court in **Brown v. Board of Education**[1] (see the boxed case summary) explicitly rejected the "separate but equal" doctrine it had upheld a half century earlier in **Plessy v. Ferguson.**[2] At the time of the *Brown* decision, 17 states and the District of Columbia required segregation by law (*de jure*) and in four others (Arizona, Kansas, New Mexico, and Wyoming) segregation was specifically allowed. Relying in part on social science research, the Court declared in *Brown* that "separate educational facilities are inherently unequal" and violate the Equal Protection Clause. The next year the Court provided further guidance on the issue. In **Brown II,**[3] the Court gave primary responsibility to federal district courts to supervise desegregation efforts, which it ordered be undertaken "with all deliberate speed."[4] Years of resistance to the implementation of these desegregation orders and litigation to determine whether desegregation was warranted and if and when desegregation has been achieved followed. Litigation involved not only school districts in the *de jure* states but also numerous districts throughout the nation where housing patterns, the deliberate drawing of school district boundaries, and other factors had created *de facto* segregation. The effort of the courts was matched by Congressional action in passing antidiscrimination legislation, the first and most important being the Civil Rights Act of 1964, and providing increased federal financial support to education. Legislation and financial support combined to create a "carrot and stick" mechanism that increased the pace of school desegregation.

BROWN v. BOARD OF EDUCATION OF TOPEKA

Class action suits were brought on behalf of African American students in the states of Kansas, South Carolina, Virginia, and Delaware to obtain admission for those students to public schools on a nonsegregated basis. The plaintiffs appealed directly to the U.S. Supreme Court from the separate federal district courts' holdings that race-based segregation of public school students was constitutional under the "doctrine of separate but equal" as enunciated in **Plessy v. Ferguson.** The U.S. Supreme Court held that the segregation of students in public schools on the basis of race violated the equal protection guarantees of the Fourteenth Amendment. The Court expressly overturned **Plessy v. Ferguson,** stating "the doctrine of 'separate but equal' has no place in the field of public education, since separate educational facilities are inherently unequal." It concluded that when a state decides to provide public education, it is a right that must be made available to all on equal terms.

Go to the Companion Website at **http://www. prenhall.com/underwood**, select Chapter 10, choose Cases module, and click on **Brown v. Board of Education of Topeka** to read the entire opinion of the court.

Desegregation steadily progressed over the next two decades. African American parents and children relied on the Fourteenth Amendment to challenge admission and transfer policies, testing practices, tracking, inferior facilities, and discriminatory expenditure patterns. African American teachers used Title VII to challenge hiring practices, testing and certification requirements, and promotion and transfer policies that discriminated against and disproportionately impacted African American employees. However, by the mid- to late 1980s the pace of desegregation had slowed as a result of changes in economic and community demographics in many urban areas and a growing reluctance by a more conservative federal judiciary to impose and enforce desegregation remedies (over 500 court-ordered and voluntary desegregation plans have been eliminated). Within a decade the quarter century of progress that had been made in integrating African American students was lost. Moreover, the segregation of Hispanic students had become even greater than that of African American students. In 2000 over 75% of Hispanic students and 70% of African American students attended schools in which over 50% of the students were minority, and 37% of each attended schools that were 90% to 100% minority.[5]

Diversity Programs

In an attempt to combat this resegregation, many school districts have implemented policies that strive to provide a diverse learning environment. School districts that have never been under court-ordered desegregation are experimenting with programs to combat racial isolation. Districts that were once under court supervision to desegregate, but have since obtained unitary status (a court ruling that the district has officially eliminated the effects of past discrimination), are continuing their desegregation plans and diversity programs. Still others, those who promised the government that they would change (a consent decree), are revisiting their plans.

Schools typically offer several justifications for a policy decision promoting racially diverse classrooms. One justification is that when students with different backgrounds, outlooks, values, and beliefs come together in public schools all students benefit from the interaction. Another is that racially isolated schools tend to be underfunded and produce poor academic results for minority students, with the ultimate negative economic impact on the community. The fundamental argument is that diverse learning environments are necessary to prepare children for success in later life in our diverse American society. Among the programs that districts employ to promote diversity in the workplace and classroom are those described on page 189 in the block Common Programs Used to Achieve Diversity.

Despite the apparent benefits of promoting racial diversity, the efforts of many school districts, especially those involving the forced busing of students or the involuntary transfer of teachers, have been subject to legal challenges. Legal challenges to school district race-conscious policies assert that the policies violate the Equal Protection Clause. When courts consider challenges to district diversity policies, they begin the examination from the premise that by considering student race the school district has in effect classified students by race. Hence, if students have been classified by race the court may apply the strict scrutiny level of review. Using this level of review the court will uphold racial classification only if it can be shown to meet the two "prongs" of the strict scrutiny analysis: (1) The classification is necessary to achieve a compelling state interest, and (2) the classification is "narrowly tailored" enough to meet the interest without creating overly burdensome negative consequences for those outside the classification.

Affirmative Action

Among the more controversial strategies to promote diversity is *affirmative action*. The principle of affirmative action holds that prohibiting discrimination is not enough; what is needed are affirmative steps to admit, recruit, hire, and retain individuals who are underrepresented in the workforce and student body.

In two higher education affirmative action cases (**Grutter v. Bollinger**[6] and **Gratz v. Bollinger**[7]), the Supreme Court held that trying to achieve racial diversity is a compelling state interest that may justify a voluntary affirmative action plan; however, the plan must be narrowly tailored to remedy the past discrimination (see the boxed case summary on page 190).

COMMON PROGRAMS USED TO ACHIEVE DIVERSITY

Attendance Zones

Attendance zones may be drawn to maximize the likelihood of racial diversity.

Transfer Policies

These include policies that allow students to transfer only from schools in which they constitute a racial majority to schools in which they would be in the minority. Ordinarily, transfer policies and other student assignment devices do not involve the total exclusion of children but merely their assignment to a school other than their first choice.

Magnet Schools

Usually these are schools that emphasize a particular academic program, such as math or science or the visual and performing arts. It can also mean a school that has been enhanced with extra programmatic offerings or beautified facilities attractive to parents and students.

Admission to Elite or Special Academies

Admissions policies at elite or special academies sometimes include race as a factor in admission to maintain or to improve racial diversity. In these policies, race is usually just one of a number of factors in the admissions decision.

Controlled Choice

These programs defy the conventional geographic structure by allowing parents to select among several schools for their child to attend. Policy makers project that diversity will occur naturally due to the capacities of the various schools and the racial blend of the controlled choice attendance zones.

Interdistrict Transfer Programs

These programs allow entrance to or exit from the district for purposes of desegregation. Interdistrict transfer programs now operate in various metro areas in the Northeast, South, and Midwest.

GRUTTER v. BOLLINGER

The United States Supreme Court upheld the University of Michigan Law School's diversity admissions program by a 5–4 vote. The Court ruled that diversity in higher education is a compelling state interest, which may allow a school to consider a student's race in making admission decisions in a carefully constructed admissions program. Writing for the majority, Justice Sandra Day O'Connor concluded that the school's objective to "enroll a 'critical mass' of minority students" avoided the constitutional sins of racial quotas or racial balancing. The *Grutter* opinion stressed that the University of Michigan Law School considered each applicant individually, weighing all of the attributes the student would bring to the school, not only the student's race. For this reason, the Court found that the law school's approach met the narrowly tailored prong of strict scrutiny—that is, it considered race no more than absolutely necessary to achieve the goal of educational diversity.

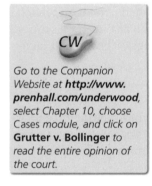

Go to the Companion Website at *http://www. prenhall.com/underwood*, select Chapter 10, choose Cases module, and click on **Grutter v. Bollinger** to read the entire opinion of the court.

Even though these cases involved higher education, the lower courts have applied the reasoning of *Gratz* and *Grutter* to student assignment cases in which K–12 school districts make race-based student assignment decisions to achieve diversity. In a case involving the public schools, the Fifth Circuit Court of Appeals has ruled that a Louisiana school district's magnet school's admission policy, which takes an applicant's race into account as a factor, violates white applicants' equal protection rights, despite the fact that the district is under a desegregation consent decree.[8] The school had adopted a race conscious policy for admission to the magnet school. Admission to the school was competitive, but out of all applicants who satisfied the initial qualifications, priority was given to siblings of current students and African American applicants who would otherwise attend a school with over 90% African American enrollment. All other qualified applicants were ranked by their standardized test scores. Separate rankings were maintained by race so that racial mix of 50% white and 50% African American students, plus or minus 15 percentage points could be maintained. The appeals found the program was unconstitutional since it was not narrowly tailored and was essential a quota system.

In another case involving the use of race as a factor in its student assignment plan, **Comfort v. Lynn School Committee**,[9] the First Circuit Court of Appeals upheld a school district's voluntary desegregation plan that featured a student assignment plan that allowed students to attend neighborhood schools. Race became a factor only when a student wanted to transfer to another school. The district would permit the transfer only if it would not increase the racial imbalance at either the sending or the receiving school. The court agreed that achieving racial and ethnic diversity in its school populations was a compelling interest, and that the student assignment plan was narrowly tailored to achieve this goal because the plan dealt with noncompetitive transfers, avoided the use of quotas, and was of a finite duration.

The courts have applied a similar rationale in reviewing employee affirmative action plans. In **Wygant v. Jackson Board of Education,**[10] the U.S. Supreme Court overturned a Michigan school district's collective bargaining agreement that provided for the release of White employees with greater seniority than Black employees in order to preserve the percentage of minority teachers employed prior to the layoffs. The Court ruled that affirmative action plans must be designed to remedy location-specific past discrimination, not general societal discrimination. That is, first, evidence must exist that remedial action is necessary, and second, the plan must be narrowly tailored to remedy the past discrimination. The Third Circuit Court of Appeals ruled similarly in **Taxman v. Board of Education of Piscataway,**[11] finding that the retention of an equally qualified Black teacher over a White teacher to preserve racial diversity was unconstitutional. That case was accepted for review by the United States Supreme Court, but was settled before the Court made a decision.

EMPLOYMENT DISCRIMINATION

Title VII

Title VII prohibits employers from discriminating on the basis of race, color, religion, gender,[12] or national origin. Title VII covers both intentional discrimination and actions that have a disproportionate adverse effect on members of a protected class. It encompasses recruiting, hiring, promotion, and compensation practices as well as fringe benefits and other terms and conditions of employment. It also prohibits employers from limiting, segregating, or classifying employees in a way that tends to deprive an individual of employment opportunities or adversely affects employment status because of race, color, sex, religion, or national origin. Employers are prohibited from retaliating against an employee who exercises rights under Title VII.

Teachers typically bring two types of employment discrimination claims under Title VII: *disparate treatment,* which requires that the plaintiff prove that he or she is a member of a group protected by Title VII and was treated less favorably than others by some employment practice or policy; and *disparate impact,* which requires that the plaintiff show that an employment practice or policy has a more severe impact on a protected class than others. A disparate treatment claim places the burden of proof squarely on the plaintiff. The plaintiff must first demonstrate a

Title VII of the Civil Rights Act of 1964 prohibits discrimination on the basis of race, color, or national origin in federally assisted programs and activities.

42 U.S.C. § 2000d

prima facia case of discrimination. This means that the plaintiff must show that he or she (1) was a member of a group protected by Title VII, (2) is qualified for the position in question, and (3) was treated less favorably than another by a particular employment practice. If the plaintiff can establish these facts, the employer can still rebut the claim by articulating a nondiscriminatory reason for the practice. This means that the employer must show that the challenged practice is job related and justified by a legitimate business goal. If the employer meets this burden of proof, the burden of proof shifts back to the plaintiff to show that the articulated reason is a mere pretext for intentional discriminatory intent. Intent is very difficult to prove. In 1982 the Supreme Court said discriminatory intent can be established only by demonstrating actual motive and cannot be presumed from employment data that show something less than intent.[13]

The other type of Title VII claim, *disparate impact,* is based on employment practices that appear to be neutral, but actually have a more severe impact on protected groups. Proof of intent is not necessary to prove discrimination based on disparate impact. According to the Supreme Court decision in **Griggs v. Duke Power Company**[14] (see the boxed case summary), which the Civil Rights Act of 1991 strengthened, if the claimant can show that an employment practice or policy results in a disparate impact on a protected class, the burden shifts to the employer to demonstrate that the challenged practice or policy is job related and consistent with business necessity. Even if the employer does offer a business necessity for a discriminatory practice, the claimant may still prevail by showing that the district could serve its interest by means that are not discriminatory. For example, a female applicant for a high school biology teaching position in Arizona filed a sex discrimination suit against the school district on the basis that its requirement that applicants for the teaching position also have the ability to coach varsity softball had a disparate impact on women.[15] Although the board admitted the coupling of the two positions did have a disparate impact on women, it defended the practice by maintaining its business necessity. In considering this defense, the

Go to the Companion Website at *http://www. prenhall.com/underwood*, select Chapter 10, choose Cases module, and click on **Griggs v. Duke Power Company** to read the entire opinion written by the court in this case.

GRIGGS v. DUKE POWER COMPANY

An employer required job applicants to either have a high school education or pass two standardized tests. Neither of these requirements was directed or intended to measure the ability to learn or to perform job tasks. The practice was challenged as discriminatory to African American applicants who were disproportionately eliminated from consideration due to this job requirement. The Supreme Court held that the requirement was discriminatory if the employer could not show that the requirement was significantly related to successful job performance. Job requirements that have a disparate impact on a protected group are permissible only if they are demonstrably a reasonable measure of job performance.

court maintained that to be successful the district must show compelling business purposes and that there were no acceptable alternative practices or policies available that would better accomplish the business purpose advanced. Because the board was unable to demonstrate that less discriminatory alternatives had been attempted when, in fact, substantial evidence existed that alternatives were available, the appellate court held for the plaintiff and remanded the case to the lower court for a determination of damages.

If an employee is successful in a discrimination complaint, the court may order a stop to the discriminatory practice, the reinstatement or hiring of the employee, the payment of attorneys fees, or any other just remedy the court decides is necessary to rectify the situation.[16] However, remedies may be limited if the complainant is able to show discrimination was a factor in the employment decision, but the employer is able to prove it would have made the same decision even if discrimination were not a motivating factor.[17]

Equal Pay Act

The Equal Pay Act[18] prohibits gender-based wage discrimination. According to the Equal Pay Act, equal pay and benefits must be provided to men and women for the same job or for jobs that require equal skill, effort, and responsibility. Equal Pay Act claims frequently involve questions of whether positions are comparable enough to be "equal work."

In the past many schools actually did pay male and female teachers on a different basis but school districts have eliminated these clear acts of discrimination. However, questions still arise in other types of positions. For example, in **Gokay v. Pennridge School District**[19] a female human resource director successfully made an Equal Pay Act claim when she was replaced with a man who had similar credentials but was paid at $10,000 more than her salary. Questions of equal pay have also arisen in regard to extra duty assignments. For example in **Burkey v. Marshall County Board of Education**[20] the district regularly paid the coaches for girls sports (who were all female) half of what it paid the coaches for boys sports (who were all male). The court ordered the district to equalize the pay for the positions.

DISABILITY DISCRIMINATION

As discussed in chapter 8, Section 504 of the Rehabilitation Act and the Americans With Disabilities Act (ADA) both prohibit discrimination on the basis of disabilities. They prohibit discrimination in recruiting, the application process, hiring, advancement, training, benefits, compensation, termination, and contractual relationships. Under Section 504 and the ADA a person has a disability if he or she

1. has a physical or mental impairment that substantially limits one or more major life activities;
2. has a record of being substantially impaired; or
3. is regarded as being substantially impaired.

Just claiming a disability is not sufficient to qualify as a "person with a disability" even if the employer has acknowledged the disability to the extent of attempting to provide accommodations for the alleged disability. For example, in **Cigan v. Chippewa Falls School District**[21] Ms. Cigan had been a physical education teacher in the district for 30 years. In the last years of her employment she alleged various disabilities including arthritis, bursitis, degenerating spinal discs, scoliosis, and spondylitis. The district made accommodations for her, but finally the superintendent requested that she retire. The court did not find that she was protected by the ADA because there was no proof that one or more of her major life activities was impaired, and she was not protected as being regarded as having a disability even though the district had provided accommodations for her in the past.

Antidiscrimination statutes do not protect individuals who currently engage in illegal drug use, but do protect nonusing drug addicts and alcoholics. For example, in **Martin v. Barnesville Exempted Village School District Board of Education**,[22] a school custodian was disciplined for using alcohol on the job. The court found that the ADA offered him no protection, particularly because the discipline was not directed at his status as an alcoholic, but at his behavior of consuming alcohol on school premises contrary to district policy.

Antidiscriminal rules differ somewhat for those who have a contagious disease or infection that is a direct threat to the health and safety of others. As mentioned in chapter 2, in **School Board of Nassau County v. Arline**[23] the Supreme Court held that a teacher, who was disabled due to a history of tuberculosis, was protected by Section 504 and overturned her dismissal. But the Court also found the district could remove her from the classroom if there were a significant risk of infection. It set out the following considerations to determine whether it must accommodate an individual with a contagious condition or whether such an accommodation presents an undue burden on the district or makes the individual not qualified for the position: (1) the nature of the risk (how the disease is transmitted), (2) the duration of the risk (how long the carrier is infectious), (3) the severity of the risk (what the potential harm is to third parties), and (4) the probabilities the disease will be transmitted and will cause varying degrees of harm. In applying these considerations in **Doe v. DeKalb County School District**,[24] the court upheld a district's decision not to allow an HIV positive teacher to supervise a self-contained classroom for students with severe behavior problems. The district considered the risk of transmitting the disease to these students due to frequent physical encounters was "significant" as compared to teaching a regular education classroom.

If an employee or applicant does qualify as a person with a disability, is otherwise qualified to perform the essential functions of the job, and satisfies the job-related requirements, the school must make reasonable accommodations for him or her. In general it is the responsibility of the individual with the disability to inform the employer that an accommodation is needed. If the need for accommodation is not obvious, the employer may request documentation of the disability.

Reasonable accommodations might include such measures as providing special equipment or devices, job restructuring, modification of work schedules, or transfer or reassignment. However, the law does not require employers to modify the essential functions of a position or to lower or substantially modify their school district standards to accommodate a person with a disability.[25] Nor does the employer have to provide the accommodation if to do so would cause the employer undue hardship. Also, a requested accommodation that conflicts with seniority rules under ordinary circumstances is not a reasonable accommodation.[26]

Employers found in violation of Section 504 and/or the ADA may be ordered to reinstate or promote the employee, provide back pay, litigation expenses, and/or compensatory damages. In reasonable accommodation claims, damages are not recoverable if the employer demonstrates good-faith efforts to make reasonable accommodations in consultation with the person with a disability.

SEX DISCRIMINATION

Sex discrimination is prohibited not only under Title VII but also under Title IX of the Education Amendments of 1972,[27] which prohibits sex discrimination by public and private education institutions receiving federal funds. The provisions of Title IX are similar to those of Title VII and apply to both teachers and students. Since it went into effect in 1975 numerous legal challenges have arisen over exactly what is an "educational program or activity" and the requirements to ensure that females are not being discriminated against in these programs or activities.

Sexual Harassment

Sexual harassment lawsuits are serious threats to schools in terms of legal liability, damage to the learning environment, and loss of community support. Sexual harassment is considered a form of sex discrimination under Title VII for employees and under Title IX for students.

Sexual harassment is usually described in two ways: *Quid pro quo sexual harassment,* which occurs when an individual with authority makes threats or promises to give or withhold something of value in exchange for sexual favors, and hostile environment sexual harassment. *Hostile environment sexual harassment* is not as blatant, occurs when the sexual behavior, remarks, and so forth are severe enough to negatively affect the learning environment, making it hostile, intimidating, or offensive.

In **Franklin v. Gwinnett**[28] (see the boxed case summary), which involved the sexual harassment of a student by a teacher, the Supreme Court recognized that sexual harassment, if sufficiently severe, persistent, or pervasive, can create a hostile environment for the victim that limits the student's ability to benefit from, or participate in, an educational program or activity in violation of Title IX.

FRANKLIN v. GWINNETT COUNTY PUBLIC SCHOOLS

A student claimed that a coach had sexually harassed her both verbally and physically even to the point of coercive sexual intercourse. The student sued the school under Title IX for sexual harassment claiming money damages. The United States Supreme Court held that students may obtain money damages under Title IX for intentional acts of discrimination. The Court stated that a teacher's sexual harassment of a student because of her sex constituted a type of "discrimination" that would violate Title IX.

Go to the Companion Website at **http://www. prenhall.com/underwood**, select Chapter 10, choose Cases module, and click on **Franklin v. Gwinnett County Public Schools** to read the entire opinion of the court.

In employment situations the critical inquiry is whether the sexual conduct is unwelcome. It is not sexual harassment if both parties agreed to the conduct.[29] However, when the issue is sexual harassment of *students* by *adults*, the U.S. Department of Education's Office of Civil Rights (the federal office that has authority over Title IX compliance) has said that welcomeness and consent are not the issue. Sexual contact between an adult employee and an elementary student is assumed not to be consensual.[30] In cases involving secondary students, there is a "strong presumption" that sexual contact is not consensual.

In reviewing allegations of student harassment the Office of Civil Rights (OCR)[31] and the courts look at a number of factors to determine whether hostile environment sexual harassment has occurred. These include

- the degree to which the conduct affected one or more students' education;
- the type, frequency, and duration of the conduct;
- the identity of and relationship between the alleged harasser and the victim or victims of the harassment;
- the number of individuals involved;
- the age and sex of the alleged harasser and the victim or victims of the harassment;
- the size of the school, location of the incidents, and context in which they occurred; and
- other incidents at the school.

In sexual harassment situations involving employment, the courts look to see whether[32]

- the conduct was verbal or physical or both;
- the conduct was physically threatening or humiliating;
- the conduct was repeated;
- an inappropriate remark was an isolated incident;
- the conduct was hostile and patently offensive;
- the alleged harasser was a coworker or supervisor;
- others joined in perpetrating the harassment; and
- the harassment was directed at more than one individual.

Courts use all of these factors in combination to make a determination; the facts of each situation are very important in determing whether sexual harassment has occurred.

Same-Sex Sexual Harassment. Sexual harassment can occur even when the people involved are of the same gender[33] (see the boxed case summary of **Oncale v. Sundowner Offshore Services**). Same-sex harassment claims do not require a gay or lesbian context. The crucial issue is whether members of one sex are exposed to disadvantageous terms or conditions of employment to which members of the other sex are not exposed. Actionable same-sex harassment might be motivated by sexual desire, but could also be based on other sex-related motivations.

ONCALE v. SUNDOWNER OFFSHORE SERVICES

A gay man was subjected to a recurrent harassment by his coworkers on the oil rig. He quit his job because of the harassment. The Supreme Court unanimously held that same-sex harassment is actionable under Title VII. The Court said that the issue is not the sex of the harasser or whether the words used by the harasser have sexual content or connotations. The issue is whether members of one sex are exposed to disadvantageous terms or conditions of employment to which member of the other sex are not exposed. A plaintiff need not prove that the conduct was motivated by sexual desire. However, a plaintiff must prove that the conduct was not merely tinged with offensive sexual connotations but actually constituted discrimination because of gender.

Sexual Orientation Harassment. Sexual harassment based on sexual orientation[34] is actionable under Title IX. Guidance from the OCR states that "sexual harassment directed at gay or lesbian students that is sufficiently serious to limit or deny a student's ability to participate in or benefit from the school's program constitutes sexual harassment prohibited by Title IX."[35] Courts have ruled that schools have an obligation to protect gay and lesbian students. For example, in

*Go to the Companion Website at **http://www. prenhall.com/underwood**, select Chapter 10, choose Cases module, and click on **Oncale v. Sundowner Offshore Services** to read the entire opinion of the court.*

Nabozny v. Podlesny[36] a gay male student's having been subjected to years of taunts and threats at school ultimately ended in violence. He was spat upon, urinated upon, subjected to a mock rape in a class of 20 students, and beaten and kicked resulting in internal injuries. School administrators had repeatedly failed to act to stop the harassment, telling the student that he should expect such treatment if he was going to be gay and that "boys will be boys." The court found that the district had a responsibility to protect the student and had failed to do so. The court required the district to pay almost $1 million in damages to the student.

Sexual Harassment of Students by Other Students. The vast majority of student sexual harassment that occurs in the schools is student-to-student harassment. In fact, some studies have shown that as many as 80% of students experience some form of sexual harassment, usually student-to-student, at school.[37] Maintaining the "deliberate indifference" standard for employee harassment of students set forth in *Gebser*, in its 1999 decision in **Davis v. Monroe**[38] the Supreme Court said that schools may be held responsible for peer sexual harassment when school officials are deliberately indifferent or fail to respond to end student peer sexual harassment of which they have actual knowledge (see the boxed case summary).

DAVIS v. MONROE COUNTY BOARD OF EDUCATION

Aurelia Davis brought a case on behalf of her 10-year-old daughter, alleging that over the course of 5 months, a 5th-grade student had sexually harassed her daughter by attempting to touch her breasts and genital area, rubbing against her sexually, and repeatedly saying he wanted to have sex with her. The plaintiff and her daughter alleged that they had complained about each incident when it occurred, but the school refused to take meaningful action. Mrs. Davis further alleged that the continued harassment and the school's failure to respond affected her daughter's ability to receive an education, as evidenced by the girl's grades dropping and a suicide note that she wrote. The United States Supreme Court held that schools are liable for damages in private actions brought under Title IX when school officials are deliberately indifferent to student peer sexual harassment of which they have actual knowledge. To prevail a plaintiff must show the following: (1) Gender-oriented conduct that is "severe, pervasive, and objectively offensive" occurred; (2) the harassment had the impact of denying a student's education; (3) the district had "actual knowledge" of the harassment; and (4) the district responded with "deliberate indifference."

The Court in *Davis* did recognize that not all unwelcome physical harassment nor all offensive comments are sexual, and that students often engage in

*Go to the Companion Website at **http://www. prenhall.com/underwood**, select Chapter 10, choose Cases module, and click on **Davis v. Monroe County Board of Education** to read the entire opinion of the court.*

"insults, banter, teasing, shoving, pushing, and gender specific conduct that is upsetting to the students subjected to it" but that do not rise to the level of conduct to impose liability. To rise to the level of possible liability, the student-to-student sexual harassment must be as follows: "so severe, pervasive, and objectively offensive, and that so undermines and distracts from the victims' educational experience, that the victims are effectively denied equal access to an institution's resources and opportunities."[39] Guidance in determining what sexual harassment is, and what it is not—a kiss on the cheek by a first grader—is provided by the U.S. Department of Education's guidelines, *Sexual Harassment Guidance: Harassment of Students by School Employees, Other Students, or Third Parties.*[40]

The concepts discussed in regard to sexual harassment and protection against sexual harassment are similar in their application to other forms of harassment. That is, schools must also ensure there is no harassment on the basis of race, religion, or disability. As an example see the In the News feature.

IN THE NEWS . . .

A former Newbury Park High School (CA) student has filed suit in federal district court claiming he was the target of anti-Semitic harassment by the school's baseball coach. The suit alleges that the verbal harassment went on for over a year, with Conejo Valley Unified School District (CVUSD) officials failing to take any meaningful steps to stop it. Samuel Goldstein was a member of Newbury Park's football and baseball teams coached by John Marsden. Samuel's complaint claims that he was the butt of several anti-Semitic jokes made by the coach and teammates. Samuel's parents contend that school officials failed to take action against Mr. Marsden even after assuring them that he had been disciplined. Mr. Marsden eventually was suspended by CVUSD in September 2003. The suit alleges that even after his suspension he continued to attend school events, where he stirred up students, parents, and other coaches by telling them that the Goldsteins were responsible for his dismissal. As a result, the Goldsteins claim, every time they attended a football game they were subjected to verbal abuse from parents and students. In addition, Samuel claims that a student threatened to kill him because of his family's role in Mr. Marsden's removal and that school officials failed to take any disciplinary action against the student. The suit seeks unspecified damages.

Source: From "Former Student Files Suit Claiming Anti-Semitic Harassment by Baseball Coach," by Amanda Covarrubias, July 2004, *Los Angeles Times.* http://www.latimes.com/news/education

School District Liability for Sexual Harassment of Students. In the lead Supreme Court decision, **Gebser v. Lago Vista**[41] (see boxed case summary on page 200), the Court held that a school district was liable under Title IX for sexual harassment of a student by a school employee if school officials knew that the harassment was occurring and failed to respond or were deliberately indifferent to the harassment.[42]

GEBSER v. LAGO VISTA INDEPENDENT SCHOOL DISTRICT

A male teacher carried on a sexual relationship with an eighth-grade female student. The sexual contact took place off school grounds and was unknown to the school district until discovered by happenstance by a police officer. The teacher was terminated and his license was revoked. During the time the sexual relationship was taking place, the district had neither an official grievance procedure for sexual harassment complaints nor a formal antiharassment policy. The student filed suit against the school district and the teacher, raising claims under Title IX along with several state law claims.

The United States Supreme Court upheld the school district's position that someone with authority to address the discrimination must have actual knowledge of a teacher's sexual harassment and fail to respond adequately before the district could be held liable under Title IX. The official's failure to respond to known harassment must amount to "deliberate indifference" before liability can be imposed.

*Go to the Companion Website at **http://www. prenhall.com/underwood**, select Chapter 10, choose Cases module, and click on **Gebser v. Lago Vista Independent School District** to read the entire opinion of the court.*

For example, in **P.H. v. School Dist. of Kansas City, Mo.,**[43] the court found the district had no "actual notice" that the teacher was sexually abusing a student. Other teachers complained that the teacher was spending too much time with the student, the student was frequently tardy and absent from class, and his grades were suffering. However, none of these complaints indicated suspicions of sexual abuse. When the vice-principal confronted the teacher the teacher offered a plausible explanation—both he and the student were both involved in numerous student organizations.[44]

Single-Sex Instruction

The debate concerning coeducation at the elementary and secondary level that began in the 1800s continues to this day. Then, as now, the debate has centered on the difference in abilities and needs of boys and girls, and whether a coeducational environment is more conducive to learning for either or both groups of students.

Educators have argued that separating classes based upon gender, especially if participation is voluntary, can improve the performance of both genders. Those who support single-gender instruction report that it can improve test scores, attendance, and student behavior among both groups. With fewer pressures of coeducational interaction, students can focus more on academic success and career goals. Single-gender education promotes self-confidence and leadership qualities in females and males alike. Female students benefit from greater teacher attention and increase skill levels in such areas as math and science. Many studies have recognized that single-gender instruction, even if for only one class a day, can have a beneficial effect on educating and socializing students. Teachers can tailor the education program around unique learning styles.

On the other hand, many other advocacy groups and researchers have argued that it is misguided and harmful to segregate students on the basis of gender, even with the intent to respond to current classroom inequities. To them, this type of segregation is as invidious as that struck down in **Brown v. Board of Education.** Rather than allow educators to use gender segregation as part of the educational methodology, these advocates argue that the classroom should be transformed into a learning environment that is friendly and beneficial to both genders.

Currently public schools cannot have single-sex schools in which enrollment is mandatory or in which an equivalent single-sex opportunity does not exist for both genders. An early major decision involving single-gender education is **Vorcheimer v. School District of Philadelphia.**[45] The City of Philadelphia had maintained an all-male academic high school (Central) and an all-female high school (Girls), along with a number of coeducational high schools. The single-gender schools had been maintained by the city for over 120 years, and attendance at the institutions was voluntary. The boys' school and the girls' school were academically equivalent. The plaintiff, a female high school student, requested an injunction requiring her admittance to the all-male school. She argued that the male-only admissions policy at Central was discriminatory. The Third Circuit Court of Appeals upheld the system, finding no equal protection violation. On appeal, the United States Supreme Court allowed the Third Circuit's decision to stand because the Court split its ruling 4 to 4 on whether the practice was unconstitutional.[46] (In cases of a tie vote in the Supreme Court the lower court's decision is left in place.)

In 2005 the U.S. Department of Education adopted new regulations to allow school districts to create single-sex classrooms and schools.[47] Previous Department of Education regulations on this subject reflect the long-held interpretation that Title IX of the Education Amendments of 1972 prohibits school districts from maintaining single-sex classrooms or schools except in limited circumstances, such as physical and sex education classes. The new regulations (excerpted on page 202) allow elementary and secondary schools to offer voluntary single-sex classes within a coeducational school as long as both sexes are treated fairly and equally. However, districts that offer an entire single-sex school for one gender are not required to offer the same for the other gender, as long as they offer an equal educational opportunity to both genders.

The benefits of single-gender instruction have been and will continue to be the subject of debate. Reasonable people can disagree about its merits. Yet, single-sex instruction and single-sex institutions are clearly on the rise. In 1996 only 4 public schools in the United States offered single-sex educational opportunities. By 2004 that number had increased to 143.[48]

> **SINGLE-SEX CLASSES AND SCHOOLS**
>
> - *Single-sex classes.* Under the current regulations school districts can offer single-sex classes in very limited circumstances. Under proposed regulations a school district may offer a single-sex class as long as it meets three conditions. First, the school district must be able to show that an important governmental or educational objective is met by offering a single-sex class. Second, the district must implement the objective evenhandedly. Third, the district must offer a substantially equal coeducational class in the same subject.
> - *Single-sex schools.* Current regulations allow school districts to operate single-sex schools as long as districts operate single-sex schools for both sexes that have comparable courses, services, and facilities. Under the proposed rules districts will be able to offer single-sex schools as long as they offer substantially equal opportunities to students of the other sex in a single-sex school, a single-sex educational unit (or a school within a school), or a coeducational school.

GUIDING LEGAL PRINCIPLES

- The Equal Protection Clause, federal statutes and regulations, state laws, local ordinances, and district policies all prohibit schools from engaging in discrimination. These antidiscrimination rules that protect various classes of individuals apply to school district education programs as well as employment practices and decisions.
- The courts have developed a three-tier approach to equal protection:

  Strict scrutiny. If the government classification is based on race or national origin or materially impacts a fundamental right (voting, criminal appeals, interstate travel), courts apply strict scrutiny. This means the law will be validated only if it is necessary to achieve a compelling governmental interest.

  Intermediate scrutiny. Courts apply middle-level scrutiny to classifications based on gender and alienage. This type of review requires that the governmental objective be "important" and that the means chosen be "substantially related" to achieving that objective.

  Rational basis review. All other challenged classifications are subjected to a deferential level of review in which a court will determine whether the classification bears a rational relationship to a legitimate governmental purpose.

- In addition to constitutional protections, a number of federal and state statutes prohibit discrimination on the basis of race, sex, gender, religion, national origin, age, and disability.
- The Supreme Court has held that racial segregation in the public schools is unconstitutional.
- To make classifications of students based on race, even for the purposes of increasing diversity, the classification must be necessary to a compelling state interest (improving diversity) and must be narrowly tailored to achieve that end.
- Sexual harassment is considered a form of sex discrimination and is prohibited, including quid pro quo and hostile environment harassment.
- Schools can be held responsible for sexual harassment at the hands of teachers and students if they knew of the behavior and failed to respond.
- Single-sex classes or schools are acceptable only if participation is voluntary and equal opportunities are offered to both genders.

YOU BE THE JUDGE

Go to the Companion Website at *http://www.prenhall.com/underwood*, select Chapter 10, choose the You Be the Judge *module and click on the name of the case for more information about the case and the court's decision and rationale.*

A Long and Lonely Road

Wayne County School District (UT) encompasses a large and sparsely populated geographical area. The district operates a number of buses to transport students to and from school. State administrative rules require a minimum of 10 students to create a new bus route or route extension. If there are not enough students, the district pays parents the cost of transporting their students. A family sought to get a bus route altered to pick up their children. Wayne County considered the feasibility of creating a route closer to the students' home but concluded that it was more cost-efficient to continue to reimburse the parents for the cost of transporting the students to the existing bus stop. The parents sued. They argued that the district discriminated against their children in violation of their children's equal protection rights. The argued that the district should have to treat all students the same regarding bus transportation. The district agreed that the decision was based on efficiency of time and money.

Questions for Discussion and Reflection

1. Is there a possible discrimination claim every time a district treats one student different from another?
2. What do you think the parents would have to prove to win their case?

3. Do you believe this school district violated the equal protection rights of these students by refusing to establish a new bus route that would have provided the students with bus service from the county road nearest their home?

Visit the Companion Website for a more detailed description of the facts in the case **Labrum v. Wayne County School Board.**

* * *

More Than Just a Bad Lunch

An Asian American student allegedly was subjected to race-based peer harassment starting with his fourth-grade year at W. S. Boardman Elementary School (NY). In addition to enduring verbal taunts, he was physically assaulted on several occasions. Both the student and his mother complained more than once to the school's principal. Each time, the principal interviewed the students accused of misconduct and disciplined them. The student claimed that, in one incident, a school lunchroom monitor used racist language, called him and his family "crazy," and threatened his life. Although witnesses verified that the monitor called him crazy, they denied hearing any remarks of a racial nature or threatening his life. The principal gave the monitor a warning and placed a letter regarding the incident in her personnel file. The parent sued the district and the lunchroom monitor for racial harassment as an equal protection violation.

Questions for Discussion and Reflection

1. What standard would the court apply when deciding this discrimination case, strict scrutiny or rational basis?
2. In your opinion should the district be found liable for the racial harassment of the student?
3. Does the district have a different responsibility for the actions of the other students than for the lunchroom monitor? Support your response.

Visit the Companion Website for a more detailed description of the facts in the case **Yap v. Oceanside Union Free School District.**

* * *

Tiebreakers

Seattle School District Number 1 operates 10 public high schools that vary significantly in terms of quality. The school district has never been segregated by law. However, due to Seattle's racially imbalanced housing patterns, if Seattle's children were simply assigned to the high schools nearest their homes, a significant racial imbalance would exist in the schools. To prevent segregation and to promote racial diversity in its high schools, the school board adopted a multistep, open choice student assignment plan. Under this plan, if a high school has more applicants than seats, four tiebreakers are used to determine which students to admit. The first tiebreaker gives a preference to students with siblings already attending the requested school. If a school is still oversubscribed after applying this first tiebreaker, the school district proceeds to a second tiebreaker, which is based entirely on race. Ultimately, the school district's use of this racial tiebreaker determines where about 10 percent of applicants will be admitted. Once all students of the preferred racial category are admitted to an oversubscribed high school, any remaining "ties" are broken by resort to a third variable: distance. Although a fourth tiebreaker exists—a random lottery—it is rarely invoked because distances are calculated to one hundredth of a mile for purposes of the preceding tiebreaker. Parents Involved in Community Schools (PICS), a group of parents whose children were denied assignments to their schools of choice, sued the district, alleging that the use of race as a tiebreaker was unconstitutional.

Questions for Discussion and Reflection

1. What arguments could the school make in defending this system?
2. What other tiebreakers could you use to make this system more defensible under the Constitution?
3. How do you think the court would rule in this case?

Visit the Companion Website for a more detailed description of the facts in the case **Parents Involved in Community Schools v. Seattle School District No. 1.**

MORE ON THE WEB

Go to the Companion Website at **http://www.prenhall.com/underwood**, select Chapter 10, choose the More on the Web *module to connect to the site mentioned.*

The U.S. Department of Education, Office of Civil Rights (OCR) is the agency charged with the enforcement of civil rights laws. Visit the OCR website at http://www.ed.gov/ocr. Under "Topics A–Z," find and click on "Sexual Harassment," then "Sexual Harassment Resources." Look under "Frequently Asked Questions" to see how the OCR defines sexual harassment and what it can do to help eliminate sexual harassment against students. Also under "Sexual Harassment Resources," download the "Checklist for a Comprehensive Approach to Addressing Harassment." Ask a teacher or administrator with whom you have contact for his or her responses to the standards posed as they relate to his or her school.

ENDNOTES

1. 347 U.S. 483 (1954).

2. 163 U.S. 537 (1896).

3. *Brown v. Board of Education of Topeka,* 349 U.S. 294 (1955).

4. Ibid.

5. Orfield, G. (2001). *Schools more separate: Consequences of a decade of resegregation.* Cambridge, MA: Harvard University, The Civil Rights Project.

6. *Grutter v. Bollinger,* 539 U.S. 306 (2003).

7. *Gratz v. Bollinger,* 539 U.S. 244 (2003).

8. *Cavalier v. Caddo Parish School Board,* No. 003039 (5th Cir. March 1, 2005).

9. No. 03-2415 (1st Cir. June 16, 2005).

10. 476 U.S. 267 (1986).

11. 91 F.3d 1547 (3rd Cir. 1996), *cert. granted,* 521 U.S. 1117, *cert. dismissed,* 522 U.S. 1010 (1997).

12. Title VII does not cover discrimination based on sexual orientation. See, e.g., *Higgins v. New Balance Athlet. Shoe, Inc.* 194 F. 3d 252 (1st Cir. 1999); *Rene v. MGM Grand Hotel,* 243 F. 3d 1206 (9th Cir. 2001). Some states and local jurisdictions have laws, ordinances, or policies that prohibit discrimination based on sexual orientation in the employment context.

13. *Pullman-Standard v. Swint,* 456 U.S. 273 (1982).

14. 401 U.S. 424 (1971).

15. *Civil Rights Division of the Arizona Department of Law v. Amphitheater Unified School District No. 10,* 680 P.2d 517 (Ariz. App. 1983).

16. 42 U.S.C. § 2000e–2005g (2005).

17. *See Desert Palace, Inc. v. Costa,* 539 U.S. 90 (2003).

18. 29 U.S.C. § 206d (2005).

19. 2004 WL 257085 (E.D. Pa. 2004).

20. 513 F. Supp. 1084 (N.D. W.Va. 1981).

21. 388 F.3d 331 (7th Cir. 2004).

22. 209 F.3d 931 (6th Cir. 2000).

23. 480 U.S. 273 (1987).

24. No. 97-8915 (11th Cir. July 17, 1998).

25. *Southeastern Community College v. Davis,* 442 U.S. 397 (1979).

26. *U.S. Airways v. Barnett,* 535 U.S. 391 (2002).

27. 20 U.S.C. § 1681 (2005).

28. 502 U.S. 60 (1992).

29. *Meritor Savings Bank,* 477 U.S. 57, 69 (1986).

30. U.S. Department of Education, Office for Civil Rights (OCR). (2001). *Revised Sexual harassment guidance: Harassment of students by school employees, other stu-*

dents, or third parties. Retrieved January 19, 2001, from http://www.ed.gov/offices/ OCR/shguide/shguide.pdf

31. Ibid.

32. *See Harris v. Forklift Systems,* 510 U.S. 17 (1993); *Clark County School District,* 532 U.S. 268 (2001).

33. *Oncale v. Sundowner Offshore Services,* 523 U.S. 75 (1998).

34. For a full discussion of the rights of gay and lesbian students, see *Dealing with legal matters surrounding students' sexual orientation and gender identity.* Retrieved May 3, 2005, from www.nsba.org/site/docs/34600/34527.pdf

35. U.S. Department of Education, Office for Civil Rights (OCR). (2001). *Revised sexual harassment guidance: Harassment of students by school employees, other students, or third parties.* Retrieved January 19, 2001, from http://www.ed.gov/offices/ OCR/shguide/shguide.pdf

36. 92 F.3d 446, 455–456 (7th Cir. 1996); also *Montgomery v. Indep. Sch. Dist. No. 709,* 109 F. Supp.2d 1081 (D. Minn. 2000).

37. American Association of University Women (AAUW). (2001). *Hostile hallways: Bullying, teasing and sexual harassment in school.* Washington, DC: AAUW Educational Foundation.

38. 536 U.S. 629 (1999).

39. *Davis v. Monroe County Board of Education,* 526 U.S. 629 (1999).

40. U.S. Department of Education, Office of Civil Rights. (1997). *Sexual harassment guidance: Harassment of students by school employees, other students, or third parties.* Washington, DC: U.S. Government Printing Office.

41. 524 U.S. 274 (1998).

42. *Gebser v. Lago Vista Independent School District,* 524 U.S. 274 (1998).

43. 265 F.3d 653 (8th Cir. 2001).

44. See also *Davis v. DeKalb County Sch. Dist.,* 233 F.3d 1367 (11th Cir. 2000).

45. 430 U.S. 703 (1977).

46. But see *Garrett v. Board of Education,* 775 F. Supp. 1004 (E.D. Mich. 1991). (Where the court was not convinced that excluding girls from the schools would serve to achieve the stated objective of addressing concerns regarding high unemployment rates, school dropout levels, and homicides among African American males.)

47. 69 Fed. Reg. 11276. Nondiscrimination on the Basis of Sex in Education Programs or Activities Receiving Federal Financial Assistance, 69 Fed. Reg. 11276 (proposed March 9, 2004) (to be codified at 24 C.F.R. pt. 106).

48. National Association for Single Sex Public Schools lists the 36 single-sex public schools in operation for the 2004–2005 school year. It cites the oldest operating single-sex public school as Western High School (Baltimore, MD), established in 1844. It cites 9 new single-sex public schools established in 2003 and 11 established in 2004. National Association for Single Sex Public Schools. (2004). Retrieved from http://www.singlesexschools.org/home-introduction.htm

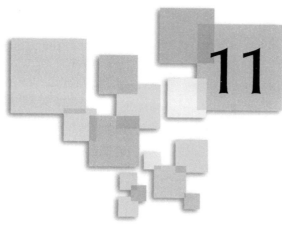

RELIGION IN THE SCHOOLS

The issue of the appropriate relationship between religion and the state has been one of the most controversial in American legal history. The experience of the nation's founders both with attempts to interfere with the free exercise of religion and with state control of religion prompted a desire to address the issue of religion in the very first amendment to the Constitution in an attempt to erect what President Thomas Jefferson called a "wall of separation between Church and State." The First Amendment to the U.S. Constitution guarantees religious freedom in two separate and distinct clauses that are often in tension with one another. The first, the Establishment Clause, prohibits the establishment of religion by the government, while the other, the Free Exercise Clause, prevents the government from infringing on an individual's free exercise of religion.

Maintaining the wall of separation without being "hostile to religion" has been the challenge faced by government officials and public school teachers and administrators. Often they find their actions challenged in the courts, and a number have reached the U.S. Supreme Court. This chapter examines how the courts have interpreted the First Amendment within the public school environment in relation to some of the most contested church–state issues. After reading this chapter you will be able to

> "Congress shall make no law respecting an establishment of religion, or prohibiting the free exercise thereof."
>
> U.S. Const. Amend. I

- Explain how challenges under the Establishment Clause are evaluated.
- Distinguish between permissible and impermissible prayer in the schools and at school-sponsored activities.

- Discuss the principles that apply to religious expression in the school.
- Explain the limits which can be placed on Religious displays, the observation of religious holidays, the distribution of religious material, and the wearing of religious attire and symbols by students and teachers.
- Elaborate on the appropriate use of religious materials in the curriculum.
- Describe the conditions under which students may be released from school to receive religious instruction.

INTERPRETATION OF THE FIRST AMENDMENT

The First Amendment Establishment and Free Exercise clauses could mean anything from simply that the government cannot establish or sponsor an official state religion to meaning that no public official or public school employee can make any reference to religion. In interpreting and applying both the Establishment and the Free Exercise clauses along this continuum, the Supreme Court has developed the tests discussed here to provide guidance to school districts and governmental entities.

Establishment Clause

In the landmark case of **Lemon v. Kurtzman**[1] (see the boxed case summary), the U.S. Supreme Court established a three-part test, since referred to as the "*Lemon* test," to determine whether a government action challenged under the Establishment Clause passes constitutional muster. To pass the test an affirmative response must be given to the first two questions, and a negative response to the third: (1) Does the action or policy have a secular legislative purpose? (2) Does its primary effect neither advance nor inhibit religion? (3) Does the policy or action foster an excessive government entanglement with religion?

LEMON v. KURTZMAN

Rhode Island and Pennsylvania enacted laws that provided for salary supplements to private sectarian schoolteachers who taught only secular courses. The laws were challenged on the ground that they violated the establishment clause. The U.S. Supreme Court analyzed the statutes by applying a three-prong test and concluded that both statutes failed to satisfy the third prong by fostering an excessive government entanglement with religion.

Three major Supreme Court decisions have since modified the *Lemon* test. Although not directly overturning *Lemon*, the Court has reinterpreted it in such a

Go to the Companion Website at **http://www. prenhall.com/underwood**, select Chapter 11, choose Cases module, and click on **Lemon v. Kurtzman** to read the entire opinion of the court.

way as to significantly affect its application. In 1985 the Court modified the *Lemon* test to ask (1) whether the actual purpose of the action is to endorse or disapprove of religion; and (2) whether, irrespective of the government's purpose, the actual effect conveys a message of governmental endorsement or disapproval.[2] In 1992 the Court added the "coercion test" to the *Lemon* and the "endorsement" test and asked whether the practice in question in effect coerced students to participate in a religious exercise.[3] In 1997 the Court focused on whether the practice in question

- resulted in government indoctrination;
- defined its recipients in relation to their religion; and
- created excessive entanglement between government and religion.[4]

No matter which test is used, the consistent theme remains that government may not actually or in appearance endorse religion.

Free Exercise Clause

The Free Exercise Clause of the First Amendment guarantees individuals the right to worship as they choose. In fact, in the landmark case in education, **Wisconsin v. Yoder**[5] (see the boxed case summary), the Supreme Court said the state could not interfere with the free exercise of religion unless it could show a compelling state interest in so doing. However, the free exercise of religion right is not absolute. Although individuals are free to believe whatever they want, they are not always free to act on those beliefs. The government may prohibit or regulate certain practices (e.g., snake handling where the state has a compelling interest in ensuring public safety).

WISCONSIN v. YODER

The U.S. Supreme Court concluded that enforcing a state compulsory attendance law against Amish children after they had completed the eighth grade, infringed on their free exercise of religious rights. The Court found that the state had no compelling interest in requiring Amish children to attend school past the time their basic educational skills had been learned.

In 1990, the Supreme Court modified its Free Exercise Clause analysis. It found that where the government practice is neutral and has only an incidental burden on religion, a compelling state interest was not required to justify the government action.[6] The following sections present a discussion of the impact of current judicial interpretations of the First Amendment on teachers and students. Particular attention is given to the issue of prayer in the schools, various forms

Go to the Companion Website at **http://www. prenhall.com/underwood**, *select Chapter 11, choose Cases module, and click on* **Wisconsin v. Yoder** *to read the entire opinion of the court.*

of religious expression, observation of religious holidays, religion in the curriculum, and the practice of releasing students during the school day to receive religious instruction.

PRAYER IN THE SCHOOL

Individual and Group Prayer

The issue of school prayer remains one of ongoing and heated dispute. In a pair of decisions in the early 1960s the U.S. Supreme Court ruled that school-sponsored prayer and Bible reading violate the Establishment Clause[7] (see the boxed case summary of **Engel v. Vitale**). However, under the Free Exercise Clause individual students and employees have a protected right to engage in individual prayer. Student-initiated prayer, individually or in a group setting, is also permitted as long as it does not result in the endorsement of religion by the school (which would run afoul of the Establishment Clause). Such prayer must also be nondisruptive and is subject to the same constraints as other student speech in the particular setting.

ENGEL v. VITALE

Students cannot be compelled to recite a state-composed prayer at school even if it is nondenominational. Nor may they be subjected to prayer under circumstances raising the perception of school sponsorship. The court ruled that "it is no part of the business of government to impose official prayers for any group of American people."

Go to the Companion Website at **http://www. prenhall.com/underwood**, *select Chapter 11, choose Cases module, and click on* **Engel v. Vitale** *to read the entire opinion of the court.*

Sometimes a fine line exists between prayer that violates the Establishment Clause and prayer that does not. The U.S. Supreme Court has noted that there is a "crucial difference between the state endorsing religious speech, which the Establishment Clause forbids, and private religious speech, which the Free Speech and Free Exercise Clauses protect."[8] The key is whether it appears that the prayer is school sponsored.

Under some circumstances courts have permitted schools to start the day with a "moment of silence" when the purpose of the activity was not just a cover to provide an opportunity for school prayer as a daily activity, as was the proven intent of the state of Alabama in **Wallace v. Jaffee** when the Alabama Supreme Court struck down a statute that mandated a moment of silence for "meditation and voluntary prayer."[9] However, the U.S. Supreme Court has declined to review and overturn a decision from the Fourth Circuit letting stand a Virginia statute that required a daily moment of silence for students to "meditate, pray, or engage in any other silent activity,"[10] on the grounds of not only the absence of legislative intent to establish religion but also its stated secular concern about violence in the schools. Since September 11, 2001, there has been a significant increase in the number of states and school districts that have adopted mandatory moments of silence.

Prayer at School-Sponsored Activities

Although it is clear that the school or teachers may not orchestrate prayer at the beginning of the day, in classes, or within the curriculum, school districts continue to wrestle with the issue of whether, and under what circumstances, prayers may be delivered at school-sponsored activities. Two of the most frequently litigated of these areas have been prayer at graduation ceremonies and at athletic events.

The Supreme Court in 1992 addressed the issue of prayers at graduation ceremonies in **Lee v. Weisman**[11] (see the boxed case summary), a case challenged a Rhode Island school's practice of allowing the principal to invite a member of the clergy to deliver a prayer at graduation exercises. The principal instructed the clergy that the prayer was to be nonsectarian and gave them a copy of "Guidelines for Civic Occasions," prepared by the National Conference of Christians and Jews. In ruling that school-organized prayer, even if voluntary and nonsectarian, violates the Establishment Clause, the Court focused on the fact that the school controlled the activity by selecting the clergy and giving directions to them. Moreover, in the opinion of the Court, the "psychological coercion" placed on dissenters to attend graduation ceremonies had the effect of government coercion of students to attend religious exercises.

LEE v. WEISMAN

The U.S. Supreme Court ruled that the school-sponsored prayer at graduation exercises violated the Establishment Clause. The Court stated that although government may accommodate the free exercise of religion, such accommodation cannot supersede the "fundamental limitations imposed by the Establishment Clause," which prevent the government from using coercion to support or encourage participation in religious exercises or worship. It rejected the school district's argument that there was no coercion because student participation in graduation ceremonies was voluntary; not to attend would require the student to miss his or her own high school graduation.

In the years since *Weisman,* the courts have clarified that if the prayer is not school sponsored, but truly a student's expression, it may be constitutional. For example, in **Adler v. Duval**[12] the Eleventh Circuit Court of Appeals held that a school policy permitting unreviewed, student-led messages at the beginning of graduation ceremonies is constitutional even though it contained no restriction

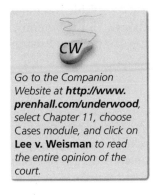

Go to the Companion Website at **http://www.prenhall.com/underwood**, *select Chapter 11, choose Cases module, and click on* **Lee v. Weisman** *to read the entire opinion of the court.*

against prayer. The court found nothing in the school policy that invited or encouraged religious messages. The court also emphasized that under this particular policy the school had no control over the content of any message delivered.

The courts have applied the *Weisman* coercion rationale in reviewing prayer at other school-sponsored activities. In **Santa Fe Independent School District v. Doe**[13] the U.S. Supreme Court held that a policy permitting student-led "invocations" before football games violated the Establishment Clause. The Court found the prayer was actually school sponsored because the messages were delivered over the school's public address system, under the supervision of school faculty, and pursuant to a policy that encouraged public prayer. Although noting that attendance at a football game is voluntary, the Court reasoned that the social pressure or personal desire to attend does not dramatically differ from that of graduation exercises, and those in attendance may not be coerced into participating in an act of religious worship. The Court also noted that the very election process itself (the student who delivered the prayer was the elected student council chaplain) ensured that minority view candidates will never prevail and that their views would be effectively silenced.

RELIGIOUS EXPRESSION

The Establishment, Free Exercise, and Free Speech clauses sometimes are in tension when individuals want to express their religious beliefs within the school. As discussed in chapter 7, outside school-sponsored contexts, student speech can be suppressed due to its content if it is disruptive, harmful, or pervasively vulgar. As was also discussed, student speech may also be limited to reasonable times, places, and manners. These general principles apply to religious expression as well.

When the speech is within the curricular context, the school may provide further restrictions, particularly to ensure that it does not appear the school is endorsing religious speech. For example, in **Bannon v. Palm Beach County,**[14] the U.S. Court of Appeals for the Eleventh Circuit ruled that a high school principal did not violate a student's First Amendment rights to free speech or free exercise by requiring that the student remove religious messages from a mural she had painted as part of a school-wide beautification project. The court found that the speech in question was school sponsored because the public would reasonably perceive the murals as bearing the school's imprimatur. Based on **Hazelwood School District v. Kuhlmeier,**[15] the court concluded that the principal could restrict the content of the mural.

The results are a little different when teacher speech is at issue; then a school's interest in avoiding the appearance of sponsoring religion (violating the Establishment Clause) more easily trumps the free speech rights of school employees. Accordingly, teachers can be directed to refrain from expressing religious viewpoints in the classroom or to students during the school day.[16] For example, the Tenth Circuit Court of Appeals found that a fifth-grade teacher's rights had not been violated when she was required to remove a religious poster from her classroom wall and stop reading the Bible at her desk during her students' silent reading period.[17]

Of course, as private individuals teachers enjoy the same religious liberties as others. However, difficulty sometimes arises in determining exactly when the teacher is acting as a private individual instead of a teacher. For example, in **Wigg v. Sioux Falls Sch. Dist.,**[18] Wigg, a third-grade teacher, wanted to participate in the student religious club meeting held after school. The principal had told her she could not participate, concerned that this would give the perception of endorsement of religion. The court disagreed and found that because the club meeting was after school and Wigg was participating as a private individual it was within her right to do so.

RELIGIOUS DISPLAYS

The courts are consistent in their ruling that displays in schools may not of **Stone v. Graham** promote or endorse religion. In keeping with the *Lemon* test, if the purpose or effect of the display is an apparent endorsement of religion, it violates the Establishment Clause. Application of the *Lemon* test led the Supreme Court to prohibit the posting of the Ten Commandments in school[19] (see the boxed case summary of **Stone v. Graham**) and a Michigan court to rule that a picture of Jesus Christ prominently displayed outside the principal's office violated the Establishment Clause.[20]

> ### STONE v. GRAHAM
>
> The U.S. Supreme Court has held that a statute requiring the display of the Ten Commandments in every public school classroom was unconstitutional. The Court focused on the intent of promoting a religious belief that had the probable effect of endorsing religion.

*Go to the Companion Website at **http://www. prenhall.com/underwood**, select Chapter 11, choose Cases module, and click on **Stone v. Graham** to read the entire opinion of the court.*

The use of a religious symbol displayed without a secular purpose will be found to violate the Establishment Clause.[21] For example, in **Doe v. Harlan County School District**[22] after a court prohibited a display that included only the Ten Commandments, the school added an assortment of other documents to the display. However, these additional documents continued to focus on religion (e.g., the presidential proclamation declaring 1983 the "Year of the Bible," a proclamation by President Lincoln designating a national day of prayer, a Kentucky statute that authorized the reading and posting of texts, and the school board resolution permitting the posting of the Ten Commandments). The court again disallowed the display noting that while the display of some of the documents might not have the effect of endorsing religion in a different context, a reasonable observer would perceive an endorsement. The court pointed out that this was particularly true because the documents had been selected and edited so the only common link between them was religion.

OBSERVING RELIGIOUS HOLIDAYS

Although there is no Supreme Court ruling on religious holidays in the public schools, the same general rule applies: Public schools may not sponsor religious practices. In practice this means that there can be recognition of a holiday, and the teacher can teach about the holiday, but any holiday program should serve an educational rather than a religious purpose. Additionally, programs should not make a child feel excluded because of his or her religion. Holiday programs in December may include religious music and themes, but these should not dominate. Any skit should emphasize cultural, rather than religious, aspects of the holiday. This does not mean that any display, program, or song that has some religious element but whose primary purpose and effect is secular would violate the First Amendment. In fact the courts have stated that to prohibit the singing of certain songs that might be religious in origin, but were sung because of their recognized musical value, would be showing hostility to religion.[23] (See the In the News feature.)

IN THE NEWS . . .

After years of legal assaults on municipal displays of Nativity scenes and Christmas observances in public schools, Christian groups are now mounting court challenges in the other direction.

From Mustang, Oklahoma, to Maplewood, New Jersey, they are filing or threatening to file lawsuits to win the inclusion of manger scenes in school plays, Christmas carols in school concerts, and Christmas trees in public buildings. . . .

Last year, a school administrator stopped Jonathan Morgan at the door to his classroom because the "goody bag" he had brought to a school party on the last day before Christmas vacation contained candy canes with a religious message attached. Titled "The Legend of the Candy Cane," it said the candy was shaped in a J for Jesus and bore a red stripe "to represent the blood Christ shed for the sins of the world."

This year, the 9-year-old and his evangelical Christian parents went straight to court. They were among four families who persuaded Judge Paul Brown, of the U.S. District Court for the Eastern District of Texas, to issue a temporary restraining order on Thursday securing their children's right to hand out "religious viewpoint gifts" at school-sponsored holiday parties.

Source: From "Evangelicals Use Courts to Fight Restrictions on Christmas Tidings," by Alan Cooperman, December 20, 2004, *Washington Post,* http://www.washingtonpost.com/wp-dyn/articles/A12388-2004Dec19.html

Holiday displays may include religious symbols. The displays should be temporary, require no active participation in any religious activity, and include diverse religious, cultural, and ethnic symbols. The displays must support valid educational goals, including understanding the diverse communities in which we live.[24] As an example, see the New York City Policy on Holiday Displays (below). Although the policy was challenged, the court upheld the policy, finding that its use was to convey an inclusive message, teaching about a variety of faiths and religious symbols, which did not violate the Free Exercise and Establishment Clauses.[25]

Students from many religious traditions may ask to be excused from classroom discussions or activities related to particular holidays. Some holidays considered by many people to be secular are viewed by others as having religious connotations. For example, some parents have challenged the observance of Halloween and the display of witches as promoting the religion of Wicca.[26]

Schools routinely grant requests to be excused from participating in holiday programs, and provisions for such requests are often part of school district policy.[27] Some parents and students may also request to be excused from discussions of certain holidays even when approached from an academic perspective.

NEW YORK CITY POLICY ON HOLIDAY DISPLAYS

New York City is a diverse multicultural community. It is our responsibility as educators to foster mutual understanding and respect for the many beliefs and customs stemming from our community's religious, racial, ethnic, and cultural heritage. In furtherance of this goal, we must be cognizant of and sensitive to the special significance of seasonal observances and religious holidays. At the same time, we must be mindful that the Constitution prohibits a school system from endorsing or promoting a particular religion or belief system.

The display of secular holiday symbols as decorations is permitted. Such symbols include, but are not limited to, Christmas trees, Menorahs, and the Star and Crescent.

Holiday displays shall not appear to promote or celebrate any single religion or holiday. Therefore, any symbol or decoration which may be used must be displayed simultaneously with other symbols or decorations reflecting different beliefs or customs.

All holiday displays should be temporary in nature.

The primary purpose of all displays shall be to promote the goal of fostering understanding and respect for the rights of all individuals regarding their beliefs, values, and customs.

Source: Skoros v. City of New York, (E.D. N.Y. 2004). Retrieved May 3, 2005, from http://www.nyed.uscourts.gov/02cv6439mdo.pdf

If focused on a limited, specific discussion, such requests may be granted in order to strike a balance between the student's religious interests and the school's interest in providing a well-rounded education.

Students as well as teachers may also request to be absent from school for religious reasons. Although the courts have generally recognized the right of school districts to place limits on the number of such absences, they have also required that reasonable accommodation be made for the exercise of staff and student religious beliefs. For example, courts have held that it is within the discretion of school districts to limit the number of paid leaves that are provided employees for religious leave, but they have found that it is a reasonable accommodation to allow employees to take unpaid leave for religious reasons.

DISTRIBUTION OF RELIGIOUS LITERATURE

Another issue developing in the courts is the school's obligation to distribute or refrain from distributing religious materials to children. Some parents are upset when their children bring home flyers promoting religious clubs and events. Others feel a school should promote all community activities, particularly religious ones. As with other issues involving religion, public schools have to walk a very narrow line. When school officials allow distribution of other literature, the same rules must be applied to the distribution of religious literature.[28] School policies may not prohibit distribution of materials on school grounds based solely on their religious content. Montgomery County Public Schools (MD) regularly distributed materials to families (by placing materials in folders to be carried home by children) for children's groups, including Boys Scouts and 4-H. But when asked to distribute materials to promote an after-school "Good News Club" (a proselytizing group), it refused, citing Establishment Clause concerns. The Fourth Circuit Court of Appeals disagreed with the districts' actions noting that the religious group would be receiving no benefit other than those afforded to other organizations. The district was ordered to allow the distribution of the materials.[29]

Wearing Religious Attire or Symbols

As discussed in chapter 7, schools have substantial discretion in adopting student dress codes. Religious messages on clothing and wearing of religious symbols can be regulated under the same rules as other student apparel. However, schools cannot adopt rules that burden students' Free Exercise Clause rights without adequate justification.[30] For example, in **Cheema v. Thompson**[31] a district refused to allow three young Khalsa Sikh children to wear ceremonial knives called "kirpans" to school. The school maintained wearing the knives violated school policy and state law on possession of weapons in school. The parents of the children claimed it was a central tenet of their religion to wear five symbols of their faith—long hair, a comb, sacred underwear, a steel bracelet, and a kirpan—at all times. The case ultimately settled in 1997 when the parties agreed to terms that made accommodations for the religious beliefs and still protected the safety of students. Under the terms of the settlement the kirpan blade had to be dulled and could not exceed two and a half inches. It had to be sewn securely into a sheath and further secured in a cloth pouch.

Attempts to regulate the wearing of religious attire by teachers also presents a challenge to school districts in maintaining the balance between the rights of the teacher and the interest of the school. A few states have statutes regarding religious garb worn by teachers in public schools. For example, statutes in both Arkansas and Tennessee specifically allow teachers to wear religious garb. On the other hand, statutes in Oregon, Pennsylvania, and Nebraska specifically prohibit the wearing of religious garb. In the states in which there is no applicable statute, courts have generally permitted teachers to wear *incidental* pieces of religious garb, finding that the wearing of religious garb or symbols (e.g., a cross or Star of David) by itself is not unconstitutional.[32] However, the courts have tended to support school districts in restricting teacher dress that is intended to carry a specific religious message. For example, in **Downing v. W. Haven Bd. of Educ.**[33] the court found no violation of the teacher's rights when she was required to change clothes or cover a T-shirt with the slogan "Jesus 2000" on it.

*Go to the Companion Website at **http://www. prenhall.com/underwood**, select Chapter 11, then choose the* Resources *module to find the state-specific statutes prohibiting religious garb.*

CURRICULUM ISSUES

Students and their parents have brought numerous First Amendment challenges to the curriculum in an attempt either to introduce religious material and curriculum or to eliminate specific courses, activities, or materials thought to be advancing religion. Although many people claim that the schools are hostile to religion and that all mention of religion is forbidden in the schools, in fact, public school curricula may include the teaching about religion or may use religious material. The Supreme Court has specifically said that the study of the Bible or of religion, when presented objectively as part of a secular program of education, does not violate the First Amendment.[34] But of course, the curriculum may neither endorse nor inculcate religion. Nor can teachers in exercising their free exercise of religion make their religious beliefs part of classroom instruction. Schools have a constitutional duty under the Establishment Clause to prevent teachers from inculcating religion.[35]

In recent years an increasing number of parents have contended that schools are using instructional materials, courses, or specific practices to promote a nontheistic or antitheistic "religion" that they refer to as "secular humanism." In cases to date the courts have rejected these arguments and have reaffirmed the position taken by the Supreme Court in 1968 in **Epperson v. Arkansas**[36] in striking down an Arkansas law forbidding instruction in evolution. According to the court, "the state has no legitimate interest in protecting any or all religions from views distasteful to them."

Although the school does not have to eliminate material found to offend a particular faith, teachers and schools cannot construct a class whose purpose is actually to inculcate or sponsor religion. For example, a school district in Mississippi offered a course entitled "Biblical History of the Middle East" on an opt-out basis as part of its curriculum. A federal court agreed with a parent that the course violated the Establishment Clause. The court found that the course (1) lacked a secular purpose, (2) had the primary effect of advancing religion, (3) led to excessive government entanglement with religion, (4) unconstitutionally endorsed fundamentalist Christianity, and (5) subjected students to subtle coercive pressure to attend the Bible classes.[37]

In instances in which parents or students find a course or part of a curriculum offensive, they often seek an exemption from the challenged course or exposure to the objectionable material. However, schools are not compelled to excuse student participation just because the family disagrees with, or dislikes, the ideas presented. The material or activity must *actually* violate the tenets of the student's religion for excusal to be mandatory. In addition, in numerous examples the courts have said that the state's compelling interest in educating regarding the particular topic (e.g., AIDS prevention and the dangers of alcohol and drug abuse) supported refusal of the religious exemption.

Finally, courts have generally recognized that students have a right to express religious beliefs in assignments within limitations. Teachers cannot require students to modify, include, or exclude religious views in their assignments. Teachers can still control students' assignments for legitimate pedagogical reasons or if they

RELIGIOUS EXPRESSION AND PRAYER IN CLASS ASSIGNMENTS IN U.S. DEPARTMENT OF EDUCATION GUIDANCE

Students may express their beliefs about religion in homework, artwork, and other written and oral assignments free from discrimination based on the religious content of their submissions. Teachers should judge such home and classroom work by ordinary academic standards of substance and relevance and against other legitimate pedagogical concerns identified by the school. Thus, if a teacher's assignment involved writing a poem, the work of a student who submits a poem in the form of a prayer (for example, a psalm) should be judged on the basis of academic standards (such as literary quality) and neither penalized nor rewarded on account of its religious content.

Source: From *U.S. Department of Education Guidance on Constitutionally Protected Prayer,* 2001, issued in conjunction with the No Child Left Behind Act. http://www.ed.gov/policy/gen/guid/religionandschools/prayer_guidance.html

give the appearance of endorsement of religion. Student work that includes religious expression, however, should be assessed under ordinary academic standards, including the criteria established for the assignment.[38] (See Religious Expression and Prayer in Class Assignments in U.S. Department of Education Guidance on page 220.) For example, in **DeNoyer v. Livonia Public Schools**[39] the court concluded that a second grader had no right to show a videotape of her singing a proselytizing religious song. The court upheld the teacher's rationale that the presentation was not in line with the assignment (developing self-esteem by giving an oral presentation), was longer than assigned, and would encourage other students to bring in long videos. In **Settle v. Dickson County School Board**[40] the court held that the teacher could give a student a zero on a research paper without violating the students' free exercise rights. The student choice of topic was the life of Jesus Christ, but the student did not meet the teacher's requirements of using at least four sources to research a topic.

RELEASED TIME FOR RELIGIOUS INSTRUCTION

Historically, many schools have released students during the school day so they can receive religious instruction. In the first case to reach the Supreme Court on this issue, **McCollum v. Board of Education,**[41] students were excused from regular public school classes to attend private religious instruction in another part of the school building. The Court ruled that this practice violated the Establishment Clause and that religious instruction may not take place on public school property during school hours. In a subsequent decision the Supreme Court held that schools may provide released time for students to accommodate their participation in religious instruction if it is off of school grounds.[42] In the years following, the courts have made it clear that schools have the discretion to dismiss students to receive religious instruction so long as they do not encourage or discourage participation, expend funds in soliciting students to attend religious classes, or penalize those who do not attend.[43]

As recently as 2004 this principle has been upheld. In **Pierce v. Sullivan West Central School Dist.**[44] the Second Circuit Court of Appeals upheld a New York statute allowing released time from public schools for religious instruction if it used no public funds and involved no on-site religious instruction.

GUIDING LEGAL PRINCIPLES

- The U.S. Supreme Court has long held that the Establishment Clause prohibits the government from (1) designating an official religion, (2) supporting a specific denomination or religion, or (3) promoting religious activity. Within the school context this means that the school may neither sponsor nor appear to endorse religious activity.

- To determine whether a government action challenged under the Establishment Clause passes constitutional muster, the school or teacher must ask whether the government action (1) has a legitimate secular purpose, (2) has a primary effect that neither advances nor inhibits religion, and (3) does not create an excessive entanglement between church and state.

- Schools must protect individuals' rights to free speech and free exercise of religion, not subject religious actions or speech to a different standard. Schools must be places that treat religion and religious beliefs with fairness and respect.

- Students have the right to pray individually or in groups or to discuss their religious views with their peers so long as they are not disruptive.

- Schools may acknowledge religious holidays, as long as there are educational purposes, and they do not appear to endorse the religious nature of the holiday.

- Study about religion in public schools is constitutional. The endorsement or inculcation of religion is not. Schools should teach about religion in a way that is objective and neutral. The school's approach must be academic, not devotional.

- Teachers must be neutral concerning religion while carrying out their responsibilities as teachers.

- Students may be released during the school day to receive religious instruction as long as it is off school grounds and is not supported or encouraged by the public school.

YOU BE THE JUDGE

Go to the Companion Website at **http://www.prenhall.com/underwood**, *Select Chapter 11, choose the You Be the Judge module, and click on the name of the case for more information about the case and the court's decision and rationale.*

Singing in the Choir

During the 1994–1995 school year, a sophomore student auditioned for and was admitted to a selective school choir. The choir was an elective credit course taught by an instructor who was a self-professed devout Mormon. The director selected almost exclusively Christian chorale music for the acappella choir's performances, frequently had the group perform at churches, and used exclusively religious music for the group's performance at the school graduation ceremony. The student, who was Jewish, objected to the selection of religious devotional songs and performing at religious sites where Christian religious symbols predominated. She filed legal action claiming a violation of the Establishment Clause and her rights under the Free Exercise Clause. The student filed suit against the school district and other related defendants, alleging that the teacher engaged in conduct that violated the Establishment and Free Exercise clauses of the First Amendment.

Questions for Discussion and Reflection

1. What arguments could the teacher make to support the selection of this music?
2. Can the student be required to attend a performance at a church? Should the choir be prohibited from performing at churches?
3. What criterion/test will the court use to evaluate the student's complaint?

Visit the Companion Website for a more detailed description of the facts in the case **Bauchman v. West High School.**

* * *

Curriculum Concerns

Lowell Elementary School (IL) used the Impressions Reading Series as a part of its supplemental reading program. The series includes works of C. S. Lewis, A. A. Milne, Dr. Seuss, Ray Bradbury, L. Frank Baum, Maurice Sendak, and other noted authors of fiction. There is a consistent theme of imagination, fantasy, and magic in some selections. Parents of a student in the school found material in the reading series objectionable, claiming it included religious concepts found in paganism, witchcraft, and Satanism. They filed an action against the district on First Amendment, Establishment Clause and Free Exercise Clause, grounds. They alleged that the materials indoctrinated their children with values directly opposed to their Christian beliefs by teaching tricks, despair, deceit, and parental disrespect.

Questions for Discussion and Reflection

1. What would the parents have to establish to have the reading selections excluded from the curriculum?
2. If students or parents object to curriculum material on religious grounds, must they be granted a religious exemption?
3. Does the First Amendment protect only mainstream religions?

Visit the Companion Website for a more detailed description of the facts in the case **Fleischfresser v. Directors of School Dist. 20.**

* * *

Bible Studies

For several years the board of education has allowed staff and students from Bryan College in Dayton, Tennessee, to conduct a program known as the Bible Education Ministry (BEM) in the county's public elementary schools. Bryan

College refers to itself as a Christian school, whose motto is "Christ Above All." The college's mission statement reads, "Educating students to become servants of Christ to make a difference in today's world." Bryan College students and faculty are required to subscribe to a "Statement of Belief" that asserts their belief in Jesus and the supreme authority of the Bible. BEM's volunteer instructors were never employed by the board. The BEM classes took place for 30 minutes, once a week, during the school day, in three county schools. The board contends that BEM's teaching has a secular purpose: to teach character development. However, many of the lesson plans used contain clearly religious themes. For example, the objective of one lesson plan for second graders was to "Teach the children God's commandments and that we should obey all of them." The lessons also sought to "teach the kids that God provides for us, even in the worst situations" and that "Jesus loves you." The parents of two elementary school students filed suit in federal district court alleging the practice was a violation of the Establishment Clause. They used the name Doe for fear of community reprisal.

Questions for Discussion and Reflection

1. How can a school offer Bible study courses that do not violate the Establishment Clause?
2. Does it make a difference in terms of a potential Establishment Clause violation whether or not the teachers were employees of the district? Why or why not?
3. Would it make a difference in the court's ruling if the classes were held off campus? After school? Explain.

Visit the Companion Website for a more detailed description of the facts in the case **Doe v. Porter.**

MORE ON THE WEB

*Go to the Companion Website at **http://www.prenhall.com/underwood**, select Chapter 11, choose the More on the Web module to connect to the site mentioned.*

The Freedom Forum, a nonpartisan foundation dedicated to free press and free speech, has developed a number of lesson plans for teaching the First Amendment to students at all levels, complete with National Standards and Benchmarks. Go to the Lesson Plan website, http://www.freedomforum.org/templates/documentasp?documentID=13588, and click on the lesson "Public Schools and Prayers: Do They Mix?" Test your knowledge of prayer in the schools and religion in the curriculum by clicking on Part 2 and taking the "School Prayer Quiz." How did you do? Read the answers provided to increase your understanding of what is allowed and disallowed.

ENDNOTES

1. 403 U.S. 602 (1971).
2. *Wallace v. Jaffree*, 472 U.S. 38 (1985).
3. *Lee v. Weisman*, 505 U.S. 577 (1992).
4. *Agostini v. Felton*, 521 U.S. 203 (1997).
5. 406 U.S. 205 (1972).
6. *Employment Division v. Smith*, 494 U.S. 872 (1990).
7. *Engel v. Vitale*, 370 U.S. 421 (1962); *School District of Abington Township v. Schempp*, 374 U.S. 203 (1963).
8. *Board of Educ. of Westside Comm. Schools v. Mergens*, 496 U.S. 226 (1990).
9. 472 U.S. 38 (1985).
10. *Brown v. Gilmore*, 258 F.3d 265 (4th Cir. 2001), *cert. denied*, 534 U.S. 996 (2001).
11. 505 U.S. 577 (1992).
12. 250 F.3d 1330 (11th Cir. 2001).
13. 530 U.S. 290 (2000).
14. 387 F.3d 1208 (11th Cir. 2004).
15. 484 U.S. 260 (1988).
16. See, e.g., *Bishop v. Aronov*, 926 F.2d 1066 (11th Cir. 1991).
17. *Peloza v. Capistrano Unified School District*, 37 F.3d 517 (9th Cir. 1994), *cert. denied*, 515 U.S. 1173 (1995).
18. 382 F.3d 807 (8th Cir. 2004).
19. *Stone v. Graham*, 449 U.S. 1104 (1981).
20. *Washegesic v. Bloomington Public Schools*, 33 F.3d 679 (6th Cir. 1994), *cert. denied*, 514 U.S. 1095 (1995).
21. *Lynch v. Donnelly*, 465 U.S. 668 (1984); *Allegheny County v. Greater Pittsburgh ACLU*, 488 U.S. 815 (1989).
22. 96 F. Supp.2d 667 (E.D. Ky. 2000). Also see *McCreary v. ACLU*,—U.S.—(2005) as it relates to posting in a county courthouse; *Van Orden v. Perry*,—U.S.—(2005) allowing the posting on statehouse grounds.
23. *Doe v. Duncanville Independent School District*, 70 F.3d 402 (5th Cir. 1995).
24. See, e.g., *Florey v. Sioux Falls School District 49-5*, 619 F.2d 1311 (8th Cir. 1980), *cert. denied*, 449 U.S. 987 (1980); *Clever v. Cherry Hill Tp. Bd. of Educ*, 838 F. Supp. 929 (D. N.J. 1993); *Sechler v. State College Area School District*, 121 F. Supp.2d 439 (M.D. Pa. 2000).
25. *Skoros v. City of New York*, F. Supp.2d (E.D. N.Y. 2004).
26. *Guyer v. School Board of Alachva County*, 634 So.2d 806 (Fla. App. 1994).
27. See *Clever v. Cherry Hill Tp. Bd. of Educ.*, 838 F. Supp. 929 (D. N.J. 1993).
28. See, e.g., *Hedges v. Wauconda Community Unit School District*, 9 F.3d 1295 (7th Cir. 1993); *Muller v. Jefferson Lighthouse School*, 98 F.3d 1530 (7th Cir. 1996), *cert. denied*, 510 U.S. 1186 (1997).

29. *Child Evangelism Fellowship of Maryland v. Montgomery County Public Schools,* 370 F.3d 589 (4th Cir. 2004).

30. See, e.g., *Cheema v. Thompson,* 67 F.3d 883 (9th Cir. 1995); *Menora v. Illinois High School Association,* 683 F.2d 1030 (7th Cir. 1982), *cert. denied,* 459 U.S. 1156 (1983); *Chalifoux v. New Caney Independent School District,* 976 F. Supp. 659 (S.D. Tex. 1997).

31. 67 F.3d 883 (9th Cir. 1995).

32. See, e.g., *Moore v. Board of Education,* 212 N.E.2d 833 (Ohio 1965); *Rawlings v. Butler,* 290 S.W.2d 801 (Ky. 1956); *City of New Haven v. Town of Torrington,* 43 A.2d 455 (Conn. 1945); *Johnson v. Boyd,* 28 N.E.2d 256 (Ind. 1940); *Gerhardt v. Heid,* 267 N.W. 127 (N.D. 1936); *Contra Zellers v. Huff,* 236 P.2d 949 (N.M. 1951); *United States v. Board of Education for the School District of Philadelphia,* 911 F.2d 882 (3d Cir. 1990); but see *EEOC v. Reads, Inc.,* 759 F. Supp. 1150 (E.D. Pa. 1991).

33. 162 F. Supp.2d 19 (D. Conn. 2001).

34. *School Dist. of Abington Township, Pa. v. Schempp,* 374 U.S. 225 (1963).

35. *Marchi v. Board of Cooperative Educational Services of Albany,* 173 F.3d 469 (2nd Cir. 1999).

36. 393 U.S. 97 (1968).

37. *Herdahl v. Pontotoc County School District,* 933 F. Supp. 582 (N.D. Miss. 1996); see also *Gibson v. Lee County School Board,* 1 F. Supp.2d 1426 (M.D. Fla. 1998). (Court ruled that Old Testament course had a secular purpose, but New Testament course violated the establishment clause.)

38. See, e.g., U.S. Department of Education Guidance, *Religious expression in public schools.* Retrieved May 3, 2005, from http://www.ed.gov/speeches/08-1995/religion.html

39. 799 F. Supp. 744 (E.D. Mich. 1992).

40. *Settle v. Dickson County Sch. Bd.,* 53 F.3d 152 (6th Cir. 1995).

41. 333 U.S. 203 (1948).

42. *Zorach v. Clauson,* 343 U.S. 306 (1952).

43. See, e.g., *Doe v. Shenandoah County School Board,* 737 F. Supp. 913 (W.D. Va. 1990); *Lanner v. Wimmer,* 662 F.2d 1349 (10th Cir.1981).

44. 379 F.3d 56 (2nd Cir. 2004).

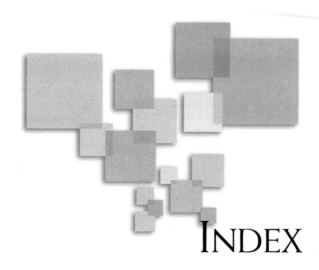

INDEX